Teaching Young Children Mathematics

Teaching Young Children Mathematics provides a comprehensive overview of mathematics instruction in the early childhood classroom. Taking into account family differences, language barriers, and the presence of special needs students in many classrooms throughout the U.S., this textbook situates best practices for mathematics instruction within the larger frameworks of federal and state standards as well as contemporary understandings of child development.

Key topics covered include: developmental information of conceptual understanding in mathematics from birth through third grade, use of national and state standards in math, including the new *Common Core State Standards*, information for adapting ideas to meet special needs and English Language Learners, literacy connections in each chapter, "real-world" connections to the content, and information for family connections to the content.

Janice R. Minetola is Associate Professor of Teacher Education at Shippensburg University, Pennsylvania.

Robert G. Ziegenfuss is Assistant Professor of Teacher Education at Shippensburg University, Pennsylvania.

J. Kent Chrisman is Professor of Early Childhood Education at Shippensburg University, Pennsylvania.

Teaching Young Children Mathematics

Janice R. Minetola, Robert G. Ziegenfuss, and J. Kent Chrisman

Routledge
Taylor & Francis Group

NEW YORK AND LONDON

First published 2014
by Routledge
711 Third Avenue, New York, NY 10017

Simultaneously published in the UK
by Routledge
2 Park Square, Milton Park, Abingdon, Oxon OX14 4RN

Routledge is an imprint of the Taylor & Francis Group, an informa business

Library of Congress Cataloging in Publication Data
Minetola, Janice R.
  Teaching young children mathematics / by Janice R. Minetola, Robert
  G. Ziegenfuss, and J. Kent Chrisman.
    pages cm
  Includes bibliographical references and index.
  1. Mathematics–Study and teaching (Early childhood)   I. Ziegenfuss,
  Robert G.   II. Chrisman, J. Kent.   III. Title.
  QA135.6.M55 2013
  372.7'049–dc23   2012046289

ISBN: 978–0–415–64159–3 (hbk)
ISBN: 978–0–415–64163–0 (pbk)
ISBN: 978–0–203–08174–7 (ebk)

Typeset in Minion
by RefineCatch Limited, Bungay, Suffolk

Printed and bound in the United States of America
by Edwards Brothers, Inc.

This textbook is dedicated to all those who aspire to teach young children by instructing them using sound, research-based, best practices in mathematics.

CONTENTS

LIST OF FIGURES

LIST OF TABLES

1

NURTURING YOUNG CHILDREN'S MATHEMATICAL DEVELOPMENT

HOW DO YOUNG CHILDREN LEARN MATHEMATICS?

This question has been the focus of many approaches, theories, and practices regarding the growth, development, and learning of young children. While children have similar feelings as adults concerning fear, pain, sadness, and joy, they are not merely miniature-sized adults; their learning needs and patterns are different (Taylor, 1999). Learning mathematics for young children should be grounded in experiences that are developmentally appropriate for a specific age group as well as the individual child, for even though a group of children may be similar in age, their developmental levels—physical, emotional, social, and cognitive—may be quite varied. Because of the variance of developmental levels in children of similar ages, educators look at general characteristics of children at different ages in planning learning experiences. They know that not all children are at the same developmental levels at the same time. Effective teachers get to know their students well and enact developmentally appropriate practices in their classrooms that help individual children reach goals that are both challenging and attainable, while at the same time, being responsive to the social and cultural context in which their students live (Copple & Bredekamp, 2009).

THEORIES VS. ASSUMPTIONS

Children from birth through the primary grades in school pass through the first three stages of intellectual development. They begin and continue to learn through their five senses—sight, hearing, taste, touch, and smell. They learn to control their body movements and continue to develop physical or body skills. They question, imitate, and practice and learn best through concrete, hands-on experiences. Although quite home-based and self-centered at first, they expand beyond these characteristics to interact with others and to explore other environments (Taylor, 1999).

Best practices in classrooms are not based on assumptions or beliefs; they are based on knowledge of how children learn and grow. Early childhood educators draw on the work of those whose theories are anchored in developmentally appropriate practice. Some of these theorists include Jean Piaget, Erik Erikson, John Dewey, and Lev Vygotsky. A brief overview of each theorist's work follows; however, you are encouraged to read more extensively in order to gain a greater understanding of the theories and how they relate to the mathematical development of young children. This section is included in this chapter to link your understanding of child development to children's mathematical thinking.

Cognitive or Intellectual Development

Jean Piaget (1896–1980) was a Swiss epistemologist whose work is described as a cognitive-development theory. He studied the cognitive or intellectual development of children and formulated a model with four stages of development. His model of intellectual development includes the following categories (Taylor, 1999) (implications for mathematical understanding in each stage are also included):

Piagetian Stages (Taylor, 1999, p. 3)

Stage 1: Sensorimotor (0–24 months of age)
Implications for Mathematical Understanding: Children in the sensorimotor stage learn through their senses. They repeat number words they hear from media such as television and from people in their environment. Some children learn to count numbers, typically from one to ten and begin to recognize some number symbols. They learn terminology related to mathematics, such as big and small. By the end of this stage children are developing the concept of object permanence, or the idea that objects exist even when they are out of sight (Charlesworth, 2005).

Stage 2: Preoperational (two–seven years of age)
Implications for Mathematical Understanding: Children in the preoperational stage are the focus of early childhood education. Although they still use their senses to learn about their world, they begin to learn through concrete, hands-on experiences. Mathematics manipulatives, or concrete objects that children can handle, become an important part of their learning experiences. For example, children need to have access to various objects in their classrooms to count, add together, and subtract from one another. They need to examine shapes, use various measuring tools, and use real-life objects such as clocks, a cash register, money, and calendars in their dramatic play areas. As children's language development continues, they begin to use more terminology related to mathematics in referring to size, weight, shape, time, and length. As children reach the later end of this stage, they use symbolic behaviors in their play. For example, a stick could represent a fishing rod, or a block could represent a toy car or train car. They begin working with classifying objects (putting things in logical groups) and seriation (putting objects in a logical sequence) (Charlesworth, 2005).

Stage 3: Concrete Operational (seven–11 years of age)
Implications for Mathematical Understanding: Children in the concrete operational stage are beginning to work with symbolic activities—the beginning of logical thought, according to Piaget (Geist, 2009). They are able to represent objects using other objects or symbols. For example, when drawing a picture representation to aid in solving a subtraction problem involving ducks on a pond, children would be

able to draw Xs or some other symbol to represent the ducks rather than draw pictures of ducks. Also, children at this stage do not need to see five objects to know what the number five represents.

Stage 4: Formal Operational (11 years of age on)

Implications for Mathematical Understanding: Children in the formal operational stage are capable of solving mathematics problems in a logical and systematic way. They begin to understand abstract mathematics concepts and solve abstract problems (Charlesworth, 2005). For example, children in this stage of cognitive development no longer need concrete manipulatives or picture representations to solve math problems. They understand that numerals represent quantities and can solve problems (add, subtract, multiply, and divide) using standard algorithms.

Social-Emotional Development

Erik Erikson's work (1902–1994) focused on eight stages of psychosocial development, in which each stage is characterized by a positive and negative attribute (Bickart, Jablon, & Dodge, 1999). The four stages listed below relate to young children's psychosocial development. Implications for mathematical understanding are included for each stage.

Erikson Stages (Taylor, 1999, p. 4)

Birth–one year: Trust vs. Mistrust

Implications for Mathematical Understanding: In any academic area, the ability to trust oneself is important, and this is especially true in mathematical thinking. Trust or mistrust has the potential of affecting their attitudes towards adults, including their teachers, as they grow and develop (Taylor, 1999).

One–three years: Autonomy vs. Shame and Doubt

Implications for Mathematical Understanding: This is the stage when children are learning to become self-sufficient. They are learning to walk, feed themselves, use the toilet, and engage in other adult-like activities. Depending on the attitudes of caregivers towards children's development in these areas, children can learn to feel good about themselves or doubt their abilities (Taylor, 1999).

Three–six years: Intuitive vs. Guilt

Implications for Mathematical Understanding: During this stage, children are engaged in adult-like activities as they are experimenting with their world (Taylor, 1999). Attitudes and feedback they receive from caregivers can directly relate to children's feelings of confidence in their ability to work with mathematical concepts such as numbers, shapes, and patterns, or they learn to feel guilty about their inabilities.

Seven–11 years: Industry vs. Inferiority

Implications for Mathematical Understanding: Children in this stage are product-oriented and want to do well and feel confident in their abilities. If children feel confident in learning mathematics, they will take risks, problem solve, and take on mathematical challenges. This in turn helps them learn and grow mathematically. Children in this stage who do not feel confident in their abilities to do mathematics shy away from risk-taking and problem solving. They learn to dislike mathematics because they have feelings of inferiority and the attitude of "I can't do it" (Bickart et al., 1999).

In working with young children, it is important for teachers to make daily decisions that help children meet success and progress in a healthy manner so positive attributes are developed as opposed to negative ones. Children need to learn to trust, develop confidence and adequacy in their abilities, and to become self-sufficient as they engage in adult-like activities. These abilities are critical learning, practicing, and using mathematics throughout the child's life.

INQUIRY-BASED LEARNING

John Dewey (1859–1952) has had a tremendous influence on education in the United States. He believed that schools should teach children to think by engaging them in hands-on, inquiry-based learning experiences. He believed that education should involve community experiences and also involve physical activity and free play (Ryan & Cooper, 2007; Taylor, 1999). Examples of hands-on projects and inquiry-based math learning experiences will be included in each of the following chapters.

SOCIO-CONSTRUCTIVISM

Lev Vygotsky (1896–1934) was a contemporary of Piaget, whose work was unpublished until after his death. He stressed the importance of language and social and cultural context in helping children develop thinking skills. His work emphasizes the social nature of learning and the importance of scaffolding children's learning through teacher–child and child–child relationships. He wrote about the Zone of Proximal Development (ZPD) in emphasizing these relationships—the zone being the "distance between the child's ability to solve problems independently compared to his ability to solve them with the assistance of someone more competent than he" (Taylor, 1999, p. 5). Vygotsky also believed that learning was at the heart of a child's development; in other words, learning leads development.

Two implications for mathematical learning with young children from Vygotsky's theory are that children can learn mathematical concepts and operations from other children if the daily activities are planned for such interactions, and mathematical activities must be planned just ahead of the child's developmental level. These require ongoing assessment and careful planning. Activities and projects will be included in later chapters that highlight these two implications.

DEVELOPMENTALLY APPROPRIATE PRACTICE (DAP)

The National Association for the Education of Young Children (NAEYC) published a position statement titled *Developmentally Appropriate Practice in Early Childhood Programs Serving Children from Birth through Age 8,* adopted in 2009, that provides a framework for best practices in educating young children that promotes optimal development and learning. The position statement is grounded in research, theories of growth and development of children, and knowledge concerning effective education. The NAEYC position statement reflects a commitment to excellence and equity in educating all children.

Early childhood practitioners make many daily decisions concerning goals for children's learning and how to help them achieve these goals. In making sound decisions, practitioners need to consider knowledge about general, age-related characteristics of children, knowledge about individual children, and knowledge about the cultural and social context in which individual children live. These pieces of knowledge are essential in guiding early childhood practitioners in planning appropriate learning experiences for individual children that will support them as they progress in learning and growing (Copple & Bredekamp, 2009).

The NAEYC position statement identifies 12 well-supported principles for educating young children. These include:

1. All the domains of development and learning—physical, social and emotion, and cognitive—are important, and they are closely interrelated. Children's development and learning in one domain influence, and are influenced by, what takes place in other domains.
2. Many aspects of children's learning and development follow well-documented sequences, with later abilities, skills, and knowledge building on those already acquired.
3. Development and learning proceed at varying rates from child to child, as well as at uneven rates across different areas of a child's individual functioning.
4. Development and learning result from a dynamic and continuous interaction of biological maturation and experience.
5. Early experiences have profound effects, both cumulative and delayed, on a child's development and learning; and optimal periods exist for certain types of development and learning to occur.
6. Development proceeds toward greater complexity, self-regulation, and symbolic or representational capacities.
7. Children develop best when they have secure, consistent relationships with responsive adults and opportunities for positive relationships with peers.
8. Development and learning occurs in, and are influenced by, multiple social and cultural contexts.
9. Always mentally active in seeking to understand the world around them, children learn in a variety of ways; a wide range of teaching strategies and interactions are effective in supporting all these kinds of learning.
10. Play is an important vehicle for developing self-regulation, as well as for promoting language, cognition, and social competence.
11. Development and learning advance when children are challenged to achieve at a level just beyond their current mastery, and also when they have many opportunities to practice newly acquired skills.
12. Children's experiences shape their motivation and approaches to learning, such as persistence, initiative, and flexibility; in turn these dispositions and behaviors affect their learning and development.

(Copple & Bredekamp, 2009, pp. 11–15)

DEVELOPMENTALLY APPROPRIATE PRACTICES IN MATHEMATICS

The National Association for the Education of Young Children and the National Council of Teachers of Mathematics published a joint position statement titled *Early Childhood Mathematics: Promoting Good Beginnings* (adopted in 2002; updated in 2010) which affirms "that high-quality, challenging, and accessible mathematics education for three–six-year-old children is a vital foundation for future mathematics learning" (p. 1). Within the joint statement are ten recommendations for providing mathematics instruction that is of high quality for young children. Recommendations include:

1. Enhance children's natural interest in mathematics and their disposition to use it to make sense of their physical and social worlds
2. Build on children's experience and knowledge, including their family, linguistic, cultural, and community backgrounds; their individual approaches to learning; and their informal knowledge
3. Base mathematics curriculum and teaching practices on knowledge of young children's cognitive, linguistic, physical, and social-emotional development
4. Use curriculum and teaching practices that strengthen children's problem-solving and reasoning processes as well as representing, communicating, and connecting mathematical ideas
5. Ensure that the curriculum is coherent and compatible with known relationships and sequences of important mathematical ideas
6. Provide for children's deep and sustained interaction with key mathematical ideas
7. Integrate mathematics with other activities, and other activities with mathematics
8. Provide ample time, materials, and teacher support for children to engage in play, a context in which they explore and manipulate mathematical ideas with keen interest
9. Actively introduce mathematical concepts, methods, and language through a range of appropriate experiences and teaching strategies
10. Support children's learning by thoughtfully and continually assessing all children's mathematical knowledge, skills, and strategies.

(adopted in 2002; updated in 2010, p. 3)

GENERAL CHARACTERISTICS OF CHILDREN BIRTH TO AGE THREE

Children in the "birth to age three" category are operating in Piaget's sensorimotor and preoperational stages. Learning involves discovering the many facets of the world around them, the five senses being the tools through which they learn. They watch, touch everything within reach, and, oftentimes, taste what they touch. From the time they are born, infants listen intently to the sounds and voices in their environment and begin to imitate the sounds they hear; soon they begin to utter words, then phrases, and finally sentences. They begin rote repetition of number words as they mimic what they hear.

Mathematically, children around the age of six months begin to develop a sense of object permanence, or the realization that objects exist even though they cannot be seen. This is important for mathematics, since most mathematics is based on the idea that objects exist outside of our perception (Geist, 2009). Children at the sensorimotor stage lack the ability to represent an object with a mental or written symbol; however, this ability develops through children's imaginative play. Geist (2009) states, "Vygotsky proposed that children's use of imagination helped them to detach the thought or idea of the object from the actual object" (2009, p. 53).

Children in the preoperational stage begin using objects to represent other objects. For example, a block can be used as a pretend telephone, or a stick can be a fishing rod. Children also realize that symbols and signs can stand for other things as they learn about numbers and number symbols.

According to Erikson's stages of psychosocial development, children in this age group learn to trust or not trust their caregivers. They continue to become self-sufficient or develop feelings of doubt and shame concerning their own abilities. This is a time of experimentation with adult-like activities. Children in this age group develop feelings of confidence concerning their accomplishments or begin to feel guilty about some of their inadequacies.

MATHEMATICS CONCEPT DEVELOPMENT FROM BIRTH TO AGE THREE

According to Sousa (2008), human beings are born with several innate capabilities, one of these being language, and the other being number sense. Through experiments involving infants who were just a few months old, it has been determined that they are capable of noticing the "constancy of objects and detect differences in their numerical quantities" (Sousa, 2008, p. 9). This does not mean that we should be instructing infants to count and do calculations. What it does mean is that infants do have a conception of numerosity or quantity.

Children from birth to age three are involved in the work of play as they are learning about their world. Caregivers of children in this age group can help lay a foundation for mathematical concept development in an informal way by using mathematical vocabulary appropriate for this age group (more than, less than, greater, bigger, smaller, wider, taller), use counting words, point and count real objects or objects in picture books, find number symbols, shapes, and patterns around the house or in the environment, read storybooks that involve numbers, shapes, and patterns, play with blocks and other manipulatives, involve children in play activities involving containers, water, and/or sand, and involve children in cooking adventures that include measuring. Once one begins thinking mathematically, ideas are limitless in exposing young children to the "math" all around them.

Charlesworth (2005) outlines beginning points for understanding math concepts and skills. She identifies birth to age two (sensorimotor stage) as a time of observation, problem solving, developing the concept of one-to-one correspondence, and learning about number, shape, and spatial sense. As children enter the preoperational stage they learn to count, compare, and classify as well as develop their language skills.

The National Association for the Education of Young Children position statement identifies numbers and operations, geometry/spatial relationships, and measurement as the three areas that are most important to emphasize in teaching preschool children mathematics (Copple & Bredekamp, 2009).

GENERAL CHARACTERISTICS OF FOUR- AND FIVE-YEAR-OLD CHILDREN

Adults who are around four- and five-year-old children oftentimes comment, "To only have that much energy again!" Children of this age group have lots of energy and are naturally active and curious about themselves, others, and the world around them, thus the incessant who, what, where, when, and why questions. They are willing to try new adventures, and their play is typically quite imaginative.

Although they enjoy being around and playing with other children, they are still quite egocentric in their thinking (Oesterreich, 1995). Children's egocentric thinking can be expanded to include the opinions of others as they listen to classmates' explanations or ideas concerning solutions to mathematics problems. For example, children could have various ideas concerning how to figure out how many legs there are in a barnyard containing five chickens. It would be important for teachers to elicit ideas on solving this problem from many children, so they have the opportunity to hear each other's thoughts.

Four- and five-year-old children are at Piaget's preoperational stage. Through their imaginative play, children strengthen their representational ability and their ability to think more abstractly about numbers, geometric shapes, and problem solving. Thinking intuitively, or according to what seems right, children at this stage of cognitive development do not understand adult logic. Teachers, in instructing children concerning mathematical concepts, need to understand the intuitive thought processes of this age group and provide explanations that are understandable to them.

Although varying in capabilities, four- and five-year-old children are generally eager to learn, and take pride in what they can do to the point of being boastful in showing their self-confidence. Their gross motor skills are developing and being refined through their physical activity. They are capable of "acting out" various mathematical concepts or problem solving situations. For example, children can "race" from point A to point B as they are gathering data concerning the time it takes to run or walk at a quick pace between the two points.

Attention spans are increasing to perhaps 10–15 minutes before moving on to another activity, which enables them to sit for longer periods of instructional time. Also, one can often notice interests emerging and learning preferences being exhibited.

Typical four- and five-year-old children are growing and developing physically, socially, emotionally, and cognitively. Successful prekindergarten and kindergarten programs focus on the general developmental characteristics of four- and five-year-old children and instruct them so as to capitalize on their natural curiosity, attention-span capacity, and level of activity.

GENERAL CHARACTERISTICS OF SIX-, SEVEN-, AND EIGHT-YEAR-OLD CHILDREN

Six-, seven-, and eight-year-old children are curious learners who enjoy concrete, hands-on experiences with learning. They are energetic and need opportunities in the classroom to move around. They enjoy experimenting and can learn from reflecting on what they have done. This age group enjoys imaginative play, and they can participate in puppet shows, dramatize stories, or act out word problems in mathematics. They are learning to think logically and organize concepts symbolically (Bickart et al., 1999).

Cognitively, six-year-old children are still operating in the preoperational stage of development. As they progress towards age seven, they are transitioning into Piaget's concrete operational stage of cognitive development, the stage that covers primary- and elementary-aged children. Although children in this stage are beginning to think logically, their thinking is not as systematic or abstract as the thinking of an adult. As children's logical thinking skills develop, they no longer solve problems merely using visual and perceptual information (Geist, 2009).

Important thinking capabilities, mathematically, that six-, seven-, and eight-year-old children develop include conservation, trial-and-error thinking, the ability to play games with rules, reversibility of thought, and more complex classification skills (Geist, 2009). Children who are conservers are able to take the same amount of a substance and understand that the amount of substance does not change as its shape changes. They can think logically that the amount must be the same. Children who are not able to conserve only focus on one aspect of the substance. They think that there is more or less of the substance based on appearance. Mathematically, children who conserve understand that the number 10 is still the number 10 regardless of the numeral combinations that make the number. For example, children who conserve know that $5 + 5$, $6 + 4$, $7 + 3$, $2 + 8$, $9 + 1$, and $10 + 0$ all make combinations of the number 10. They also understand that a circle is a circle regardless of its orientation in the real world. In other words, one can find circles in many different places.

Children's logical thinking allows them to approach mathematical problem solving situations using a variety of methods. If a problem does not work out one way, they can try another way to solve the problem. Children not exhibiting this flexibility in problem solving approaches try to solve a problem one way; if that does not work, they ask for help or merely give up trying to solve the problem.

With the new sense of logic exhibited in the concrete operation stage of cognitive development comes the ability to play board games and games of sports that require playing by the rules. Children learn that everything has an explanation and that things happen for a reason (Geist, 2009). This is important mathematically, as children work with numerical patterns, concepts of geometry, and algorithms for operations with numbers.

Reversibility of thought refers to a child's ability to think in two directions at the same time (Geist, 2009). For example, in thinking about a "family" of numbers that make a math fact—for example, 4, 5, and 9—children need to think about the "whole," or the number 9, and the parts that make up the number 9, the numbers 4 and 5. This is especially important, as children are working with subtraction facts. They are required to consider the "whole," or the number being subtracted from, and the part that is being subtracted from the "whole."

This ability to think in two directions simultaneously allows children the ability to classify objects using a more complex classification scheme. Children come to understand that an object can fit into or be classified into two categories. For example, in an activity involving sorting buttons, a child would be able to understand that a shank button, one sorting classification, could also fit into the classification under red buttons, a second sorting classification.

MATHEMATICS LEARNING IN THE PRIMARY GRADES

Once children enter kindergarten in most public schools, their mathematics curriculum at each grade level is determined by the school district's standards-based mathematics curriculum. A stipulation of No Child Left Behind (United States Congress, 2001) is that school districts utilizing federal funds are responsible for developing challenging state standards along with rigorous tests to assess how well children are meeting the standards. Many states are now in the process of transitioning to the *Common Core State Standards*. The National Council of Teachers of Mathematics' *Principles and Standards for School Mathematics* (2000) document is foundational in the development of state standards. The most recent document from the National Council of Teachers of Mathematics, *Curriculum Focal Points for Prekindergarten through Grade 8 Mathematics: A Quest for Coherence* (2006) is also influential in determining appropriate mathematics content for various grade levels.

HOME/SCHOOL/COMMUNITY CONNECTION

The ideal learning situation for any age group of children is to have a strong home/school connection as part of their education and general well-being. "Ongoing parental involvement—as in any subject—can provide a solid foundation for children's learning and attitudes" (Kliman, 1999). A good connection between home and school provides children with support in what they are learning and extends learning to their world outside of the classroom. Children who "practice," explore, investigate, and extend what they are learning to their home environment are being provided with the optimal educational experience.

Additionally, getting involved in the community also helps children build mathematical understanding beyond the classroom. Children need opportunities to extend what they are learning mathematically to the natural environment. They also need opportunities to get out into their neighborhoods and communities and experience local businesses and other buildings, science centers, museums, colleges and universities, and places where maps are available for them to view and utilize (Seefeldt, Galper, & Stevenson-Garcia, 2011).

It is important to provide parents and guardians with venues to share their thoughts, ideas, and the activities they do with their child to support their child's growth and development. There are many ways in which teachers can extend classroom activities and learning into the home setting and give parents/guardians a sharing voice. The following are some ways to accomplish this:

1. Family/teacher conferences
2. Weekly, bi-weekly, or monthly newsletters
3. School information websites
4. Bulletin boards and other displays
5. Take-home activities to do with family members or guardians
6. Parent-share meetings
7. Family-share websites
8. Open house
9. In some cases, home visits
10. Math family fun nights
11. Mathematical terms that families can use, discuss, and describe
12. Games and activities that can be sent home for families to play.

For more suggestions for family engagement information and activities, please see Couchenour and Chrisman (2011, pp. 237–239).

IMPLICATIONS FOR TEACHING MATHEMATICS TO BUILD CONNECTIONS

Teachers should not be afraid to be creative in finding ways to make home/school/community connections. As they plan math lessons for their students, teachers should be encouraged to think "outside the box" when it comes to homework assignments and other ways to extend what children are learning in the classroom to the real world. For example, instead of sending home a worksheet on which children will be completing patterns, ask children to look for patterns in their home environment, make a drawing of a pattern they discovered, and bring it to school the next day. The whole family can get involved in this assignment. The teacher can then have the children work with these patterns in many different ways. In this way children "own" the patterns they are describing, duplicating, and extending. Another idea would be to take children on a pattern walk around the school or community, if possible. Again, children could record the patterns they are discovering. These patterns could be displayed on a classroom bulletin board and/or shared on the classroom webpage, where applicable.

Teachers can also create hands-on storybook activities that focus on a specific math concept or skill. After reading a math-related storybook in class, the teacher would provide parents/guardians with a synopsis of the story. At home, children would review the story with family members and then complete the activity. Again, this could be an activity the whole family could enjoy.

Once teachers begin thinking creatively about the math content and skills children are learning, ideas for making home/school/community connections are endless.

CREATING A CLASSROOM FOCUSED ON DIVERSITY

We live in a multiethnic, multicultural, and multi-ability society. It is important for teachers to treat all children as individuals and be sensitive to individual needs and differences as they plan mathematics lessons for diverse populations of students. Eliason and Jenkins (2012) outline goals they see as important for teaching diverse students. These include:

1. All children must be given opportunities to reach their potential regardless of their gender, social class, religion, race, ethnic group, or physical or mental abilities.
2. All children should feel included and valued as worthy members of the class and of society.
3. Children should be helped to clarify and feel positive toward their own identity, including their sex, ethnic background, race, and physical abilities.
4. Children can learn to take the perspective of children who are different from themselves.
5. The diversity perspective should be integrated into all aspects of the school or program.

(2012, pp. 97–99)

Eliason and Jenkins (2012) state that "teachers must diligently strive to overcome intentional and unintentional . . . bias in classrooms so that *all* their students will feel important, respected, and equal to their peers" (p. 100). It is important for teachers of all age groups to make sure all children, including both boys and girls, are provided with equal opportunities and high expectations in learning mathematics. Biases can take many forms and can include stereotyping, inequitable attention, dividing students by gender or racial/ethnic groups, linguistic biases found within curriculum materials, and discriminating words heard in teacher conversations (Eliason & Jenkins, 2012). Biases can also surface in the form of behavior expectations.

The use of unfounded stereotypes concerning gender—girls are good at linguistic skills, but bad at math and science; and boys are good at math and science, but bad at linguistic skills—have no place in educational settings or in society in general. Girls and boys may show varying academic strengths at different ages, but this should not become a stereotypical rule.

Teachers, during conferences with parents/guardians, should encourage mastery of mathematics concepts and skills for all children. Some parents/guardians may attend a conference holding to the old stereotype concerning girls not being as good at learning math and science. Some females may even confess to not ever being good at math themselves, giving the impression that it is OK for girls to experience the same. Teachers have the opportunity to re-educate parents/guardians in believing that all children, including girls, can accomplish math as well as boys, and that they should have high expectations for achievement in mathematics regardless of gender, ethnic background, socio-economic status, or race.

No child should feel like he or she is invisible in the classroom. Sometimes girls or other children in the classroom are willing to take a "back seat" in learning situations and accept their passive role as the norm. Teachers should encourage active participation from each child, regardless of gender, race, ethnic background, or socio-economic status. One way to ensure that all girls and boys are experiencing equal attention is to use alternating patterns when calling on students to answer or ask questions and to participate in discussions. To ensure that all students are equally provided with opportunities to participate in learning, teachers sometimes have students' names written on popsicle sticks, which are then divided into containers labeled "girls" and "boys." A girl/boy pattern for pulling popsicle sticks can be utilized in this way. In addition to patterns of calling on students, seating arrangements should guarantee that students are mixed. Teachers should be careful in forming groups so they are not forming groups by gender, race, or ethnic background—mixed groups are always the preference.

Learning materials, curriculum materials, and manipulatives should be bias-free. Classroom pictures/posters and resource materials should provide "equal" time to genders, ethnic groups, and races. Do the pictures/posters and other materials used in the math class reflect content that is interesting and relevant to both genders and all groups of students? In other words, all children should be able to identify with materials used and displayed in the classroom.

Two areas often overlooked in considering biases are the language teachers use and math problems they create for children to solve. Oftentimes, unknowingly, teachers may refer to engineers, doctors, and mathematicians as "he" and nurses and secretaries as "she." Left unchecked, these kinds of stereotypes are projected onto students. Being young and impressionable, children come to believe them as being true. Along the same line, teachers need to make sure they create bias-neutral math problems for their students to solve.

The key to classroom equity is to treat all children with respect and sensitivity, and to have high academic and behavior expectations for all. This includes giving all children adequate "wait time" before requiring them to answer questions, and giving all children equal feedback and equal speaking and participation time.

CHILDREN WITH SPECIAL NEEDS

As a teacher of any age group of children, it is important to "see" each child as an individual person and learner. All children do not have the same capabilities or learn exactly the same way or at the same rate. In instructing a community of individual learners, a teacher needs to learn each child's "story" and meet the individual needs of each child. Oftentimes this entails making adaptations in instructional plans for individual learners, so they can participate in learning activities and not feel ostracized from the rest of the children due to a specific disability. For example, an adaptation may need to be made for a child in a wheelchair so that he or she can participate in an activity. A child constricted to a wheelchair should never be told to just watch and not be able to participate. This is true of children with any special needs.

It is important for teachers to be educated in working with children with special needs, and in planning and adapting instructional strategies and classroom management styles that best meet the needs of the diverse population of children in prekindergarten and kindergarten programs and in the primary grades in school. "A culture of equity does not mean using the same curriculum, teaching practices, or contexts with all students. What must be offered to all students are high expectations for success and opportunities to learn challenging mathematics" (NCTM, 2000, p. 1).

Ryan and Cooper (2007) identified specific disabilities among children as:

1. Specific learning disabilities
2. Speech or language impairments
3. Mental retardation (1–3 implications for teaching math)
4. Emotional disturbance
5. Health impairments
6. Autism
7. Orthopedic impairments
8. Hearing impairments
9. Developmental delays
10. Visual impairments
11. Traumatic brain injury
12. Deaf-blindness
13. Multiple disabilities.

(2007, p. 65)

IMPLICATIONS FOR TEACHING MATHEMATICS TO CHILDREN WITH SPECIAL NEEDS

An all-inclusive learning environment should be the goal of every classroom. Planning adaptations when creating math lessons for children is the norm, since children are all individual human beings, and a one-size-fits-all mentality is not appropriate in meeting the needs of a diverse population of children. Also, many children enter classrooms with an Individual Education Plan (IEP). Teachers need to make sure they are following educational plans in meeting the needs of specific students.

An important goal of mathematics education for all children, including those children dealing with disabilities, is to understand what mathematic concepts mean and be able to apply them in the context of the real world (NCTM, 2000). Miller and Hudson (2006) discuss five, evidence-based guidelines in helping children, especially those with disabilities, understand mathematic concepts. These guidelines include:

1. **Use various modes of representation by presenting concepts in multiple ways.**
   The model calls for children to first experience the concept in a concrete form using dramatization or physical actions. After children understand the concept at the concrete level, the teacher would then move them to the representational level where they would perhaps use manipulatives or draw pictures pertaining to the concept. Last, children would move to the abstract level, where they would just use numbers (Miller & Hudson, 2006).

2. **Consider and use appropriate lesson structures in helping children understand mathematical concepts.**
   There is so much for a teacher to consider in planning a math lesson for children. The teacher, using knowledge about the diverse learning needs of the students in the classroom, needs to think of the best ways to demonstrate the concept to the children and how best to use manipulatives, picture representations, and diagrams and graphs. This also includes the different ways the lesson will be presented, along with how the children will practice the concept. Will the children practice individually, in pairs, or in small groups? Lesson structures could include: the compare/contrast model in helping children recognize similarities and differences; the example/non-example model in helping children recognize and discriminate various representations of the concept (e.g., circle/not a circle); and the step-by-step model (Miller & Hudson, 2006). This model has proven to be successful with children dealing with "memory or organizational-thinking deficits" (p. 31).

3. **Consider the language particular to mathematic concepts.**
   It was once believed that learning mathematics was independent of language. Thinking in this area has changed drastically. The thinking process in solving math problems is greatly connected to the language of mathematics, which is unique to its discipline. It is important that children learn and understand vocabulary words and language specifically associated with mathematical concepts. Teachers can support the learning of math language by using pictures, gestures, and actions to depict words and concepts. They can: demonstrate the word with a physical action (walking the perimeter of a room or shape); dramatize solving a problem (I have three pencils; if I add four more pencils to the ones I already have, I now have seven pencils); drawing pictures of vocabulary words (e.g., draw various shapes in a math journal); and find pictures to represent the word (Miller & Hudson, 2006).

4. **Integrating the mathematical concepts children are learning in their classroom with real-world applications.**
   Helping children connect what mathematical concepts they are learning in their classroom to application in the real world provides legitimacy for children in why

they are learning the concept, skill, or content. Young children do not have the maturity or experience to make these connections for themselves, so it becomes the responsibility of the teacher to help them see how the mathematics they are learning is used in everyday life (Miller & Hudson, 2006). Teachers can be creative in assigning homework assignments. If possible, they can plan field trips into the community, where mathematical concepts can be applied. They can invite guests into the classroom to inform children of the ways they use math in their daily lives or in doing their jobs. Teachers, along with their students, can create their own real-world problems to solve. Finally, teachers can use technology by finding software for children that engages them in simulated, real-world problem solving (Miller & Hudson, 2006).

5. **Provide explicit instruction for children in helping them learn complex concepts.** The literature on mathematics instruction and literature pertaining to content area instruction for students with disabilities "indicates that students need explicit instruction to promote their understanding of difficult concepts and related skills" (Miller & Hudson, 2006, p. 33). Explicit instruction includes the use of an advanced organizer to provide a review of the pertinent knowledge, the objective for the day's lesson, and a rationale for learning the new content. It also includes the teacher demonstrating the concept or skill ("I do" phase); the "we do" phase, which includes a great deal of teacher support as students practice the concept or skill; and finally the "you do" phase, during which time the students practice independently (Miller & Hudson, 2006).

MATHEMATICALLY PROMISING CHILDREN

Also referred to as mathematically gifted students, these children also fall under the category of children with special needs. Wilkins, Wilkins, and Oliver (2006) emphasize the need for making accommodations in the mathematics curriculum for these children so they are appropriately challenged. Accommodations should move gifted children, as well as all children, "beyond computation into higher-order mathematical thinking processes" (p. 7).

It is important for teachers to identify children who are "mathematically promising students." Identifying children at the prekindergarten and kindergarten levels who may have high potential in mathematics may present more challenges than in higher primary grades. As teachers observe children in learning centers, the play area, or during discussion times, the following questions can be considered:

1. Does the child sort objects in ways other children do not seem to recognize or consider?
2. Does the child seem to have ability to count much higher than others (or count backwards or skip-count)?
3. Does the child provide explanations in greater detail and with more complex mathematical ideas than other children?
4. Is the child able to solve problems quicker and with less effort than other children?
5. Does the child generate multiple solutions when solving problems, participating in activities, or when engaged with peers (puzzles, constructions, drawing, representing, etc.)?

6. Does the child consistently ask why and seek deeper meaning in problem solving situations?

Specific examples may include higher skills in counting money when playing at the store center or recognizing higher numbers than other children can count. The mathematically promising students may be able to add three or more addends when others in the classroom are working on understanding adding two addends to compute a sum. Regardless of the activity, the key is, does the child stand out in the teacher's mind as academically and conceptually above the other children when involved in mathematics activities?

Additional questions to consider when observing and assessing children in grades two and three could include:

1. Does the child consistently perform high on formal, summative assessments?
2. Is the child a consistent performer on classroom quizzes?
3. When pretests are administered, does the child appear to already know the material?
4. Are the child's report grades consistently high?
5. Are former teachers in agreement that the child exceeds expectations mathematically?

It is important to hold high expectations for all children and challenge children as they are learning. This is especially important for children who have demonstrated exceptional mathematical aptitude. Adaptations to instruction may need to be made in order to challenge these children.

Types of adaptations for mathematically promising children could include:

1. Integrating mathematics with science and/or social studies
2. Making literature connections to math content
3. Engaging children in building projects
4. Encouraging children to play math games that involve strategizing to develop problem solving skills
5. Providing children with different types of logic puzzles and games
6. Involving children in collecting, tabulating, and graphing data.

(adapted from Wilkins, Wilkins, & Oliver, 2006)

IMPLICATIONS FOR TEACHING MATHEMATICS

Mathematically promising students could possibly be some of the most unchallenged learners in classrooms. It is not unusual for more capable students in mathematics to finish their work quickly and then sit quietly waiting for others to finish, help others, work ahead in workbooks, read, or do additional problems of the same type. All children, including those who are mathematically promising, need to be challenged at their level of understanding, performance, and capabilities. There are some benefits to be gleaned in having mathematically promising students help their classmates— what we can teach to others, we understand even better ourselves. This should not, however, be the major portion of mathematics instruction for these students. Using the suggestions stated above and other creative ideas, teachers could create a menu of choices for mathematically promising students so that they are continually challenged and progressing in their knowledge, understanding, and application of mathematic concepts.

ENGLISH LANGUAGE LEARNERS (ELL)

Because we live in a multicultural society, many children who are entering preschool and primary school programs may not speak English or are learning English as their second language. These children are referred to as English Language Learners (ELLs). In an inclusive community of learners, children who are learning English at any developmental level need to feel cared for, supported, and valued. As with children who have special needs or disabilities, adaptations for English Language Learners need to be made in planning program activities and instruction. Self-confidence and self-esteem in ELLs can be supported by ensuring that every possible effort is being made to help these children understand what is being said and happening in the classroom and in feeling valued as an individual learner.

IMPLICATIONS FOR TEACHING MATHEMATICS TO ENGLISH LANGUAGE LEARNERS

The same instructional strategies that were recommended for children with special needs are also appropriate in teaching mathematics to English Language Learners. To recap, five evidence-based guidelines were introduced by Miller and Hudson (2006) in teaching math concepts and skills to children with special needs. These included: using various modes of representation, considering lesson structures that best meet the needs of the students, teaching the language of mathematics, extending mathematics concept to real-world applications, and providing explicit instruction. Additionally, Garrison (1997) discusses the benefits of small-group work for emergent English speakers. Many children who are learning a second language may be hesitant in speaking in front of a classroom of peers. Small-group work affords these students a more comfortable venue in which to speak with classmates, problem solve, and share what they are learning. Having all children keep math journals is important in helping them practice communicating mathematically. A suggestion for ELLs might be to allow them to explain themselves in their native language as they are learning English. A problem-based approach in which problems are drawn from the students' backgrounds is also beneficial in teaching emergent English learners (Garrison, 1997). This approach provides context-rich problems for students, which could help to pique their interest. As with all children, English Language Learners need to understand how mathematical concepts are linked or connected and move beyond computational skills to problem solving that requires complexity of thought.

LEARNING STYLES AND MULTIPLE INTELLIGENCES

We do not all learn the same way, and we do not all have the same interests or learning preferences. Teachers need to learn how each of the children in their classrooms learns best and offer activities that contain an element of each learning style. Ryan and Cooper define learning styles as the following:

There exist a number of different theories and models of learning styles. One approach looks at four modalities for learning: visual (seeing), auditory (hearing), kinesthetic (moving) or tactile (touching) and is based on the idea that different people prefer different modes of learning . . . Other models look at learning styles for processing information. For example, some learners absorb information concretely and in a sequential manner. Other learners focus more on ideas and abstractions, while still others like to learn socially.

(2007, p. 64)

An additional consideration in planning instructional activities for children involves consideration of Howard Gardner's multiple intelligences. Gardner (1993) proclaims that linguistic and analytical abilities are only two facets of intelligence. He has identified and defined eight intelligences, which include:

1. Verbal/linguistic intelligence (ability to use language, oral and written)
2. Logical-mathematical intelligence (ability to understand causal systems; manipulate number quantities and operations)
3. Spatial intelligence (ability to visualize the spatial world in the mind's eye)
4. Bodily-kinesthetic intelligence (ability to use the whole body or parts of the body in problem solving or performing)
5. Musical intelligence (ability to operate musically)
6. Interpersonal intelligence (ability to understand other people)
7. Intrapersonal intelligence (ability to understand oneself)
8. Naturalistic intelligence (ability to discriminate among living things).

IMPLICATIONS FOR TEACHING MATHEMATICS

It is important for preservice teachers to know their personal preferred learning style(s). The reason is that, as teachers, we tend to teach the way we prefer to learn. This means that teachers who are auditory learners will have a tendency to do a lot of talking during their mathematics lessons. This may be fine for children in the classroom who learn well through listening; however, visual, kinesthetic, and textile learners could be lost as the lesson proceeds, because that is not their preferred learning style. It is important for teachers, in planning lessons, to consider the preferred learning styles of the students in the classroom and factor this information into the structure of the lesson. For example, during a mathematics lesson on basic shapes (circle, square, triangle, rectangle), a teacher would display the shapes (visual learners), talk about their characteristics or attributes (auditory learners), allow the children to handle the various shapes (textile learners), and walk around the classroom looking for the basic shapes in objects in the classroom (kinesthetic learners). This last step also connects learning about the basic shapes to real-world applications.

Likewise, teachers should analyze their personal multiple-intelligence strengths, since teachers could have a tendency to structure lessons according to their own strengths. For example, teachers with verbal/linguistic intelligence may prefer to have students discuss and then describe the function of the minute hand and hour hand on a clock in their journals. While journal writing is a worthwhile educational exercise, students could also learn about the functions of the hands on a clock through rhymes, songs, raps, or physically being one of the hands on a floor-model clock. Teachers, in knowing their students, can plan flexible mathematics lessons that tap into their students' natural, multiple-intelligence strengths.

INTEGRATING THE CURRICULUM

Integrating mathematics with other subject areas provides children with an enriching perspective on the many ways that mathematics can be applied in the real world. Geist states:

> The traditional method of learning subjects in isolation does not reflect how mathematics is used in real-life situations. Finding time during lessons or the school day to show how subjects overlap and support each other is vital to developing students that learn how to apply knowledge, not just repeat information by rote.
>
> (2009, p. 350)

Geist refers to the real-life application of mathematics as horizontal relevance (2009, p. 350). When children understand the horizontal relevance of what they are learning, they can apply their problem solving skills both within and outside the classroom. They are not just learning knowledge about mathematics for the sake of learning it; they are learning mathematics in order to be able to use it.

The resourceful teacher will find ways to integrate subject areas. These could include integrating mathematics with reading, science, social studies, music, art, technology, and physical activity. For example, a storybook read by children in a primary classroom may be a beginning point for collecting data related to the storyline, recording the data, graphing the data, and interpreting the results. There are resources available that provide teachers with ideas for integrating subject areas. These include:

Literature-Based Activities for Integrating Mathematics with Other Content Areas K-2 by Robin A. Ward
(Allyn & Bacon, 2008)
Integrating the Arts Across the Elementary School Curriculum (2nd ed.) by R. P. Gelineau
(Wadsworth Publishing, 2011)
Hands-On Math Projects with Real-Life Applications, Grades 3–5 by J. S. Muschala and G. R. Muschala
(Jossey-Bass, 2009)
Activities Linking Science with Math K–4 by J. Eichinger
(NSTA Press, 2009)

CHILDREN'S LITERATURE

Young children and storybooks belong together. Children love to have storybooks read to them, and oftentimes a favorite storybook is read over and over because of the fascination with the story and/or pictures in the storybook. Teachers of prekindergarten, kindergarten, and primary-aged schoolchildren can capitalize on young children's love of storybooks and use stories to extend or enrich what the children are learning mathematically or in any content area.

The benefits of children's literature in an instructional program are many. Whitin and Wilde (1995) proclaim that mathematics arises out of human activity and that many stories illustrate good mathematics being used. Stories often provide a context that provides meaning and understanding. Children's literature can provide a bridge between what is being learned in a classroom and the real world. Storybooks help connect mathematics to children's lives and provide mathematical reasoning from a variety of perspectives.

It is important to include storybooks that have a multicultural perspective in programs for young children. Children need to see themselves in the cultures represented in the storybooks, and they also need to see others who are different from themselves in the literature. Teachers can help children realize that people in all cultures "do" mathematics.

Throughout the mathematics content chapters in the text, Chapters 3–7, the authors use storybooks in various ways in their sample activities and lesson plans.

VOCABULARY DEVELOPMENT

With the publication of *Curriculum and Evaluation Standards for School Mathematics* by the National Council of Teachers of Mathematics in 1989, new guidelines were set for mathematics curriculum and instruction. One profound change in instruction focused on emphasizing communication; thus language has become one of the central foci when instructing children in mathematics concepts. Children are expected to speak and write mathematically about what they understand conceptually and the methods they use in solving problems. This is a new component in mathematics instruction that goes beyond just learning computational skills (Garrison, 1997).

Garrison offers suggestions to help children, especially emergent English speakers, learn mathematical content vocabulary words. She offers the following:

1. Introduce vocabulary families or groups of related words so children can make connections among the words. For example, measurement words, such as inch, foot, yard, can be introduced together.
2. Introduce vocabulary through a variety of visual methods. These could include making models, drawing diagrams or other pictures, and making displays.
3. For emergent English speakers, vocabulary words should be introduced in both English and the students' first language, when possible.
4. Use hand gestures when talking about mathematics vocabulary. For example, when talking about a triangle, a teacher can trace a 1 in the air or make 1 with his or her fingers. The children could do the same.
5. Have children pantomime or act out vocabulary words.
6. Construct and label mathematical vocabulary in the classroom.
7. Use manipulatives when demonstrating vocabulary words, and allow children to manipulate them as well.

LEARNING CENTERS

Activity ideas in subsequent chapters sometimes refer to providing specific items for children to use in a learning center. Many teachers divide the classroom into specific areas and refer to these areas as learning centers. Examples of learning centers could be a book center, computer center, writing center, block center, sand/water center, largemotor center, art center, music center, dramatic play center, table games or puzzle center, and manipulative/math center. There are many other possibilities depending on the focus of learning during a specific period of time in the classroom.

Learning centers are determined by curricular topics and child development objectives such as social, emotional, physical, cognitive, language, and creative development. Materials define the center, and children are provided with everything they need to go about using it. For example, after reading a storybook about patterns on butterfly wings, kindergarten children in a center could sort pictures of butterfly patterns, create their own wing patterns with blocks, bendable sticks or playdough, or locate wing patterns in other books and magazines. The curricular topic of the learning center is patterning; however, the children are also practicing fine motor skills and problem solving as they handle materials.

During center time, children can move from one center to another to complete the activities. Learning centers are changed periodically to reflect changes in curricular topics, to practice the standards included in the center through developmental activities (Beaty, 2009). Other ideas for math centers and math stations may be found in publications such as *Math Work Stations* (Diller, 2011).

Intentionally planning for math concepts during center times still allows for children to play with those math concepts. The benefits of play have recently been researched by Elena Bodrova and Deborah Leong (2003). Their findings indicate that play builds executive functions and self-regulation. These skills help children to organize, stay within roles (tasks), and manage their own materials and space.

ADDITIONAL RESOURCES

Teachers have a vast array of options available to them via the Internet for finding mathematics ideas and activities appropriate for prekindergarten and kindergarten children. The following are professional sites and resources to consider.

Gadzinowski, A. (2013). *Challenging exceptionally bright children in early childhood classrooms* (see chapter 7). St. Paul, MN: Redleaf.

National Council of Teachers of Mathematics (NCTM)
http://standards.nctm.org/document/eexamples/index.htm
This site provides electronic examples of age appropriate activities for young children.

http://illuminations.nctm.org/
This site offers insights into ways to illuminate the NCTM academic standards for mathematics instruction. It contains links to activities, lessons, standards, and weblinks for hundreds of exemplary online resources as identified by an editorial panel of NCTM.

National Association for the Education of Young Children (NAEYC)
http://www.naeyc.org/families/
This site is devoted to parents and guardians. The resources are meant to support them in early childhood education and parenting.

An Internet Site to Consider

http://www.jacketflap.com/index.asp

This site provides a resource for information concerning authors, illustrators, and publishers of books for children.

REFERENCES

Beaty, J. J. (2009). *Preschool Appropriate Practices* (3rd ed.). Clifton Park, NY: Delmar Cengage Learning.

Bickart, T. S., Jablon, J. R. & Dodge, D. T. (1999). *Building the primary classroom: A complete guide to teaching and learning.* Washington, D. C.: Teaching Strategies, Inc.; Portsmouth, NH: Heinemann.

Bodrova, E. & Leong, D. (2003). The importance of being playful. *Educational Leadership, Association for Curriculum and Development,* 60(9), 50–53.

Charlesworth, R. (2005). *Experiences in Math for Young Children* (5th ed.). Clifton Park, NY: Delmar Learning.

Common Core State Standards Initiative: Preparing America's Students for College & Career (2010). Released by the National Governors Association Center for Best Practices and the Council of Chief State School Officers.

Couchenour, D. & Chrisman, K. (2011). *Families, Schools, and Communities: Together for Young Children* (4th ed.). Belmont, CA: Wadsworth.

Copley, J. (2011). *The Young Child and Mathematics* (2nd ed.). Washington, D.C.: National Association for the Education of Young Children.

Copple, C. & Bredekamp, S. (Eds.). (2009). *Developmentally Appropriate Practice in Early Childhood Programs: Serving Children From Birth Through Age 8* (3rd ed.). Washington, D. C.: National Association for the Education of Young Children.

Diller, D. (2011). *Math Work Stations: Independent Learning You Can Count On, K-2.* Portland, ME: Stenhouse Publishers.

Eliason, C. & Jenkins, L. (2012). *A Practical Guide to Early Childhood Curriculum* (9th ed.). Upper Saddle River, NJ: Pearson.

Gardner, H. (1993). *Multiple Intelligences: The Theory in Practice.* NY, NY: Basic Books.

Garrison, L. (1997). Making the NCTM standards fork for emergent English speakers. *Teaching Children Mathematics,* November, 132–138.

Geist, E. (2009). *Children are Born Mathematicians: Supporting Mathematical Development, Birth to Age 8.* Upper Saddle River, NJ: Pearson.

Kliman, M. (1999). Beyond helping with homework: Parents and children doing mathematics at home. *Teaching Children Mathematics,* November, 140–146.

Miller, S. P. & Hudson, P. J. (2006). Helping students with disabilities understand what mathematics means. *Teaching Children Mathematics,* Sept/Oct, 28–35.

National Association for the Education of Young Children (NAEYC) (Adopted in 2009). *Developmentally Appropriate Practice in Early Childhood Programs Serving Children From Birth Through Age 8* (Position Statement). Washington, D. C.: Author.

National Association for the Education of Young Children (NAEYC) & National Council of Teachers of Mathematics (NCTM). (Adopted in 2002; Updated in 2010). *Early Childhood Mathematics: Promoting Good Beginnings* (NAEYC/NCTM Joint Position Statement). Washington, D. C.: Authors.

National Council of Teachers of Mathematics (NCTM) (1989). *Curriculum and Evaluation Standards for School Mathematics.* Reston, VA: Author.

National Council of Teachers of Mathematics (NCTM) (2000). *Principles and Standards for School Mathematics.* Reston, VA: Author. http://www.nctm.org/standards/content.aspx?id=4294967312.

National Council of Teachers of Mathematics (NCTM) (2006). *Curriculum Focal Points for Prekindergarten Through Grade 8 Mathematics: A Quest for Coherence.* Reston, VA: Author.

National Council of Teachers of Mathematics (NCTM) (September, 2008). "What is equity in mathematics education?" (News Bulletin). Reston, VA: Author.

Oesterreich, L. (1995). Ages & stages – four-year-olds. In L. Oesterreich, B. Holt, & S. Karas, *Iowa Family Child Care Handbook* [Pm 1541] (pp. 204–207). Ames, IA: Iowa State University Extension. (Reprinted with permission from the National Network for Child Care.) Website: http//: www.nncc.org/Child.Dev/ages.stages.4y.html

Ryan, K. & Cooper, J. M. (2007). *Those Who Can, Teach* (11th ed.). NY: Houghton Mifflin.

Seefeldt, C., Galper, A. & Stevenson-Garcia, J. (2011). *Active Experiences for Active Children: Mathematics.* Upper Saddle River, NJ: Pearson.

Sousa, D. A. (2008). *How the Brain Learns Mathematics.* Thousand Oaks, CA: Corwin Press.

Taylor, B. J. (1999). *A Child Goes Forth: A Curriculum Guide for Preschool Children* (9th ed.). Upper Saddle River, NJ: Prentice Hall.

United States Congress (2001). *No Child Left Behind.* Pub. L. 107–110. Washington, D.C.: U.S. Government Printing Office.

Whitin, D. J. & Wilde, S. (1995). *It's the Story that Counts: MORE Children's Books for Mathematical Learning, K-6.* Portsmouth, NH: Heinmann.

Wilkins, M. M., Wilkins, J. L. M. & Oliver, T. (2006). Differentiating the curriculum for elementary gifted mathematics students. *Teaching Children Mathematics*, 13 (10), 6–13.

2

MATHEMATICS CURRICULA FOR YOUNG CHILDREN, STANDARDS, AND ASSESSMENT

The National Association for the Education of Young Children (NAEYC) and the National Council of Teachers of Mathematics (NCTM), in a joint position statement (2002/2010, p. 3), have made the following recommendations related to the teaching of mathematics with young children.

In high-quality mathematics education for three- to-six-year-old children, teachers and other key professionals should:

- Enhance children's natural interest in mathematics and their disposition to use it to make sense of their physical worlds.
- Build on children's varying experiences, including their family, linguistic, and cultural backgrounds; their individual approaches to learning; and their informal knowledge.
- Base mathematical curriculum and teaching practices on current knowledge of young children's cognitive, linguistic, physical, and social-emotional development.
- Use curriculum and teaching practices that strengthen children's problem solving and reasoning processes as well as representing, communicating and connecting mathematical ideas.
- Ensure that the curriculum is coherent and compatible with known relationships and sequences of important mathematical ideas.
- Provide for children's deep and sustained interaction with key mathematical ideas.
- Integrate mathematics with other activities and other activities with mathematics.
- Provide ample time materials, teacher support for children to engage in play, a context in which they explore, and manipulate mathematical ideas with keen interest.
- Actively introduce mathematical concepts, methods and language through a range of appropriate experiences and teaching strategies.
- Support children's learning by thoughtfully and continually assessing all children's mathematical knowledge, skills and strategies.

Mathematical Thinking

Ginsburg, Lee, and Boyd (2008) have identified major factors in the development of children's thinking. One of those factors is the distinction between simply learning a few counting words and understanding the significance of numbers on a number line (and how to use them). Another major factor is the ability of some children to be aware of their mathematical thinking and to verbalize that thinking.

Consider these recommendations as you read the following sections of this chapter.

THE COMPONENTS OF EFFECTIVE MATH CURRICULA IN EARLY CHILDHOOD PROGRAMS

Ginsburg et al. (2008) have identified six major components of mathematics education typically found in early childhood programs. Table 2.1 lists these components with a brief description of each and the ways they may be used in preschool, child care or primary grades. The critique provided shows some concern about overreliance on using only one method or strategy.

The six components included in the chart may be viewed as a framework as you read the following chapters. Consider this additional information below about each component:

1. **Environment** includes materials, equipment, the daily schedule, and the interactions during the day. Preparing the environment in ways that challenge children, engage them in problem solving and provide ways to support their learning will have a significant impact on their learning of mathematical concepts.
   Implications and Examples for Teaching Mathematics:

   A. Set up specific areas in the room for math
      Examples: table games area for sequencing, counting, shapes, puzzles, etc.
   B. Math terms are visible in many areas of the classroom
      Examples: numbered cubbies, lunch count charts, graphs showing children's interests
   C. Highlight math language throughout the day
      Examples: sing songs in group times with math terms, use math terms during transition activities, take math cards/games outside

2. **Play** is often misunderstood as a powerful teaching tool. The latest research by Bodrova and Leong (2003) has shown that high-quality play provides children with self-regulation and executive functioning skills. (Self-regulation/executive functioning is defined as the ability to regulate one's own social, emotional and cognitive behaviors; Bodrova & Leong, 2007). These skills will help children focus on math concepts and better understand both the big ideas and the details.
   Implications and Examples for Teaching Mathematics:

   A. Set up multiple areas in the room that incorporate math play
      Examples: dramatic play areas with cash registers, menus with numbers, groceries with price tags, use blocks to measure and weigh, place-counting books with puppets in a library area, etc. (Bodrova & Leong, 2003)

Table 2.1 Six Components of Early Childhood Mathematics Education (ECME)

Components	Brief Description	Ways to Implement	Critique
Environment	Providing a rich variety of materials and equipment for math exploration (refer to the Environmental Rate Scale; Harms, Clifford, & Cryer, 2005).	Children's mathematical thinking is supported during multiple times of the day and places in the room.	Support for children's mathematical thinking must be extensive in the environment.
Play	Provides many valuable opportunities for mathematical intellectual development, especially in block center play.	Play can provide many materials in learning centers, group times, and small-group activities.	Must help children connect their experiences in play to mathematical forms and terms.
Teachable Moment	Teacher's observations of children's mathematical understanding.	Teacher listens, observes and notes patterns, insights, or problems in children's mathematical thinking.	Teachers need practice and developmental knowledge to use this approach.
Projects	Activities that involve measurement, space, perspective, representation, and other mathematical concepts (Katz & Chard, 2000).	Ask divergent questions and listen for children's responses. Assess children's interests and knowledge and then plan based on these factors.	Teachers must be skillful in planning, so a variety of mathematical concepts are developed and not just introduced to a variety of themes.
Curriculum	"a written instructional blueprint and set of materials for guiding students' acquisition of certain culturally valued concepts, procedures, intellectual dispositions, and ways of reasoning" (Clements & Samara, 2007, p. 36)	A guide for organizing materials and activities and help children organize their thinking about math concepts and operations.	Must be research-based and age/individual appropriate.
Intentional Teaching	The active introduction of mathematical concepts, methods, and language through a range of appropriate experiences and teaching strategies (NAEYC, 2002, p. 4).	Teachers must plan in deliberate ways.	Planning must be age appropriate and allow for discovery and construction of knowledge.

Source: based on the work of Ginsburg, Lee, and Boyd (2008).

B. Set up multiple areas outside that incorporate math play
Examples: hopscotch, math cubes for rolling on the ground with movement words and numbers, place levers, ramps, and weights in the outside environment with pads to document actions

3. **Teachable moment** is that critical time when the child is on the cusp (verge or edge) of understanding a concept. The role of the teacher is to be so in tune with each child that when the moment presents itself, the teacher can expand, enrich, or extend the learning. Of course, other adults (families) and peers can also assist in the teachable moment.
Implications and Examples for Teaching Mathematics:

A. Include times in the day for teachers to work with small groups of children to hear their ideas and language about math
Examples: time for math centers and small-group math times
B. Include places in the day for teacher to work with small groups of children for teachers to interact with materials to observe children's actions on objects
Examples: use math centers and math stations (as an example, see Diller, 2011).

4. **Projects** provide time for math concepts to be fully accommodated into children's thinking before moving on. Projects can scaffold the learning in ways that promote concept development that will be understood and remembered.
Implications and Examples for Teaching Mathematics:

A. Plan for areas in the room for practice of math concepts
Example: Set up areas that contain problem solving tasks that require children to apply the concepts that have just been taught
B. Plan for times in the day for practicing the concepts recently learned
Examples: group work for using the terms and concepts
Note: these may last for several days or weeks

5. **Curriculum** is actually what happens in the day. If the day is planned the curriculum will be planned. If the curriculum is disorganized or not developmentally appropriate, then it will not have a positive impact on the child's understanding of mathematical concepts. The most appropriate curricula engage children at their developmental level, have a mixture of play with teacher direction, include small-group instruction, and have authentic assessments.
Implications and Examples for Teaching Mathematics:

A. Use a planned curriculum that is research-based and age appropriate
Example: curriculum that uses the best information based on children's thinking about math (Examples: Creative Curriculum, Big Math for Little Kids—see list below).
B. Build in multiple times throughout the daily schedule for both explicit math instruction and also implicitly in a variety of places
Example: morning meetings that include math discussion, take home math bags for families, family math nights, etc.

6. **Intentional teaching** is a relatively new term in early childhood education but has been practiced by effective teachers for a long time. The notion focused on both the

planning and organization that must be done prior to instruction for children to learn effectively.

Implications and Examples for Teaching Mathematics:

A. Incorporation of math standards in a variety spaces in the room
   Example: Use *Common Core and State Standards* for planning activities in learning centers, small group times, whole group instruction, etc.
B. Incorporate math standards in a variety of times in the daily schedule
   Example: Specifically use songs, transitions, and problem solving math activities in many ways throughout the daily schedule
C. Assess the impact on children's understandings of the standard
   Use authentic assessment to determine if children have understood and are able to use the math concept represented by the standard.

Ginsburg et al. (2008) have also written about current curricula that are often used in preschool, child care, Head Start, etc. You may see these in classrooms, mentioned in workshops or discussed in professional development articles.

Table 2.2 Samples of Math Curricula for Young Children

Math Curriculum	Source for Further Information
Creative Curriculum(Dodge, Colker, and Heroman, 2002)	www.teachingstrategies.com
Big Math for Little Kids(Balfanz, Ginsburg & Greenes, 2003)	www.pearsonschool.com
Building Blocks(Clements & Sarama, 2007)	http//:gse.buffalo.edu/org/buildingblocks/
Measurement-Based Approach (Sophian, 2004)	www2.hawaii.edu/~csophian
Number Worlds Curriculum(Griffin, 2007)	http//:sranumberworlds.com
Mathematics Curriculum(Klein & Starkey, 2002)	http//:ies.ed.gov/ncee/wwc/reports/early_ed/
Storytelling Sagas(Casey, 2004)	www2.be.edu~caseyb/storytelling.html
High/Scope/Numbers Plus(Epstein, 2010)	http//:secure.highscope.org(then search for Numbers Plus)

ANOTHER TYPE OF CURRICULUM

In the book *Tools of the Mind: A Vygotskian Approach to Early Childhood Education*, Elena Bodrova and Deborah Leong (2007) have outlined a curriculum process that includes the following components:

Teachers systematically scaffold children's moving along the continuum of self-regulation from being regulated by others to engaging in "shared" regulation to eventually becoming "masters of their own behavior."

Children gain control of their social, emotional, and cognitive behaviors by learning how to use a variety of "*mental tools.*"

Teaching of early literacy and mathematics emphasizes building underlying cognitive competencies such as *reflective thinking* and metacognition.

Children practice self-regulated learning throughout the day by engaging in a variety of specifically designed developmentally appropriate *self-regulation activities.* Children learn to regulate their own behaviors as well as the behaviors of their friends as they enact increasingly more complex scenarios in their imaginary play in prekindergarten and in learning activities in kindergarten.

Table 2.3 provides additional applications of this curricular model.

Table 2.3 Tools of the Mind: A Vygotskian Approach to Early Childhood Education

Curricular Term	Description	Example
Scaffolding	The teacher carefully plans the next step based on the child's understanding level	Materials are placed in learning centers that are based on the child's next level math operation
Mental tools	Symbol charts, pictures, or graphic organizers are strategically placed around the room, in centers, on walls, on tables, etc.	Pictures are placed on the classroom walls that remind students how to take the next step in the problem or mathematical operation
Reflective thinking and metacognition	Ways to help children to think about their own math understanding	Writing down each step of a problem or placing pictures of the steps in order
Self-regulation activities	Practicing methods that lead to greater organizational skills	Using self-talk or mental tools to organize materials or math operations

OTHER CURRICULAR INFORMATION

Marcy Guddemi, Executive Director of the Gesell Institute of Child Development and Art Baroody, in a University of Illinois, Number Sense Project (2012), have provided additional suggestions and information about the development of mathematical thinking through the following examples of typical classroom activities:

* know where child is in developmental/learning trajectory
* games, games, and games
* manipulatives and interactions with others
* Candy Land©, Card games, dice, spinner games
* problem solving games—how to measure classroom, how to weigh things, how to build things
* bowling and keeping score
* Math Their Way (Baratta-Lorton, 1995)

Understanding children's steps of learning math concepts starting with the most simple to more complex is illustrated in Figure 2.1. This type of understanding helps teachers plan activities that are organized for the most effective instruction.

Math Learning Trajectory

8. Mentally adding 2 to 5

7. Mentally adding 0 & 1

6. Number-after equals 1 more

5. Comparison of neighboring numbers

4. Number-after knowledge

3. Increasing magnitude concept and counting-based comparisons>3

2. Meaningful object counting

1. Small number recognition

(Baroody, p. 4)

Figure 2.1 Children's Steps in Learning Math.

TECHNOLOGY AND CURRICULUM FOR YOUNG CHILDREN

The National Association for the Education of Young Children (NAEYC) and the Fred Rogers Center for Early Learning and Children's Media at St. Vincent College have collaborated on a position statement addressing issues related to the use of technology and young children. The statement is entitled *Technology and Interactive Media as Tools in Early Childhood Programs Serving Children from Birth through Age Eight* (NAEYC/ Fred Rogers Center, 2012). This statement can be found at www.naeyc.org by clicking on Position Statements and locating the title "Technology and Young Children." This document provides an excellent framework for teachers to use in the decision-making process of deciding what software to use and how it could be used in the daily schedule.

McManis and Gunnewig (2012) have developed the *Early Childhood Educational Technology Evaluation Toolkit* that is published by Hatch Early Learning. Information about this helpful instrument may be found at: www.hatchearlychildhood.com/ layoutimages/documents/ebooks/EvaluatingTechnology_ToolKit.pdf (as cited in McManis & Gunnewig, 2012).

Linder (2012) has identified the essential characteristics of Early Childhood Mathematics lessons. These are especially important to remember when using technology such as interactive whiteboards or tablets with young children:

1. Building communities and communication (use of collaborative activities)
2. Making connections (integrating other subject areas with math)
3. Representing understanding (provide a variety of ways for children to show their math work and thinking)
4. Exploring with materials (use of variety of objects for children to solve math tasks)
5. Child-centered tasks (support multiple ways of solving problems).

For sources of current software, go to Children's Technology Review at: http//:childrenstech.com.

The following are some samples of recently reviewed software:

Counting Ants Adventure
Motion Math: Hungry Guppy

Motion Math: Wings (age 4 and up)
Math Doodles (K and up)
Math Logic game (for ages 4 and up)

Websites that offer virtual manipulatives for math lessons include:

Illuminations
http://illuminations.nctm.org
Kidspiration
www.insiration.com/Kidspiration
Math Forum
http://mathforum.org
National Library of Virtual Manipulatives
http://nlvm.usu.cdu

For further information about using technology with young children, such as interactive whiteboards, computers, mobile phones, touch tables, tablets, go to these websites and online resources:

Diligo Group
http://groups.diligo.com/group/ecetech
Education Week: Digital Directions
www.edweek.org/dd.?Intc=thed
Edutopia Elementary Tech Integration Blog
www.edutopia.org/blog/meaning-tech-integration-elementary-mary-beth-hertz
Fred Rogers Center for Early Learning Environment
www.ele.fredrogerscenter.org
Hatch
www.hatchearlychildhood.com

APPROACHES TO LEARNING

In an early childhood program it is also important to understand and utilize what has come to be called "approaches to learning" (Hyson, 2008). These are general, child-centered goals to keep in mind for each child during planning and instruction of the math curriculum.

The daily experiences with young children typically encourage and support children's learning in the following ways:

Initiative, engagement, and persistence (including decision-making, persistence and task completion, self-help and independence in learning)
Curiosity and eagerness to learn (including participation in varied experiences, questioning, eagerness to learn)
Reasoning and problem solving (including flexibility and resilience, help-seeking, thinking skills)
Invention and imagination (pretending creative approaches to situations).

Table 2.4 Sample Weekly Plan

Weekly plan	Date:		
Activities:	Standards:	Approaches:	Assessment:
Meeting special needs:	Differentiation plans:	Family engagement:	Other notes:

Please note that these approaches are beyond activities and curricula. They form a broader framework that defines and supports programs and teachers in planning and instruction. These can guide programmatic decision-making and support children's thinking related to mathematics.

One way to think about and use these approaches in planning weekly curriculum activities is shown in Table 2.4.

PROFESSIONAL STANDARDS FROM THE NATIONAL COUNCIL OF TEACHERS OF MATHEMATICS (NCTM) AND THE *COMMON CORE STATE STANDARDS INITIATIVE*

Curricula, as discussed in the previous section of this chapter, can be related to the following section on standards. The content chapters in this text are aligned with professional standards from two documents published by the National Council of Teachers of Mathematics (NCTM), a non-profit professional organization for mathematics educators from preschool through higher education. *Principles and Standards for School Mathematics* was published by NCTM in 2000. This document provides mathematic standards in grade bands from prekindergarten through twelfth grade in five content areas—Numbers & Operations, Algebra, Geometry, Measurement, and Data Analysis & Probability. The grade bands include preK–2; 3–5; 6–8; and 9–12.

Curriculum Focal Points for Prekindergarten through Grade 8 Mathematics: A Quest for Coherence was published by the NCTM in 2006. Three key content points are identified at each grade level, prekindergarten through grade eight, as foci in that particular grade in the same five content areas—Numbers & Operations, Algebra, Geometry, Measurement, and Data Analysis & Probability. The document also identifies mathematical connections at each grade level that are not one of the key focus areas, but help lay a solid foundation for future studies in mathematic.

The *Principles and Standards in School Mathematics* (2000) and *Curriculum Focal Points for Prekindergarten through Grade 8 Mathematics: A Quest for Coherence* (2006) are two separate documents published six years apart; however, the National Council of

Teachers of Mathematics has aligned the standards in both documents so they are consistent.

Standards from a third document are also woven within the content chapters of the text in the same five content areas as the NCTM professional standards. The *Common Core State Standards* document was released in June 2010, by the National Governors Association Center for Best Practices and the Council of Chief State School Office. This newest initiative for English Language Arts and Mathematics standards has focused on the best state standards in developing a framework for teachers and parents in guiding children in mastering standards from kindergarten through grade 12 that will help them be successful in their chosen career or in pursuing a college education. The initiative is an effort to make mathematics curriculum "more focused and coherent in order to improve mathematic achievement in this country" (2010, p. 3).

The National Council of Teachers of Mathematics, along with three other professional mathematics organizations, released a statement on June 2, 2010, titled *Mathematics Education Organizations Unite to Support Implementation of Common Core State Standards* (NCTM/NCSM/ASSM/AMTE, 2010), supporting the goals and intent of the *Common Core State Standards* in stating that they are a "welcomed milestone in the standards movement" (2010, p. 1).

NATIONAL COUNCIL OF TEACHERS OF MATHEMATICS PROCESS STANDARDS

In *Principles and Standards for School Mathematics* (2000), the National Council of Teachers of Mathematics (NCTM) identified five process standards that are important in a mathematics program. These same five process standards are embraced in the *Common Core State Standards* (NCTM et al., 2010). The process standards include:

1. Problem solving
2. Reasoning and proof
3. Communication
4. Connections
5. Representation.

The following are explanations of each process standard found in *Principles and Standards for School Mathematics* (NCTM, 2000; excerpted and paraphrased):

Problem Solving
Problem solving is an integral part of all mathematics learning and so it should not be an isolated part of the mathematics program . . . Problem solving means engaging in a task for which the solution method is not known in advance. In order to find a solution, students must draw on their knowledge, and through this process, they will often develop new mathematical understandings (p. 52).

Reasoning and Proof
Mathematical Reasoning and Proof offer powerful ways of developing and expressing insights about a wide range of phenomena . . . People who reason and think analytically tend to note patterns, structure, or regularities in both real-world

situations and symbolic objects; they ask if those patterns are accidental or if they occur for a reason; and they conjecture and prove . . . Students should see and expect that mathematics makes sense (p. 55).

Communication

Communication is an essential part of mathematics and mathematics education. It is a way of sharing ideas and clarifying understanding . . . The communication process also helps build meaning and permanence for ideas and makes them public (p. 59).

Connections

Understanding involves making connections . . . By emphasizing mathematical connections, teachers can help students build a disposition to use connections in solving mathematical problems, rather than see mathematics as a set of disconnected, isolated concepts and skills (p. 63).

Representation

Students should understand that written representations of mathematical ideas are an essential part of learning and doing mathematics. It is important to encourage students to represent their ideas in ways that make sense to them, even if their first representations are not conventional ones (p. 66).

Young children should be given frequent opportunities to engage in problem solving that is developmentally appropriate for their level of knowledge and understanding. Problems to be solved can arise from children's questions or be posed by the teacher. Problems could also arise from situations within the classroom environment. Children should participate in conversations and discussions that require them to make predictions and consider various solutions to the same problem. Children learn to think in diverse ways by listening to others' perspectives.

As children are engaged in problem solving appropriate for their age and developmental level, they should be required to reason why they think a certain solution would work or is correct, and communicate their thoughts to others. An example of a question to use frequently with young children is, "Why do you think so?"

The *Common Core State Standards* (National Governors Association Center for Best Practices/Council of Chief State School Office, 2010) document includes a second strand of process standards specified in the National Research Council's report "*Adding it Up:* adaptive reasoning, strategic competence, conceptual understanding . . . procedural fluency . . . and productive disposition" (2010, p. 6). Infused in the *Common Core State Standards* are eight Mathematical Practices that include:

1. Make sense of problems and persevere in solving them.
2. Reason abstractly and quantitatively.
3. Construct viable arguments and critique the reasoning of others.
4. Model with mathematics.
5. Use appropriate tools strategically.
6. Attend to precision.
7. Look for and make use of structure.
8. Look for and express regularity in repeated reasoning.

(2010, p. 22)

ASSESSMENT OF CHILDREN'S LEARNING

There are different types of assessments that are used for different purposes and reasons. In thinking about assessments broadly, they can be divided into two categories—formal and informal. Formal assessments include standardized assessments and screening assessments. Informal assessments include classroom assessments such as observations, running records, anecdotal records, checklists, work samples, interviews with children, and portfolios. Informal assessments can be thought of as formative in nature; they are used on a daily or weekly basis to assess the progress students are making in learning competencies and skills. Formal assessments are summative in nature; they are administered at the end of a unit of study or at the end of the academic year to assess how the standards have been met. Important decisions are made by teachers and others based on the results of formal testing. Standardized, formal testing is limited in early childhood and is mostly used to identify potential disabilities and make decisions on how best to meet an individual child's needs (Eliason & Jenkins, 2012).

Education in the 21st century is a time of standards-based instruction, assessment, and accountability. Under stipulations laid forth in No Child Left Behind, signed into law by President George W. Bush in 2001 (U.S. Congress, 2001), schools are required to prove that children are learning what teachers are teaching. Beginning in the primary grades, children at various grade levels are required to take state exams that are based on the particular state's academic standards in order to assess what children are actually learning. This, of course, varies by state.

What is the purpose of assessing children's learning? According to the National Association for the Education of Young Children position statement, assessment has four specific and beneficial purposes that include:

1. Plan and adapting curriculum to meet children's developmental and learning needs
2. Helping teachers and families monitor children's progress
3. Evaluating and improving program effectiveness
4. Screening and identifying children with disabilities and special need

(Copple & Bredekamp, 2009)

One achievement test or state exam at the end of a school year does not necessarily meet the four purposes of assessing children's learning. Besides, assessment of children's learning should be ongoing, not just measured at one point in a school year. Outside of achievement tests and state exams, then, how do we assess what young children are learning as a result of instructional programs? Assessment of learning should consist of checklists for observations, performance rubrics, anecdotal records, running records, portfolios of children's work, and, in primary grades, a few pencil and paper tests. It is important at these ages not to compare children, but to guide each child in growing and developing as an individual learner, as they have been doing since the day they were born. Children's growth and development can be measured by general expectations for various age groups, but not in labeling children by comparing one child to another.

Following are brief definitions of the recommended assessments for young children mentioned in the preceding paragraph:

Checklists for Observations

Checklists provide a structured way to observe children of a particular age group in expected skills, knowledge, and behaviors. An example of such a check list is given in Table 2.5, using just a few outcomes that may be accomplished for early math learners.

Table 2.5 Performance Rubrics

Evaluation of students	Superior	Satisfactory	Needs Improvement
When counting, the last number equals the quantity	Student can count a series of objects and understands when asked that the last number represents the quantity. Student can exceed beyond 10 items.	Student can count a series of objects and understands when asked that the last number represents the quantity. Student is limited to first 10 items.	Student struggles to count a series of objects and lacks understanding when asked with regard to the last number representing the quantity.
Count to 10 or more	Student can count well beyond 10 into double digits.	Students can count to 10 quickly with little hesitation and slightly beyond 10.	Student is unable to count easily to 10.
Count on from a given starting point	Student can count on from number between 1 and 10 and larger numbers.	Student can count on from number between 1 and 10.	Student cannot count on from number between 1 and 10 or struggles and is not fluent with this skill.
Count backwards	Student easily counts backward from 10 and is able to do from larger numbers.	Student easily counts backward from 10.	Student cannot count backward from 10.
Recognize number patterns	Student can easily recognize more complex number patterns such as see how the numbers between 1 and 11, 2 and 20, 3 and 30 relate. Children may recognize a sequence of numbers (e.g. 4, 5, 6) and can extend the pattern in such as the next couple of numbers in a sequence of even numbers and can extend the pattern.	Student can recognize some simple number patterns such as a simple sequence of numbers such as 4, 5, 6 . . . and can extend the pattern.	Student cannot recognize some simple number patterns such as simple sequences of numbers.
Understand the part-part whole relationships	Students recognize simple and more complex parts as to how they relate to the whole number.	Students understand the relationship between simple two parts and the whole number.	Students have difficulty relating the parts to wholes.

Performance Rubrics

Performance rubrics provide a structured way to determine a child's level of performance in expected skills, knowledge, and behaviors. Examples of levels of performance are: "Exceeds Expectations," "Meets Expectations," and "Below Expectations"; or "Superior," "Satisfactory," "Needs Improvement." Each designation level needs to be thoroughly defined so each child is assessed accurately. Table 2.6 shows some key words in developing rubrics for your children using the *Common Core State Standards* or the NCTM *Focal Points* as a guide, depending on the age of the children being assessed. *Common Core State Standard* or NCTM *Focal Point*: children associate number words with quantities.

Table 2.6 Types of Recommended Assessments for Young Children

Outcome/ Standard	Can identify the number of objects in a set by counting and recognition	Can associate number words with specific quantities	Can count from 1 to 10
Rachael			
José			
Janelle			
Roosevelt			

Anecdotal Records

Anecdotal records are reports of performance or behavior written after the occurrence. These reports should be rich in description to provide a clear picture of the child's abilities, behaviors, and skills. Using sticky notes attached to a clipboard, here is an example of what you might include:

Richard is having difficulty recognizing quantities without counting. He begins by counting at one and does not recognize that there are 6 items unless he counts. Names for numbers are difficult for him.

Running Records

Running records are accounts written in "real time" as a child is engaged in an activity or performing a task or skill. The record depicts what the child actually did and said. Taking a single child or several children in succession, make notes similar to writing in a diary as to the progress, interactions, problem solving skills, attitude, or other relevant observations. Again, it is helpful to gear the records toward the accomplishment of a specific expected mathematics outcome, standard, or focal point.

Portfolios

Portfolios are collections of each child's work. If accurately created, a portfolio shows a child's progress over time (Bickart, Jablon, & Dodge, 1999). A portfolio is a useful discussion tool for parent conferences. Included in the portfolio can be work samples, drawing and pictures, projects, quizzes or tests, teacher records where appropriate, and any other information which will enable the child and the parent to establish the progress in learning mathematics.

ASSESSING PREKINDERGARTEN AND KINDERGARTEN CHILDREN'S DEVELOPMENT AND LEARNING

It would be developmentally inappropriate to assess prekindergarten and kindergarten children's development and learning through the use of paper and pencil tests. Other means are used to monitor children's progress in all areas (emotional, physical, cognitive, and social) and evaluate the effectiveness of programs. To assess young children it is of utmost importance to find out what they know and then scaffold or support them to the next level. Assessment is an ongoing process, and in order to be developmentally appropriate, teachers need to engage children in conversations, observe them, use checklists, write anecdotal records, and gather information from families (Jacobs & Crowley, 2010).

Additionally, it is important to assemble portfolios of each child's work, which will provide documentation of what a child knows and can do and also show the progress each makes over a period of time. Portfolios can contain samples of a child's work, including writing and artwork. It could also contain pictures of a child's constructions, and video and audio recordings. These samples of a child's work are authentic assessments in that they provide a picture of what the child can do with the skills he or she is acquiring as these skills relate to real-life situations (Jacobs & Crowley, 2010).

When appropriate and feasible, a specialist might observe individual children in the classroom setting and keep a running record of behaviors or performance as children are engaged in a task. It is important for teachers to collaborate with families in setting goals for children and in helping children meet these goals.

In some school districts kindergarten children are assessed at the end of the school year through a pencil and paper achievement test. Children do not necessarily read the test for themselves. Rather, they follow along in their test booklets, number by number, as the teacher instructs them as to what to find within each set of choices for each question. In school districts where kindergarten children are tested in this manner, it would be important to give the children experiences with this type of testing so they are familiar with the format of the test.

ASSESSING CHILDREN'S DEVELOPMENT AND LEARNING IN THE PRIMARY GRADES

It is much more prevalent in the primary grades to assess children's learning through pencil and paper tests. This traditional method of assessment, however, should not be the only ongoing assessment tool. Teachers need to continue to observe children for growth and development in all areas—physical, emotional, social, and cognitive—as they are engaged in the daily activities of a school day. They should consistently engage students in conversations, use check lists, keep anecdotal records, and gather information from families. As students become more skilled in writing their thoughts on paper, teachers can ask students to explain their solution to a mathematics problem or write about their understanding of a particular mathematics concept.

Utilizing a variety of assessment types is as important in mathematics as it is with other subject areas. The assessment process should reflect the variety of ways children learn. Following are sample types of assessments:

Traditional Tests

Traditional tests which assess the outcomes for a particular unit can be modified from the traditional way they have been conducted. Historically, tests were administered once, and if a child did not do well the teacher still moved on to the next unit of study. This traditional testing process does not model real-world testing practice. Law Board exams, medical certification exams, and teacher certification exams can all be taken multiple times until the candidate demonstrates the required level of competencies. Thus, an important modification to traditional testing is to offer students retests. Children can be given a second or third opportunity to learn critical mathematics concepts. Initial assessments should be signed by the parents/guardians and misinformation corrected prior to taking a retest. This process informs parents/guardians and provides them with an opportunity to help their child; it gives children a chance to experience success and improve their grade, and it gives the teacher a second or third opportunity for their students to meet the learning outcomes.

Traditional tests should have a performance component, a section where students are asked to show their work and communicate what they have learned. Higher level thinking such as communication of process and error analysis should be conducted beginning at a young age.

Oral Assessments of Performance Tasks

Simple, informal, oral recitations by children can help teachers assess individuals on performance tasks. The following sample rubric can be used to assess children's understanding of the concepts in the graphic model (see Figure 2.2).

Table 2.7 A Sample Rubric

Key words for levels (do not include this block in final rubric)	Exceeds Expectations or Superior	Meets Expectations/ Satisfactory	Does Not Meet Expectations or Needs Improvement
Sample key words to discern differences (do not include this block in final rubric)	Above expectations, complete understanding, exemplary, easily and with confidence; comprehensive; insightful understanding; high degree of competency	Completion of task; minor errors; mostly understood; adequate	Significant lack of understanding; does not understand the concept; makes multiple mistakes; weak; inadequate
José Marquita			

Figure 2.2 Graphic Model.

Self-Assessment

This is an area that is often overlooked in all subject areas, yet provides useful information. Simple questions asked of students as to what they understand and do not understand may give teachers important information as to where specific children are in their process of learning mathematical concepts. Questions could include:

1. Tell me all you know about _____ (fractions, counting, shapes, etc.).
2. What part of dividing numbers do you not understand?
3. Have you ever used a fraction in real life? If so, where? Do you understand what a fraction is?
4. Do you find subtraction of numbers difficult? If yes, what is difficult for you?
5. Folding a paper in fourths or blocking for children, have them fill in the four blocks according to some specific math topic.

Figure 2.3 Self-Assessment Model.

Projects

Ideas for projects are limitless. Projects should extend and enrich mathematics and provide a way for students to "use" the mathematical concepts they are learning. Examples of projects could include taking class surveys, individual surveys, recording weather data, and other ideas gleaned from the interests of students.

Visual Presentations

Providing students opportunities to demonstrate knowledge through artwork can begin at an early age. As children become more sophisticated, the visual presentations can take the form of posters, graphic representations and other creative forms.

Labs

Math labs work well for students when they are assigned to work together as a group. Labs can be used to assess if students understand the concepts as a group, can follow procedures, understand mathematics related directions, and have problem solving capabilities.

Vocabulary Assessment

Many students can become confused on tests due to their lack of misunderstanding of assessment directions or math content vocabulary rather than their understanding of math concepts. Math tests often become reading tests instead of assessments of what students know and understand mathematically. Thus, vocabulary development of mathematics terms and words commonly found in assessment directions are necessary components of math instruction. This knowledge should also be assessed along with understanding of math concepts and skills. This is important for all students, but particularly important for emergent English Language Learners and children with learning disabilities.

Online Assessments

Most math program companies provide test-maker software, which allows teachers to generate assessments to match outcomes. These are most helpful if assessments are correlated to lesson plan development and matched to specific outcomes and standards. Resources such as these enable teachers to create multiple formats of summative tests.

Math Program Assessments

These pre-teaching and summative assessments are provided as part of the math program purchased by a school district. They can provide valuable feedback regarding specific skills and knowledge both before and after a math unit is taught. Most programs math companies offer are standards-based.

Portfolio Assessment

Portfolio assessments should continue through the primary grades as well. Portfolios provide documentation of a child's progress over time and can be useful in parent/ teacher conferences in providing evidence to support what the teacher shares with families concerning their child's abilities, growth, and development.

REFERENCES

Balfanz, R., Ginsburg, H. P. & Greenes, C. (2003). The big math for little kids: Early childhood mathematics programs. *Teaching Children Mathematics*, 9(5), 264–268.

Baratta-Lorton, M. (1995). *Math Their Way*. CA: Center for Innovation in Education.

Baroody, A. (2012). *University of Illinois Number Sense Project*. Institute of Education Science, U.S. Department of Education grant, as cited in Guddemi, M., PowerPoint presentation accessed on October 20, 2012. www.gesellinstituteworkshops.org/Guddemi

Bickart, T. S., Jablon, J. R. & Dodge, D. T. (1999). *Building the Primary Classroom: A Complete Guide to Teaching and Learning*. Washington, D.C.: Teaching Strategies, Inc.; Portsmouth, NH: Heinemann.

Bodrova, E. and Leong, D. J. (2003). Chopsticks and counting chips: Do play and foundational skills need to compete for the teacher's attention in an early childhood classroom? *Beyond the Journal, Young Children on the Web* (May): 1–8.

Bodrova, E. & Leong, D. J. (2007). *Tools of the Mind: The Vygotskian Approach to Early Childhood Education* (2nd ed.). Columbus, OH: Merrill/Prentice Hall.

Casey, B. (2004). Mathematics problem-solving adventures: A language-arts based supplementary series for early childhood that focuses on spatial sense. In D. Clements, J. Sarama, & M. A. DiBaise (Eds.), *Engaging Young Children in Mathematics: Results of the Conference on Standards for Pre-school and Kindergarten Mathematics Education*. Mahwah, NJ: Erlbaum Associates.

Clements, D. H. & Sarama, J. (2007). Effects of a preschool mathematics curriculum: Summative research on the Building Blocks Project. *Journal for Research in Mathematics Education*, 38(2), 136–163.

Common Core State Standards Initiative: Preparing America's Students for College and Career (2010). Washington, DC: National Governors Association Center for Best Practices/Council of Chief State School Officers.

Copple, C. & Bredekamp, S. (Eds.) (2009). *Developmentally Appropriate Practice in Early Childhood Programs: Serving Children From Birth Through Age 8* (3rd ed.). Washington, D. C.: NAEYC.

Diller, D. (2011). *Math Work Stations: Independent Learning You Can Count on, K-2*. Portland, ME: Stenhouse.

Dodge, D. T., Coker, L. & Heroman, C. (2002). *The Creative Curriculum for Preschool* (4th ed.). Washington, DC: Teaching Strategies, Inc. Boston, MA: Pearson.

Eliason, C. & Jennins, L. (2012). *A Practical Guide to Early Childhood Curriculum* (9th ed.). Upper Saddle River, NJ: Pearson.

Epstein, A. (2010). The what and how of early math learning. *HighScope* 28(2). Ypsilanti, MI: HighScope Publications.

Ginsburg, H. P., Lee, J. S. & Boyd, J. S. (2008). Mathematics education for young children: What it is and how to promote it. *Social Policy Report* 22(I): 3–23.

Griffin, S. (2007). *Number Worlds: A Mathematics Intervention Program for Grades PreK–6*. Columbus, OH: SRA/McGraw-Hill.

Guddemi, M. (2012). *Math Development in Children Ages 3 to Grade 3*. Gesell Institute. Accessed online on 10 November.

Harms, T., Clifford, R.M. & Cryer, D. (2005). *Early Childhood Environment Rating Scale—Revised*. New York: Teachers College Press.

Hyson, M. (2008). *Enthusiastic and Engaged Learners: Approaches to Learning in the Early Childhood Classroom*. New York, NY: Teachers College Press; Washington, DC: NAEYC.

Jacobs, G. & Crowley, K. (2010). *Reaching Standards and Beyond in Kindergarten: Nurturing Children's Sense of Wonder and Joy in Learning*. Thousand Oaks, CA: Corwin.

Katz, L. & Chard, S. (2000). *Engaging Children's Minds: The Project Approach*. Stanford, CT: Ablex Publishing.

Klein, A. & Starkey, P. (2002). *Pre-K Mathematics Curriculum*. Glenview, IL: Scott Forman.

Linder, S. M. (2012). Building content and communities: Developing a shared sense of early childhood mathematics pedagogy. *Journal of Early Childhood Teacher Education*, 33(2), 109–126.

McManis, L. D. & Gunnewig, S. B. (2012). Finding the education in educational technology with early learners. *YC Young Children*, 67(3), 14–24.

National Association for the Education of Young Children (NAEYC)/Fred Rogers Center (2012). *Technology and Interactive Media as Tools in Early Childhood Programs Serving Children Birth Through Age 8*. Bridgeport, CT: NAEYC/Fred Rogers Center for Early Learning and Children's Media, St. Vincent College.

National Council of Teachers of Mathematics (NCTM) (2000). *Principles and Standards for School Mathematics*. Reston, VA: Author.

National Council of Teachers of Mathematics (NCTM). (Adopted in 2002; Updated in 2010). *Early Childhood Mathematics: Promoting Good Beginnings* (NAEYC/NCTM Joint Position Statement). Washington, DC: Authors.

National Council of Teachers of Mathematics (NCTM) (2006). *Curriculum Focal Points for Prekindergarten Through Grade 8 Mathematics: A Quest for Coherence*. Reston, VA: Author.

National Council of Teachers of Mathematics (NCTM), National Council of Supervisors of Mathematics (NCSM), the Association of State Supervisors of Mathematics (ASSM), and the Association of Mathematics Teacher Educators (AMTE) (2010). *Mathematics Education Organizations Unite to Support Implementation of Common Core State Standards (A Joint Public Statement)*. Reston, VA: Authors.

Sophian, C. (2004). Mathematics for the future: developing a Head Start curriculum to support mathematics learning. *Early Childhood Research Quarterly*, 19(1), 59–81.

US Congress (2001). *No Child Left Behind*. Pub. L. 107–110. Washington, D.C.: U.S. Government Printing Office.

3

NUMBERS AND OPERATIONS

CHAPTER OUTCOMES

After reading this chapter, teacher candidates will be able to:

- ➤ Explain numbers and operations standards for prekindergarten-aged children.
- ➤ Explain numbers and operations standards for kindergarten-aged children.
- ➤ Explain numbers and operations standards for first grade through third grade children.
- ➤ Describe numbers and operations activities that are developmentally appropriate for prekindergarten-aged children.
- ➤ Describe numbers and operations activities that are developmentally appropriate for kindergarten-aged children.
- ➤ Describe numbers and operations activities that are developmentally appropriate for first through third grade children.
- ➤ Explain how early numbers and operations activities lay a foundation for future, higher mathematical understanding, reasoning, and problem solving.
- ➤ Explain how children's literature can be used to support learning of numbers and operations concepts.
- ➤ Describe the types of adaptations that could be planned for English Language Learners (ELL) and children with special needs that might help them acquire concepts of numbers and operations.
- ➤ Describe the types of adaptations that could be planned to challenge gifted children in this content area.
- ➤ Explain how to involve families/caregivers in supporting the acquisition of concepts of numbers and operations at home.

OVERVIEW OF CONCEPT DEVELOPMENT

Conceptual development of numbers begins as children begin to understand the meaning of whole numbers and can use this understanding in meaningful ways. Children first count by rote with no meaning attached to the numbers they are repeating. They begin applying one-to-one correspondence when counting objects as they learn that "one number name is given or matched to one and only one object in a set being counted" (Copley, Jones, & Dighe, 2010, p. 741). They learn to recognize the number of objects in a set by counting or visually recognizing a number in a set without counting (subitizing). Young children learn that the last number counted tells "how many" in a set (cardinality principle) and that number words refer to specific quantities. In working with sets of objects, children engage in activities that require them to count, create, order, and compare sets, thus learning the terms "more than" and "less than." As children progress in their understanding of numbers, they create strategies for solving problems (NCTM, 2006; *Common Core State Standards*, 2010).

As children enter kindergarten their counting experiences are extended in a variety of ways. They count numbers strung in a line, arranged in area models or arrays, and scattered in nonuniform ways. Children learn to write number symbols from 1 to 20 to represent quantities and compare written numerals between 1 and 10. They count to 100 by 1s and 10s, and they learn to count on from a number other than 1. For example, they learn to begin on the number 7 and count forward. They count backwards and begin understanding that each successive number in counting refers to a quantity that is one larger than the previous number. To begin developing an understanding of addition and subtraction, children model simple putting together and separating situations with objects (*Common Core State Standards*, 2010; NCTM, 2006).

Children in first grade develop strategies for adding and subtracting whole numbers using a variety of models, learn to add and subtract within 20, and understand the relationship between addition and subtraction. They continue to work with the concept of "counting on" in combining numbers, are expected to count to 120, and learn place-value grouping of 10s and 1s in analyzing two-digit numerals. They continue reading and writing numerals, add up to three whole numbers, and use their understanding of numbers to solve problems (*Common Core State Standards*, 2010; NCTM, 2006).

Children in second grade are expected to develop quick recall of basic addition and related subtraction facts within 20. They learn to estimate sums and differences and add and subtract multi-digit numbers. They develop efficient procedures for addition and subtraction including the standard algorithms. Their number knowledge includes skip counting by 5s, 10s, and 100s, reading and writing numerals to 1,000, understanding place value concepts up to 1,000, and comparing numbers using equal-to, more-than, and less-than symbols (*Common Core State Standards*, 2010; NCTM, 2006).

At the third-grade level, children learn the meaning of multiplication and division of whole numbers as they use representations—equal-sized groups, arrays and area models—and multiply and divide within 100. As children multiply and divide whole numbers, they develop an understanding of the relationship between multiplication and division. Understanding of place value concepts extends to 10,000, and children are expected to use all four operations (addition, subtraction, multiplication, and division) in solving problems. Children's understanding of numbers includes the development of fractions as numbers (*Common Core State Standards*, 2010; NCTM, 2006).

BUILDING CONCEPTS OF NUMBERS AND OPERATIONS AT THE PREKINDERGARTEN LEVEL

Conceptual understanding of numbers and how they relate to the real world is foundational to future understanding of higher-level mathematics. Understanding whole numbers, what a number represents, what it means to count objects, and how sets can be represented by number symbols are all important first steps. This includes being able to match and compare number sets, counting from 1 to 10 and beyond, and being able to identify a number of objects from 1 to 5 by sight (subitizing). Extensions of these activities can include counting much higher and being able to count backwards or to count by multiples of small numbers (Bahr & de Garcia, 2009).

Prekindergarten children learn mathematics through the use of manipulatives and hands-on activities. In practical terms, this means that children begin with real objects they know and understand. Among the tools used in early mathematics learning are dot plates, ten frames, number lines, blocks, geo boards, and various types of cubes and counters.

Conservation of number is an important concept for children to develop. Children who can conserve know that 10 objects is still 10 objects regardless of how they are arranged. As children learn conservation of number, they progress from intuitive thought to logical thought and become more flexible in their perceptions of others' ideas and their perspective of the real world.

Learning math vocabulary, being able to communicate mathematically, and applying mathematical thinking to real-world situations and problem solving is an important component of mathematics learning. Children need to process their knowledge and understanding of mathematics. They need to understand the process of structure in their world as it relates to mathematics, and practice using the tools of mathematics to create logical arguments and attend to precision.

Cross-curricular practices or integrating content areas, and making connections among mathematical concepts is supported as children practice skills in basic numbers through the use of real data, geometry, and basic algebra concepts. This extends to comparing, sorting, counting shapes, and counting sides on geometric figures. As children verbally describe their decision-making strategies, they begin to develop conceptual understanding in mathematics.

Copley et al. (2010) state, "Although young children naturally begin to develop some informal mathematical understandings, many more opportunities to learn more school-based or formal mathematics need to be provided" (p. 744).

Copley et al. (2010) have outlined various strategies teachers can employ that can contribute to children's numerical understanding. These strategies include:

1. Practice counting using a variety of learning styles and representations.
2. Provide a variety of materials to help children develop an understanding of quantity.
3. Model counting strategies.
4. Model comparing the number of objects in two sets.
5. Identify everyday situations in which to use ordinal numbers.
6. Make obvious mistakes so that children can identify the errors.

7. Illustrate and model a variety of problems that involve combining, separating, sharing, or set-making.
8. Act out operation stories.
9. Use [children's] books to encourage numerical reasoning.
10. Encourage children to tell stories about *how many*.
11. Publish number books.
12. Create a numerically rich environment.

(pp. 744–745)

CONTENT STANDARDS FOR PREKINDERGARTEN

Numbers and Operations is the first content area defined in the NCTM document *Principles and Standards in School Mathematics* (2000). It is a key concept in *Curriculum Focal Points for Prekindergarten Through Grade 8 Mathematics: A Quest for Coherence* (NCTM, 2006) at all grade levels including prekindergarten. The *Common Core State Standards* (2010) begins at the kindergarten level, so there are no standards in this document for prekindergarten programs; however, Numbers and Operations standards are an important focus for grade levels contained in the document.

Content standards in the NCTM document *Principles and Standards in School Mathematics* (2000) are not presented by individual grades or age levels, but are grouped in age or grade bands. The first group of standards spans numbers and operations expectations from prekindergarten through grade 2. These include:

Understand numbers, ways of representing numbers, relationships among numbers, and number systems count with understanding and recognize "how many" in sets of objects:

- use multiple models to develop initial understandings of place value and the base-ten number system;
- develop understanding of the relative position and magnitude of whole numbers and of ordinal and cardinal numbers and their connections;
- develop a sense of whole numbers and represent and use them in flexible ways, including relating, composing, and decomposing numbers;
- connect number words and numerals to the quantities they represent, using various physical models and representations;
- understand and represent commonly used fractions, such as ¼, ⅓, and ½.

Understand meanings of operations and how they relate to one another:

- count with understanding and recognize "how many" in sets of objects;
- use multiple models to develop initial understandings of place value and the base-ten number system;
- develop understanding of the relative position and magnitude of whole numbers and of ordinal and cardinal numbers and their connections;
- develop a sense of whole numbers and represent and use them in flexible ways, including relating, composing, and decomposing numbers;

- connect number words and numerals to the quantities they represent, using various physical models and representations;
- understand and represent commonly used fractions, such as ¼, ⅓, and ½.

Compute fluently and make reasonable estimates:

- develop and use strategies for whole-number computations, with a focus on addition and subtraction;
- develop fluency with basic number combinations for addition and subtraction;
- use a variety of methods and tools to compute, including objects, mental computation, estimation, paper and pencil, and calculators.

(www.nctm.org/standards/)

The following NCTM Focal Points are the recommended content emphases for mathematics in prekindergarten. It is essential that these focal points be addressed in contexts that promote problem solving, reasoning, communication, making connections, and designing and analyzing representations. As a key concept in the NCTM *Focal Points and Connections* (2006), numbers and operations is defined as the following:

- Understand the meaning of whole numbers.
- Recognize the number of objects in small groups by counting and not counting (sight recognition).
- Understand that numbers refer to quantities.
- Use one-to-one correspondence by matching and comparing number amounts and counting to 10 and beyond.
- Understand that the last number stated is how many they count.
- Order sets by the number of objects in them.
- Create strategies to solve problems.

(2006, p. 11)

PREKINDERGARTEN OUTCOMES
Prekindergarten Outcome #1: Children Can Identify the Number of Objects in a Set by Counting and by Recognition
Children associate number words with specific quantities.

Sample Activity #1
In this activity children will work on counting the number of objects in a set and associating number words with specific quantities using picture cards. Eventually, children should be able to recognize the number of objects without counting (subitizing). Flash cards with common objects students will recognize and geometric shapes can range from 1 to 5 and then up to 10 objects on a card. The number symbol and number word should be included on the reverse side (Figure 3.1).

Clocks:

5   Five

Cartoon characters:

4   Four

Girls:

7   Seven

Bears:

3   Three

Figure 3.1 Examples of Flash Cards for Counting and Recognizing Numbers and Number Words.

Sample Activity #2

Children associate number words with specific quantities. For this activity, children will match number symbols/number words cards with quantities on dot cards, object cards, and geometry cards (Figure 3.2).

Dot Cards:

Object Cards:

Geometry Cards:

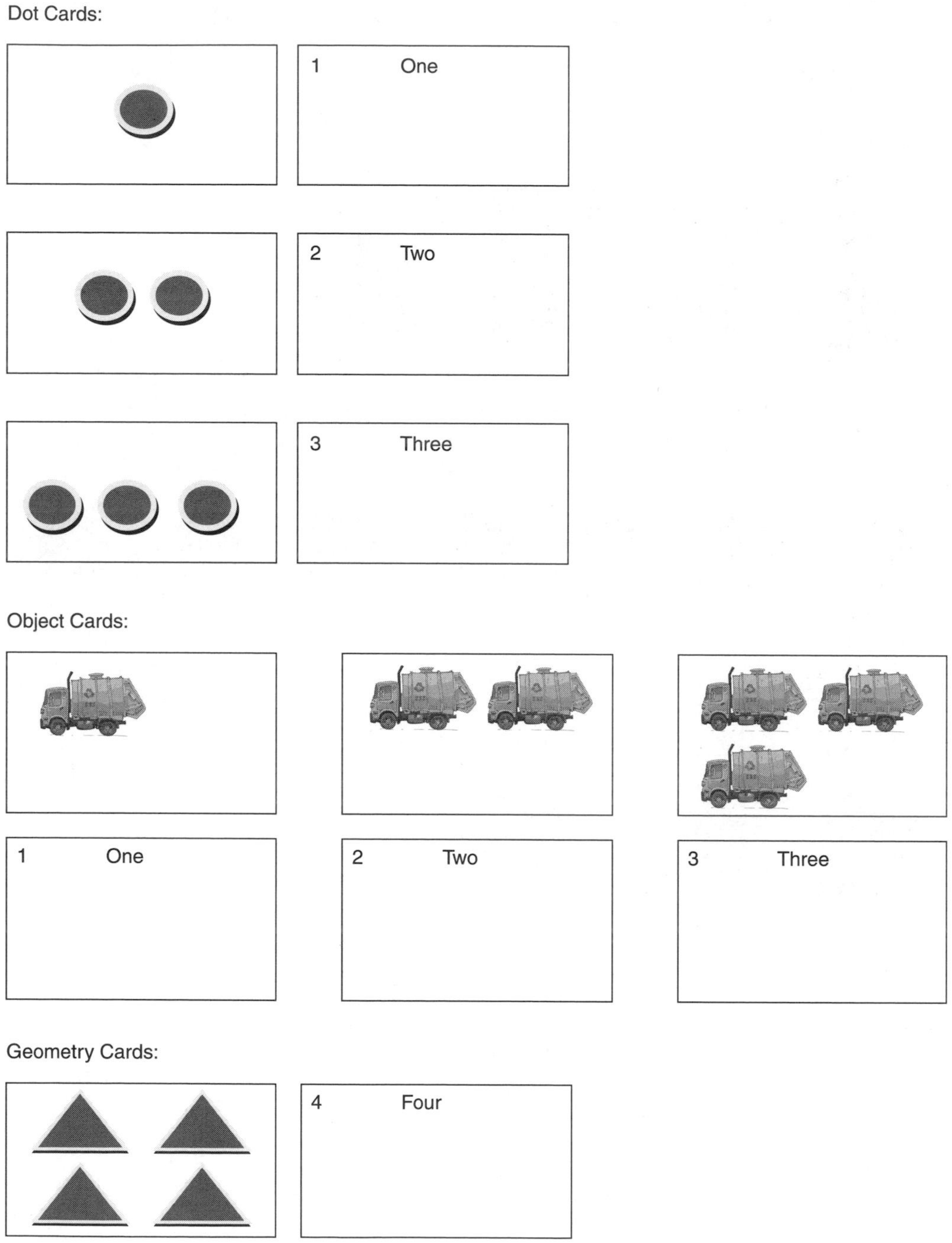

Figure 3.2 Examples of Dot, Object, and Geometry Cards for Counting and Number Symbol and Number Word Recognition.

Prekindergarten Outcome #2: Children Count to Ten or More

Opportunities to count are endless. Children become proficient at counting by experiencing counting activities in a variety of contexts. They can count objects on pre-made cards as described in previous activities. They can count real-world objects, and numbers of people and things they find in their environment.

Another context which provides counting experiences for young children is in collecting data from questions children ask or questions that would be of interest to them. As children are working with numbers, they can make predictions and also use comparing terminology as "greater than" and "less than' in comparing sets of objects.

Sample Activity #1: Data Collection/Counting Activity

Ideally, questions for collecting data should come from the children; however, teachers may need to model "I wonder . . ." type questions to get them thinking in that direction. For example, after reading a story about a dog, the teacher could pose this question: I wonder how many of us have a dog as a pet? Data could be collected in a variety of ways. One way would be to ask children to stand and line up to be counted if they have a dog for a pet. Another way would be to have children raise their hands if they have a dog for a pet.

Sample Activity #2: Graphing/Counting Activity

Data that are collected from the teacher's and the children's "I wonder . . ." questions can be placed on a simple graph for children to count. For example, data can be collected on the various pets that children have, and the data can then be placed on a simple graph. Children could practice their counting skills by counting spaces on the graph Data collection activities could be used to introduce the idea of making a prediction. Children could be asked to make a prediction about "I wonder . . ." questions and then collect data and count to determine the results. Ideas for data collection include:

Colors: What is your favorite color? (Prediction: What color do you think is the favorite of most people in the class?) Let's begin by naming colors . . . red, blue . . . How many of you like red the most? How many like blue? Let's count together . . .

Desserts: What is your favorite dessert? Let's see what people like to eat for dessert. Let's take a poll. How many like ice cream? How many like cake? Let's count the number of the students who like . . .

Favorite Food: What is your favorite lunch or breakfast food? (Prediction: What do you think most people in the class will name as their favorite food for breakfast/lunch?)

Colors of Clothing: What colors are people wearing today? (Prediction: What color do you think most people are wearing today?) Let's count the number of students who are wearing blue . . .

Sample Activity #3: Measurement/Counting Activity

Children should be provided with numerous opportunities to measure objects using nonstandard units of measure (paper clips, erasers, pennies, clothes pins, etc.). For example, children could be provided with a length of string. Using a nonstandard unit of measure, children would lay the unit along the string to determine the length of the string in that unit. Children should be encouraged to measure the same length of string using a different unit of measure and compare the results.

Sample Activity #4: Geometry and Counting/Comparing Activity

In this activity, children practice one-to-one correspondence while reinforcing basic geometric shape recognition and geometry vocabulary. Children can use picture cards or geometric shape manipulatives. How many red squares are there? Count the squares. Is there the same number of blue circles as red squares? Is one number more than the other, or less than the other number? How many squares and circles are there altogether? Let's count the squares and circles (Figure 3.3).

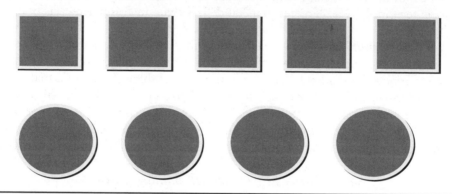

Figure 3.3 Counting and Comparing Using Geometric Shapes.

Prekindergarten Outcome #3: Children Compare Quantities to Determine Answers to Problems

Sample Activity

Materials needed for this activity include a variety of two-dimensional figures. The following question could be posed to the children: "Miss Piggy needs to buy a table. She wants to buy the table with the most number of sides. Help Miss Piggy decide which table to buy. Count the number of sides and decide which table has the most sides" (Figure 3.4).

Figure 3.4 Counting/Comparing Sides on Geometric Shapes.

CONTENT STANDARDS FOR KINDERGARTEN

In the NCTM *Focal Points* (2006), numbers and operations for kindergarten children is described as follows:

- Write numerals to represent quantities.
- Solve quantitative problems by counting, creating a set with a given number of objects, comparing, and ordering sets of numerals.
- Use cardinal and ordinal meaning.
- Model simple joining and separating situations with objects.
- Choose, combine, and apply effective strategies for answering questions.

(2006, p. 12)

The following kindergarten standards are listed in the *Common Core State Standards* (2010):

Kindergarten Standard #1: Know number names and the count sequence.
1a. Count to 100 by ones and by tens.
1b. Count forward beginning from a given number within the known sequence.
1c. Represent a number of objects with a written numeral 0–20.

Kindergarten Standard #2: Count to tell the number of objects.
1a. Understand the relationship between numbers and quantities: connect counting to cardinality:

— When counting objects, say the number names in the standard order, pairing each object with one number name and each number name with one object
— Understand that the last number name said tells the number of objects counted
— Understand that each successive number name refers to a quantity that is one larger

1b. Count to answer "how many?" questions about as many as 20 things arranged in a line, a rectangular array, or a circle, or as many as 10 things in a scattered configuration; given a number from 1 to 20, count out that many objects.

Kindergarten Standard #3: Compare numbers.
1a. Identify whether the number of objects in one group is greater than, less than, or equal to the number of objects in another group.
1b. Compare two numbers between 1 and 10 presented as written numerals.

(2010, p. 11)

KINDERGARTEN OUTCOMES

Kindergarten Outcome #1: Represent Quantities by Counting or Writing Whole Numbers

Conceptual understanding of numbers continues as children count sets of objects, begin to subitize or recognize the number of objects in a set without counting, say and write numbers, and compare and order numbers. Counting manipulatives, writing numerals, and learning appropriate vocabulary terminology should develop simultaneously. Seeing and counting number sets visually, saying the number of objects in the set, and having children create their own sets will support this learning and understanding.

There are endless opportunities to have children count objects, write number symbols to represent the size of the set, compare the size of sets and order sets from the least to greatest or greatest to least. It is important, as children are counting, that they say the number names in the correct or standard order and assign just one number name to each object in a set. As children are asked "How many did you count?" questions, they come to understand that the last number counted represents the total number of objects in the set (cardinality principle).

Children's experiences with counting should extend to being able to count up to 20 objects in a row or arranged in a circle or rectangular array. Likewise, they should practice counting up to 10 objects that are scattered, developing a system for counting each object only once.

Children are also extending their rote counting skills as they practice counting from 1 to 100 by ones and by tens. Rote counting should be supported by using a number line or hundreds chart so that meaning for the numbers children are saying can be developed.

While developing the counting concepts, it is important to have children make real-world connections. Thus counting sets should include objects the children see in their environment. This could include counting toys, desks, shoes, pictures, colors, crayons, cups, pencils and many other objects. Children can also do counting related to measurement and distance: number of steps to the playground; number of steps from their desks to the pencil sharpener/water fountain/rest room, etc.

Kindergarten Outcome #2: "Counting on" from a Given Number

As children become proficient in counting, they are able to "count on" from a given number instead of needing to begin counting with the number 1.

Sample Activity

Before the activity, the teacher would need to prepare paper fish with a piece of sticky-backed magnet attached to the mouth of the fish. A number would be written on each fish. The teacher would also need to prepare a "fishing rod" using a stick and string with a magnet attached to the end of the string. Children would take turns fishing for a number, stating the number and then counting on three to five more numbers in order that come after the number on the fish. For example, if a child catches a "7" fish, he or she would say "7, 8, 9, 10, 11, 12."

Kindergarten Outcome #3: Understanding that Each Successive Number Name Refers to a Quantity that is One Larger

It should not be assumed that as children experience various counting experiences they automatically understand the "plus 1" relationship of successive numbers. Children need experiences in developing this understanding.

Sample Activity

Materials needed for this activity include small manipulatives such as centimeter cubes, small baskets or other containers, a large, class-sized number line from 0 to 10, and paper flowers that can be taped to the number line. The number line should be displayed at the front of the instruction area so all children could see it. Each child would have a small pile of the manipulatives at his or her work area to represent pretend flowers, and a basket or other container to collect the manipulatives. Children could pretend that they are picking flowers as they collect the manipulatives.

The teacher would begin by having the children notice that there are no flowers in their baskets, thus the number zero has no flowers on it. The teacher would ask the children to pick one flower to place in their baskets, thus one flower more than zero is one flower. The teacher would tape one paper flower to the number line above the number 1. She or he would then ask the children to pick one more flower to place in their baskets. One more flower added to the basket makes two flowers. The teacher would then tape two flowers above the number 2 on the number line. The activity would continue this way until the children have 10 flowers in their baskets. As children are asked to "pick flowers," the terminology "one more" would be reinforced.

The activity could be extended by giving each child a pile of manipulatives and a number line. Children would place the number of "flowers" above the numbers on the number line beginning with zero to represent that number. Each time the child adds a flower, he or she would be encouraged to say, "And one more makes . . ."

Kindergarten Outcome #4: Children Create Sets with a Specific Number of Objects
Sample Activity

Materials needed for this activity include 10 paper stars or other manipulatives, number-word cards from zero to ten, and numeral cards from 0 to 10 for each child. Children would create sets of stars as directed by the teacher. They would then locate the number-word card and numeral card that goes with the set of stars they created. For example, children are asked to create a set of four stars. They would lay out their stars and find the number 4 and the word four to go with the set (Figure 3.5).

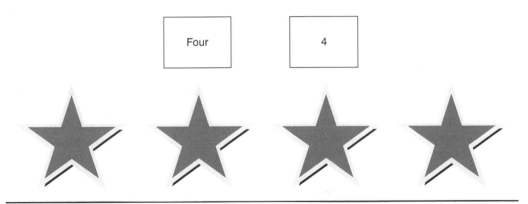

Figure 3.5 Creating Specific-Numbered Sets.

Kindergarten Outcome #5: Compare Quantities in Sets of Objects
Sample Activity

In this activity, children would be asked to form sets for comparison purposes. The teacher would select children with different-colored clothes, different shoes, etc., and have these children form a set. Children would count the number of children in each set and find the respective numbers on the class number line. They would be asked to compare the sets using the terminology "the same or equal," "more than," or "less than." The children forming the sets would then be asked to "pair up" to determine if the number in the sets is the same or different. Visually, children should be able to see if the sets are the same or equal, or if one set is greater or less than the other.

The activity could be extended by providing the children with two different types of manipulatives. Children would be directed to create one set with one type of manipulative and a second set with the other type of manipulative. Sets would be counted, paired, and compared using the appropriate terminology (Figure 3.6).

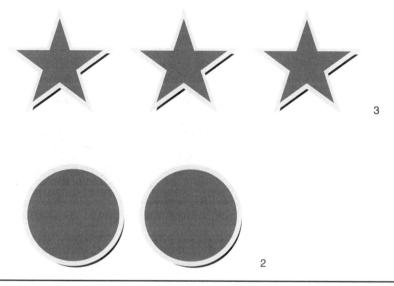

Figure 3.6 Comparing Sets.

When children become proficient in comparing numbers in different sets, they are ready to compare written numbers from 0 to 10. If children have difficulty comparing written numbers, they can use manipulative or the number line to reinforce their thinking concerning whether two written numbers are equal or one is less than or greater than the other.

Kindergarten Outcome #6: Combine or Separate Sets to Answer Quantitative Problems

Sample Activities

Combining sets provides a foundation for children in understanding the concept of addition. In the example in Figure 3.7, a child counts the number of objects in the each set, combines the two sets, and then counts how many altogether. As children become proficient in "counting on," they should be able to say "3" to represent the first set, and then "4, 5" to get a total of 5 in all.

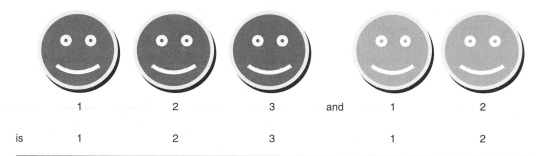

Figure 3.7 Comparing Sets.

Likewise, children begin to understand the concept of subtraction by separating sets. In Figure 3.8, a child separates a set of five smiley faces into a set of two smiley faces and another set of three smiley faces.

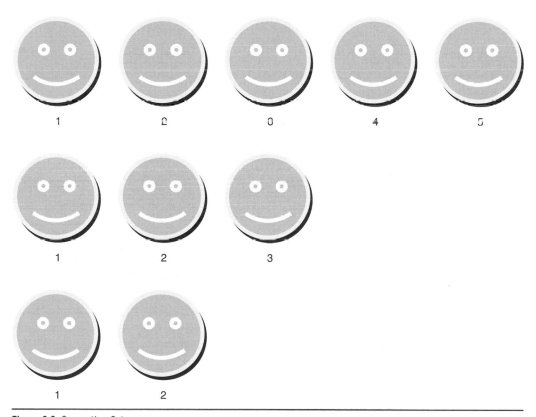

Figure 3.8 Separating Sets.

Kindergarten Outcome #7: Count Both Forward and Backward

Sample Activity

As children are becoming proficient in counting, they also practice counting backward. They begin by rote counting backward from 10 to 1. Once rote counting backward has been established, children apply this knowledge to counting combined sets both forward and backward. In Figure 3.9, a child has combined three sets (a set of 2, a set of 4, and a set of 3). The child then practices counting the combined sets forward—"1, 2, 3, 4, 5, 6, 7, 8, 9"—and then backward—"9, 8, 7, 6, 5, 4, 3, 2, 1."

Figure 3.9 Counting Combined Sets Both Forward and Backward.

CONTENT STANDARDS FOR GRADE 1

In the NCTM *Focal Points* (2006), standards for numbers and operations for grade 1 include:

> • Developing understanding of addition and subtraction.
> • Developing strategies for basic addition facts and related subtraction facts.
> • Use a variety of models, including discrete objects, length-based models (e.g., lengths of connecting cubes), and number lines, to model "part-whole," "adding to," "taking away from," and "comparing" situations to develop an understanding of the meanings of addition and subtraction and strategies to solve such arithmetic problems.
> • Understand the connections between counting and the operations of addition and subtraction (e.g., adding two is the same as "counting on" two).
> • Use properties of addition (commutative and associative) to add whole numbers, and they create and use increasingly sophisticated strategies based on these properties (e.g., "making tens") to solve addition and subtraction problems involving basic facts.
> • By comparing a variety of solution strategies, children relate addition and subtraction as inverse operations.
>
> (2006, p. 13)

The following grade 1 standards are listed in the *Common Core State Standards* (2010):

> **Grade 1 Standard #1:** Represent and solve problems involving addition and subtraction:
> **1a.** Use addition and subtraction within 20 to solve word problems involving situations of adding to, taking from, putting together, taking apart, and comparing with unknowns in all positions.

1b. Solve word problems that call for addition of three whole numbers whose sum is less than or equal to 20.

Grade 1 Standard #2: Understand and apply properties of operations and the relationship between addition and subtraction:
2a. Apply commutative and associative properties of addition.
2b. Understand subtraction as an unknown-addend problem.

Grade 1 Standard #3: Add and subtract within 20:
3a. Relate counting to addition and subtraction.
3b. Add and subtract within 20, demonstrating fluency for addition and subtraction within 10.

Grade 1 Standard #4: Work with addition and subtraction equations:
4a. Understand the meaning of the equal sign, and determine if equations involving addition and subtraction are true or false.
4b. Determine the unknown whole number in an addition or subtraction equation relating three whole numbers.

Grade 1 Standard #5: Extend the counting sequence (Count to 120 starting at any number less than 120; write numerals and represent a number of objects with a written symbol).

Grade 1 Standard #6: Understand place value
6a. Understand that the two digits of a two-digit number represent amounts of tens and ones:

- 10 can be thought of as a bundle of ten ones – called a "ten"
- The numbers from 11 to 19 are composed of a ten and one, two, three, four, five, etc.
- The numbers 10, 20 ... 90 refer to one, two ... nine tens (and zero ones)
- Compare two two-digit numbers with the symbols for equal to, greater than, and less than

Grade 1 Standard #7: Use place value understanding and properties of operations to add and subtract:
7a. Add within 100 using concrete models or drawings and strategies based on place value, properties of operations and/or the relationship between addition and subtraction.
7b. Given a two-digit number, mentally find 10 more or 10 less than the number; explain the reasoning used.
7c. Subtract multiples of 10 in the range 10–90 from multiples of 10 in the range 10–90 (positive or zero differences).

(2006, pp. 15–16)

GRADE 1 OUTCOMES

Grade 1 Outcome #1: Extend the Counting Sequence to 120 by Starting at Any Number Less Than 120

Sample Activity

There are many opportunities for children to practice extending their counting skills. As children extend their counting knowledge, it is important for them to become aware of patterns in counting. They could do this using a hundreds chart. For example, children should notice that all the numbers in a particular column, say column 3, have a 3 in the 1s place—13, 23, 33, 43, 53, etc. Likewise, all numbers in a particular row, say the 20s row, have a 2 in the 10s place—21, 22, 23, 24, 25, etc. A chart of numbers, extended to 120, would be valuable in providing children with a visual of how these numbers are extended from the hundreds chart (Figure 3.10).

1	2	3	4	5	6	7	8	9	10
11	12	13	14	15	16	17	18	19	20
21	22	23	24	25	26	27	28	29	30
31	32	33	34	35	36	37	38	39	40
41	42	43	44	45	46	47	48	49	50
51	52	53	54	55	56	57	58	59	60
61	62	63	64	65	66	67	68	69	70
71	72	73	74	75	76	77	78	79	80
81	82	83	84	85	86	87	88	89	90
91	92	93	94	95	96	97	98	99	100
101	102	103	104	105	106	107	108	109	110
111	112	113	114	115	116	117	118	119	120

Figure 3.10 Extending the Hundreds Chart to 120.

Grade 1 Outcome #2: Read and Write Numbers; Understand that Two-Digit Numbers Represent Tens and Ones; Understand Place Value

Sample Activity #1

The teacher and children can create a bulletin board or math wall, which depicts numerals, showing how they are constructed using 10s and 1s (Figure 3.11).

Sample Activity #2

All that is needed for this activity are trade books or other books that have at least 120 pages in them, whiteboards or other type of board, markers or chalk, and erasers or rags to use for erasing. The teacher could begin the activity by having the children find a certain page number by giving them only 100, 10s, and 1s information. For example, the teacher could say: Find the page number that has 7 tens and 2 ones. The children would locate page 72 in their books and write this number on their boards. On the count of three, each child would turn his or her board for the teacher to view. Individual help

8, eight

14, fourteen (one ten and 4 ones)

36, thirty-six (3 tens and 6 ones)

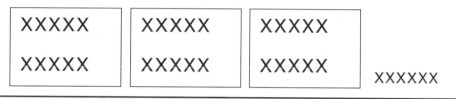

Figure 3.11 Bulletin Board or Number Wall Ideas.

could be given as required. After the boards are wiped clean, the teacher would continue the activity in the same way.

An extension of this activity could be to have children open their books to any page and write that number on their boards. Displaying the boards so the teacher can view them, he or she would ask specific children how many 10s and 1s (or 100) are needed to construct this number. Children could also depict their number by drawing a 100, 10s and 1s representations on their boards.

Sample Activity #3

Children can partner up in using number cards that depict the construction of numbers using ones and tens. Partner #1 takes a card and holds it up so Partner #2 can see only the number 15. Partner #2 reads the number and explains the number of 10s and 1s needed to construct the number 15 (1 ten and 5 ones) (Figure 3.12).

Grade 1 Outcome #3: The Numbers 10, 20, 30, etc. are Represented by 1, 2, 3, etc.
10s and Zero 1s; Understand Place Value; Read and Write Numbers

Children can find the numbers 10 through 100 on the 100s chart. They should be familiar with these numbers as they practice counting to 100 by 10s. Children should notice the pattern in this column of numbers in that each begins with a certain number of 10s, and each has no 1s. The bulletin board or number wall in the classroom should depict these numbers. These numbers can also be included in the "find-the-page" activity described previously and should be included in the number cards.

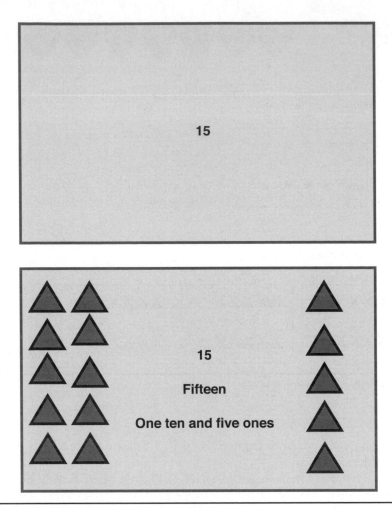

Figure 3.12 Number Cards Depicting Tens and Ones Construction.

Sample Activity #1

Children should have access to manipulatives, including base-ten blocks and snap cubes to use in constructing numbers. As they construct numbers using these manipulatives and blocks, their understanding of the meaning of number is strengthened.

Sample Activity #2

In preparation for the activity, the teacher would fill 10 lunch-sized paper bags each with a different number of base-ten blocks, representing a wide range of numbers. Bags should be numbered. Recording sheets should also be prepared with pictures of bags numbered from 1 to 10. Pairs of children would get a bag, dump out the contents, separate the manipulative into 10s and 1s, and write the number inside the bag on the recording sheet that corresponds to the numbered bag containing the 10s and 1s. For example, a pair of children getting bag #6 find 4 10s and 7 1s inside the bag. They would then record the number 47 inside bag #7 on their recording sheets. After contents are back in the bags, they should be passed around until all pairs have counted the manipulatives in all bags.

Grade 1 Outcome #4: Use Place Value Understanding and Properties of Operations to Add (Commutative and Associative Properties) and Subtract; Understand the Concepts of Addition and Subtraction

Sample Activities: Commutative Property of Addition

Teachers could use the children themselves to lay a foundation for the commutative property of addition. For example, the teacher could choose five boys and three girls to line up side by side – B B B B B G G G. The teacher would "write 5 boys + 3 girls = _____" on the board. Everyone would count the total number of children together; the teacher would write the number "8" on the space as the answer. The lined up children would then change places – G G G B B B B B, and the teacher would write "3 girls + 5 boys = _____" on the board. Again the children would count the total number of children and the teacher would write an "8" on the line. After a few more examples, the children should be asked for their thoughts. Eventually they should come to realize that, no matter how the children are lined up, the total number of children is the same.

To extend this activity, children could be given two different colors of snap cubes. The teacher would ask them to arrange their snap cubes in a specific arrangement, write the equation, and count the number of cubes. For example, children could be asked to snap three red cubes together and then add six blue cubes. Children would write "3 red + 6 blue = 9 cubes." The children would be asked to rearrange their cubes, write the equation, and count the number of cubes—"6 blue + 3 red = 9 cubes." The number of cubes for each equation should be the same.

Children could also work with other objects as they create a foundation for the commutative property of addition (Figure 3.13).

3 dogs + 2 turtles is the same as or 'equal to' 2 turtles + 3 dogs

Figure 3.13 The Commutative Property of Addition.

Sample Activities: Associative Property

The associative property of addition could be introduced using children to demonstrate the concept (Figure 3.14). The teacher could choose children according to the color of clothing they are wearing that day. For example, the teacher could choose two children

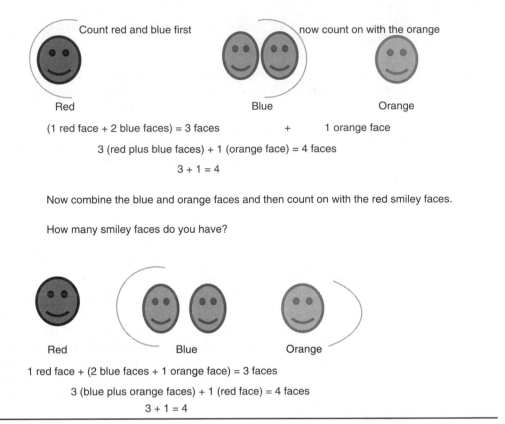

Figure 3.14 A Depiction of the Associative Property of Addition.

wearing red, three children wearing blue, and one child wearing green. Using a make-shift set of parenthesis (a hoola hoop cut into two pieces), the teacher would have two other children put parenthesis around the two children wearing red and the three children wearing blue—(2 children and 3 children). On the board the teacher would write "(2 + 3) + 1 = _____." The children would first add the number of children in parenthesis and then add the one child wearing green for a total of six children. The teacher would then have the parenthesis changed to encase the three children wearing blue and the one child wearing green, and write "(3 + 1) + 2 = _____" on the board. The children would be instructed to add the number of children in parenthesis first and then add the two children wearing red, for a total of six children.

Children should practice this concept using three sets of numbers and changing the parenthesis in calculating solutions.

Grade 1 Outcome #5: Add and Subtract within 20 Using Models, Discrete Objects, and Connecting Cubes; Use Strategies as Counting on, Making Tens, and Decomposing Numbers

Children develop conceptual understanding of addition and subtraction by drawing plural representations and using models and manipulatives. As conceptual understanding continues to develop, children should learn strategies for adding and subtracting within 20. Children can practice adding doubles (1 + 1, 2 + 2 . . . 10 + 10) and making tens.

Learning to make tens (1 + 9, 2 + 8, 3 + 7, 4 + 6, 5 + 5) is an important strategy to develop as children add columns of numbers. Children could practice "making-tens games" to become proficient at this strategy.

Sample Activity #1: Making-Tens Game

Remove all face cards from two regular decks of cards or create your own number cards. Each player in the group is dealt seven cards. Children play the making-tens game with the rules either from "Old Maids" or "Go Fish." As children make combinations of tens in their hands, they can lay down the cards when it is their turn. The game continues until one player is out of cards.

Grade 1 Outcome #6: Comparing Numbers for Addition or Subtraction

Sample Activity #1: Whose Number is Larger or Smaller?

The making-tens game described previously can be modified as a comparison game for pairs of children to play. Each child would need a deck of regular cards minus the face cards. After the decks are shuffled, each player's cards would be stacked face-down in front of the child. To play the game, each child turns over the top two cards from their respective decks and adds the numbers together or subtracts the numbers, depending on which skills the children are practicing. The children then decide whose total is larger (or smaller). The child with the largest total (or smallest) keeps all the cards. The game continues until one child has all the cards or until game time is over.

An extension of this card game would involve providing a "greater-than" sign, a "less-than" sign," and an "equal" sign for each pair of players. The child with the greater total would place the appropriate sign between the two sets of totaled cards. Each player would read the constructed number sentence from the perspective of his or her cards. For example, if Player #1 has a total of 14 and Player #2's total is 7, Player #1 would place the "greater-than" sign between the cards and state, "14 is greater than 7." Player #2 would state, "7 is less than 14." Children can self-check their comparisons using a hundreds chart or a number line.

Sample Activity #2

As children become more skilled at comparing numbers, they can draw numbers from a container and place the appropriate signs between the numbers to compare them. Children can self-check their comparisons using a hundreds chart or a number line.

Grade 1 Outcome #7: Reinforcing Addition and Subtraction Facts within Ten; Finding Unknown Wholes; Decomposing Numbers; Understanding the Relationship between Addition and Subtraction Facts

Sample Activity #1: Fact Families

Fact families are numbers that are associated with each other in forming addition and subtraction facts. For example, the numbers 5, 2, and 7 form a fact family. From their knowledge of fact family relationships, children can write: "5 + 2 = 7; 2 + 5 = 7; 7 − 2 = 5; and 7 − 5 = 2."

Materials for this activity include paper, writing implements, and a bag or other container of fact families. Pairs of children would draw a fact family from the container and then write the two addition facts and two subtraction facts using the numbers in the fact family. Children could self-check their calculations using two different-colored snap cubes (e.g., red and yellow). For example, in using the fact family 6, 3, and 9, children would write: "6 + 3 = 9; 3 + 6 = 9; 9 − 6 = 3; and 9 − 3 = 6." They would then use six red snap cubes and three yellow snap cubes to test their number sentences.

Knowledge of fact families is a tool that can be used in decomposing numbers in addition or subtraction problems. For example, in adding 5 + 7, if children know that 5, 3, and 2 form a fact family, they can decompose 5 into a 3 and 2. Using the strategy of making a ten, they can add the 3 + 7 to get 10 and then add the 2 to get a total of 12.

Sample Activity #2: Flash Cards

Moving memorized math facts from short-term to long-term memory takes practice. For most learners, 15 repetitions or more are required to move new learned material to long-term memory. Most teachers recognize that this transition requires more than 15 repetitions. Thus practice with flash cards provides the repetition needed for such reinforcement but only after the concept has been developed through the use of hands-on practice. Practicing with flash cards helps children develop instant recall of math facts.

Oftentimes children are given too many flash cards to work with at one time. This can be overwhelming to children and cause frustration. Teachers should limit the number of math facts practiced at one time to a maximum of seven to ten cards for proficient math students with enhanced memory skills and three to five cards for other children. Stacks of cards children are practicing should include known facts along with unknown facts to also help prevent frustration.

Grade 1 Outcome #8: Understanding Subtraction Problems as Unknown Addend Problems; Finding Missing Wholes

Children's understanding of fact families is beneficial in understanding subtraction problems as missing addend problems. For example, when it is understood that 5, 3 and 8 go together to form a fact family, children can find the missing addend from a conceptual perspective. Children can use this knowledge in completing the following equations:

8 − 3 = _____ This problem can be solved by finding the number that makes eight when added to three (5 + 3 = 8).
8 − 5 = _____ This problem can be solved by finding the number that makes eight when added to five (3 + 5 = 8).

Sample Activity: Find the Missing Addend

This activity can be used in a whole-group setting. Materials needed for the activity include blank Bingo cards, markers, and a container of subtraction fact equations. Children would write one number, 0 through 9, in each space on their cards. The teacher or a child would draw a subtraction fact equation from the container. Children would be encouraged to determine which number, when added to the number being subtracted makes the total. For example, if the equation 7 − 4 is pulled from the container, it would be determined that 4 + 3 makes 7. The children would chant, "Four plus three equals seven." They would cover a number 3 on their cards. The game is played until a child or children make Bingo.

Grade 1 Outcome #9: Working with Equations

Sample Activity: True-or-False Equation Game

Materials needed for this game include either Tic Tac Toe sheets or blank Bingo cards on which children write either "true" or "false" in each of the spaces, markers to cover spaces, and a container of equations such as: $8 = 6$; $10 = 5 + 4$; $9 = 9$; $5 + 3 = 5 + 3$; $5 + 3 = 10 - 2$, etc. As children draw an equation, they would need to decide whether it is true or false. If the equation is true, the children would cover a "true" word on their sheets. If the equation is false, they would cover a "false" word. The objective of the game, besides working with equations, is to get Tic-Tac-Toe, or Bingo.

Grade 1 Outcome #10: Represent and Solve Addition and Subtraction Problems

It is important for children to use object manipulatives, snap cubes, or base-ten blocks when solving addition and subtraction problem so they develop conceptual understanding of the process. Children could also draw pictures, draw representations, and use equations to find solutions.

Sample Activity #1: Using Models to Solve an Addition Problem

The following problem could be presented to pairs of children to solve using base-ten blocks: "Ms. Brown has 14 children going on a trip to the zoo, and Mr. White has 12 students going on the same trip. Show, using the base-ten blocks, how you could determine how many students in all are going to the zoo and then write the equation."

The children should practice counting by tens and then counting on the ones for a total of 26 students (Figure 3.15).

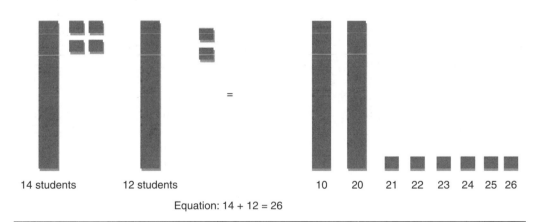

14 students   12 students   =   10   20   21   22   23   24   25   26

Equation: 14 + 12 = 26

Figure 3.15 Using a Model to Solve an Addition Problem.

Sample Activity #2: Using Models to Solve a Subtraction Problem

The children could be presented with the following subtraction problem and asked to solve it using representational drawings: "There are 18 children in our classroom. Today three children are absent. Draw a picture using circles to represent the children in our class that shows how many children are here today. Solve the problem and write the subtraction equation" (Figure 3.16).

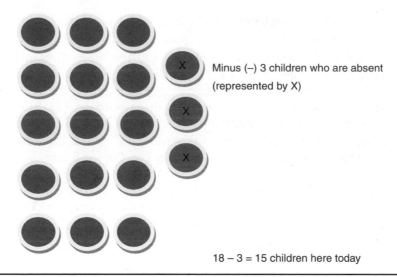

Minus (–) 3 children who are absent (represented by X)

18 – 3 = 15 children here today

Figure 3.16 Drawing Representations to Solve a Subtraction Problem.

Grade 1 Outcome #11 Finding 10 More or 10 Less (Mentally)

Before children can add 10 or subtract 10 from a given number mentally, they need to understand patterns on a hundreds chart. Children need to understand that moving down a column on the hundreds chart means that 10 numbers were added to the previous number in the column. For example, in looking at the "6" column, going down the column under "6" means that 10 numbers are added to advance to 16, 10 more numbers are added to advance to 26, and 10 more numbers are added advance to 36, etc. Likewise, when traveling up a column on the hundreds chart, 10 numbers are subtracted from the previous number in the column. For example, beginning on 85 and moving up the column to 75, 10 numbers are subtracted from 85 to move to 75. Once children have a mental picture of this pattern, they should be able to start on any number and either add or subtract 10 from that number.

Sample Learning Center Activity: Name My New Number Activity

Materials needed for this activity include a container of numbers from 1 to 100, a die, a generic game board, a hundreds chart, and a constructed paper die with "10 more" or "10 less" printed on the six faces of the die. To play the game, a child would roll the "regular' die and move that many spaces on the game board. He or she would then pull a number from the container; this is the starting number. Next, he or she would roll the paper die and either add 10 or subtract 10 mentally from the starting number, depending on the outcome of the die roll. When the new number is stated, the other player would check the hundreds chart to see if the new number is correct. If the new number is correct, the child would remain on the space on the game board; if the number is not correct, the child would go back to the previous space. Children would take turns playing the game until one child reaches the finish line.

CONTENT STANDARDS FOR GRADE 2

In the NCTM *Focal Points* (2006), numbers and operations for grade 2 is described as follows:

- Developing an understanding of the base-ten numeration system and place-value concepts.
- Develop an understanding of the base-ten numeration system and place-value concepts (at least to 1,000). Understanding of base-ten numeration includes ideas of counting in units and multiples of hundreds, tens, and ones, as well as a grasp of number relationships.
- Comparing and ordering numbers.
- Understand multi-digit numbers in terms of place value, recognizing that place-value notation is a shorthand for the sums of multiplies of powers of 10 (e.g., 853 as 8 hundreds + 5 tens + 3 ones).
- Develop quick recall of addition facts and related subtraction facts and fluency with multi-digit addition and subtraction.
- Understanding of addition to develop quick recall of basic addition facts and related subtraction facts . . . Children develop, discuss, and use efficient, accurate, and generalizable methods to add and subtract multi-digit whole numbers.

(2006, p. 14)

The following grade 2 standards are listed in the *Common Core State Standards* (2010):

Grade 2 Standard #1: Represent and solve problems involving addition and subtraction: use addition and subtraction within 100 to solve one- and two-step word problems . . . use drawing and equations with a symbol for the unknown number to represent the problem:

Grade 2 Standard #2: Add and subtract within 20: by the end of grade 2, know from memory all sums of two one-digit numbers.

Grade 2 Standard #3: Work with equal groups of objects to gain foundations for multiplication.
3a. Determine whether a group of objects (up to 20) has an odd or even number of members.
3b. Use addition to find the total number of objects arranged in rectangular arrays with up to 5 rows and up to 5 columns; write an equation to express the total as a sum of equal addends.

Grade 2 Standard #4: Understand place value.
4a. Understand that the three digits of a three-digit number represent amounts of hundreds, tens, and ones

— 100 can be thought of as a bundle of ten tens.
— The numbers 100, 200, 300, etc. refer to one, two, three, etc. hundreds (and with 0 tens and 0 ones).

4b. Count within 1,000; skip-count by 5s, 10s, and 100s.

4c. Read and write numbers to 1000 using base-ten numerals, number names, and expanded form.
4d. Compare two three-digit numbers based on meanings of the hundreds, tens, and ones digits, using greater than, less than, and equal signs to record the results of comparisons.

Grade 2 Standard #5: Use place value and properties of operations to add and subtract:
5a. Fluently add and subtract within 100 using strategies based on place value, properties of operations, and/or the relationship between addition and subtraction.
5b. Add up to four two-digit numbers.
5c. Add and subtract within 1,000 using concrete models or drawings and strategies based on place value, properties of operations, and/or the relationship between addition and subtraction; relate the strategy to a written method.
5d. Mentally add or subtract 10 or 100 to a given number 100–900.
5e. Explain why addition and subtraction strategies work.

(2010, p. 19)

GRADE 2 OUTCOMES

Grade 2 Outcome #1: Fluently Add and Subtract within 20 Using Mental Strategies; Know from Memory All Sums of Two One-Digit Numbers

Sample Activity

Children develop quick recall of addition number facts and related subtraction facts through repeated practice and playing games that require them to use these facts as part of the game process. Children can use flash cards to practice math facts; however, practicing too many unknown math facts at one time can cause stress and frustration for children. Children of similar abilities can help each other learn their math facts. In order to pair children, the teacher will need to administer individual addition and subtraction math fact tests. Once children are paired, the following methods of practice can be used:

1. Children need guidance in assembling stacks of 10 math fact cards to practice. The stack should consist of three unknown math facts and seven known facts. It would be beneficial to place fact family math facts together, so children learn the connections between the numbers. For example, if children need to practice $7 + 8 = 15$ and $8 + 7 = 15$, than their flash cards should also include $15 - 7$ and $15 - 8$, since 7, 8, and 15 form a fact family.
2. Flash cards should have the same math fact on both sides of the cards, so both children practice the facts simultaneously.
3. One child would flash the cards to the other, and then they would change roles.
4. When the unknown math facts become known, new unknown cards should replace these and discard three known facts so the stack of flash cards remains at 10.

Grade 2 Outcome #2: Children Grasp the Concept of the Base-Ten Numeration System to 1000; Making and Reading Numbers to Three and Four Digits

There are various activities that can be used to help children develop a conceptual understanding of the base-ten numeration system.

Sample Activity #1

A set of base-ten blocks is an important manipulative for children to use in forming representations of numbers. Children use the blocks to form number representations on place-value mats. The set of blocks includes cubes of 1,000, flats of 100, strips of 10, and unit cubes for ones (Figure 3.17).

Each child should have his or her own place-value mat. Children could share sets of base-ten blocks. The teacher or children could decide on a number, within 1,000, to represent with the blocks. Children represent the number with the base-ten blocks and then write the number on a piece of paper or recording board. For example, children could form the number 853 by laying out eight one-hundred flats in the hundreds column, five sticks of ten in the tens column, and three unit cubes in the ones column. They would then write "853" on their papers or recording boards. Under the numbers, children would write the value of each digit—800, 50, 3—and then place a plus sign (+) between the numbers—800 + 50 + 3—to demonstrate that these numbers, added together, equals 853. This is referred to as expanded form. Next, children could practice writing the number words under the expanded form—"eight hundred fifty-three."

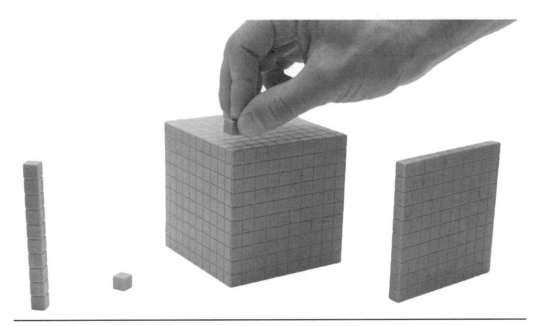

Figure 3.17 Base-Ten Blocks and Place-Value Mat.

Sample Activity #2

To help children make sense of large numbers, it is important to relate these numbers to the real world. Children would be asked to find examples of large numbers as they are used in books and magazines, on billboards, and on television shows. As children collect these numbers and bring them to the classroom, they should engage in discussions concerning the magnitude and use of the numbers. Using representation of base-ten blocks, children would draw a "picture" of the number, write the number, write the number in expanded form, and write the number words. These real-world numbers could be displayed around the classroom.

Sample Activity #3

Fill a jar with objects—candy corn, marbles, buttons, etc. Have each child estimate the number of objects in the jar, record his or her estimate on the chart, and write the number in expanded form. The chart could be displayed in the classroom (Figure 3.18).

Student name	Guess/estimate	Thousands	Hundreds	Tens	Ones
Han	125	0	1	2	5
			100	20	5
Maria	999		9	9	9
			900	90	9
Beth	427		4	2	7
			400	20	7

Figure 3.18 Determining Numbers and Writing Them in Expanded Form.

Sample Learning Center Activity

In preparation for this learning center activity, each child would be assigned a different number within 1,000. Using three note cards, the children would write the number on one card, the expanded form of the number on the second card, and the number words on the third card. Pairs of children could then exchange cards to check for accuracy. Cards would be collected and double-checked by the teacher before placing them in the learning center. As groups of children are assigned to the learning center, they would shuffle the cards, lay them out, face-up, and match the cards. Working as a team, the children would check each other's matches for accuracy.

Grade 2 Outcome #3: Comparing and Ordering Numbers within 1,000
Sample Activity #1

Before children can effectively compare and order numbers, they need to have a conceptual understanding of the meaning of the numbers in place-value form. For example, in comparing 457 and 324, children need to see the 457 as composed of four hundreds, five tens, and seven ones, and 324 as composed of three hundreds, two tens, and four ones. Once children are able to decompose and represent numbers in this way, they can easily compare and order them.

To help children develop this understanding they should first form the numbers they are comparing on place-value mats. This way, children can physically compare the numbers. They can transition to underlining numerals in the numbers to compare them. For example, in comparing 79 and 65, children would underline both numerals in the tens place – 7 6 and 6 5. This helps children focus on the number of tens in each number. If the number of tens is the same – e.g., 97 and 94—then children would underline the numeral in the ones place – 9 7 and 9 4—and then compare the numbers. They can use this procedure in comparing numbers and in ordering numbers.

Sample Activity #2

Materials needed for this activity include a container of numbers within 1,000 and a set of signs—"greater than," "less than," and "equal." Each child would draw a number from the container and read the numbers. Children would take turns deciding which sign to place between the two numbers. Children would monitor each other's decisions.

Grade 2 Outcome #4: Understanding the Meaning of 100
Sample Activity

Pairs of children would need base-ten blocks (one flat of a hundred, 10 strips of 10, and 10 unit cubes), a place-value mat, and die. The objective of the game is to reach 100 after collecting ten strips of ten. The children would take turn rolling the die and begin placing unit cubes in the ones column on the place-value mat. As 10 unit cubes are collected, they would be "traded" for a strip of ten. At various intervals of time, the teacher could call "Stop." He or she would ask pairs of children what number they have formed on their place-value mats to this point. For example, a pair of children may have four strips of ten and two ones, so they would state that they have made the number 42. They teacher would then have the children continue the game. They game should be played long enough so each pair of children reaches 100. This game would help children understand 100 as 10 sticks of ten or one flat of 100 with no tens or ones.

Grade 2 Outcome #5: Count to 1,000; Count to 1,000 by 5s, 10s, and 100s; Mentally Add or Subtract 10 or 100

As instructional tools, teachers would prepare booklets for children, the pages of which are arranged in hundreds charts. For example, page 1 would display a hundreds chart from 1 to 100; page 2 would display a hundreds chart from 101 to 200; page 3 would display a hundreds chart from 201 to 300. This pattern would continue until the last page displays a hundreds chart from 901 to 1,000. The booklets could be used to help children determine the pattern in counting from 1 to 1,000. Children could also use their booklets to make sense of the skip-counting patterns. To aid children with skip-counting patterns, they could color in yellow both the fives column and tens column on all of the hundreds charts. Next, they could draw a black circle around all the numbers in the tens column on all of the hundreds charts, and outline each hundred box on the hundreds chart in red. The booklets provide a scaffolding tool for children until they understand counting patterns and can count without the aid of the booklets.

Grade 2 Outcome #6: Mentally Add or Subtract 10 or 100 from a Given Number

The booklets from the previous outcome can provide a scaffolding tool as children learn to mentally add or subtract 10 or 100 from a given number.

Sample Activity

Materials needed for this activity include a container of numbers within 1,000, recording paper, writing implements, and two prepared paper dice. One die would have "+ 10 or "+ 100" written on each of the six faces of the die. The other die would have "− 10" or "− 100" written on each of the six faces of the die. Before playing the game, the children would decide whether they are going to focus on adding 10 or 100 or subtracting 10 or 100 during that particular game. Pairs or small groups of children would take turns drawing a number from the container; this is the given number. The same child who drew the given number would roll the appropriate die and follow the directions in either adding 10 or 100 to the given number or subtracting 10 or 100 from the given number. Children could check each other for accuracy by using their booklets. Each child would keep tally marks to indicate correct answers. After each child has had five or so turns, the pair or group of children could play the same game using the other die. At the end of the games, children could compare the tally marks they accumulated during the games.

Grade 2 Outcome #7: Add and Subtract Within 1,000; Explain Why Strategies Work

Ideally children should be given the opportunity to develop their own sense-making strategies for adding and subtracting within 1000; however, this is not always possible depending on the instructional setting. Teachers can introduce various strategies to children and provide them with the opportunity to use the strategy that makes sense to them.

Sample Strategy #1

Children can add and subtract numbers using base-ten blocks and place-value mats. For addition, children would form both numbers on the place-value mats and then combine and "trade" as required. For example, each group of ten units would be traded for a strip of ten; each group of ten tens would be traded for a flat of a hundred; and ten hundreds would be traded for a cube of a thousand. Once children understand addition using the base-ten blocks, they could draw representations of the blocks on paper to depict the numbers they are adding and follow the same process. Once children understand the regrouping process, they should be able to perform the algorithm on paper without the blocks or drawing representations.

For subtraction, children would form only the larger of the two numbers using the base-ten blocks on the place-value mats. The number being subtracted would be depicted using number cards. Children should begin by only performing subtraction problems that do not require regrouping. For example, in subtracting 427 from 639, children would form 639 using the base-ten blocks on the place-value mat. They would then find the number cards 4, 2, and 7 and place them in the appropriate columns on the mat—the 4 goes in the hundreds column, the 2 in the tens column, and the 7 in the ones column. The number cards show children how many in each column need to be subtracted.

When children are competent in subtracting using base-ten blocks and number cards, they should be shown how to regroup using the base-ten blocks. For example, in subtracting 237 from 692, children would form 692 using the base-ten blocks on the place-value mats. They would lay the 2, 3, and 7 number cards in the appropriate columns on the mat. Noticing that seven ones cannot be subtracted from two ones, the children would need to trade a strip of ten for 10 unit cubes and place these cubes in the ones column with the two cubes that are already there. Now the children would be able to subtract seven ones from 12 ones. When children understand the regrouping process using base-ten blocks, they should draw representations on paper, and then eventually perform the algorithm without the aid of blocks or drawings.

Algorithms involving regrouping require time to develop understanding. Children should not be performing an algorithm he or she does not understand.

Sample Strategy #2: Partial Sums

In this strategy, children find partial sums and then add these together to determine a final sum. This strategy reinforces place value. For example, in adding 54 and 37, children could first add the 50 and 30 (tens) together to get 80, and then add the 4 and 7 (ones) together to get 11. They would then add 80 + 11, to get a sum of 91 (Figure 3.19)

Children could also use the partial-sums strategy in adding three-digit numbers. See the example in Figure 3.20.

Sample Strategy #3: Partial Differences

Calculating partial differences in subtraction problems is a strategy that children could use. See the examples in Figure 3.21 for subtracting 27 from 79 and subtracting 146 from 239.

```
   54
 + 37
   80
 + 11

   91
```

Figure 3.19 Adding Two-Digit Numbers Using Partial Sums.

```
  1 4 7
+ 6 4 2
  7 0 0
    8 0
+     9
  7 8 9
```

Figure 3.20 Adding Three-Digit Numbers Using Partial Sums.

79

− 27

50(70 − 20) + 2(97) = 52

239

−146

100(200 − 100) − 10(30 − 40) + 3(9 − 6)
90(100 − 90) + 3 = 93

Figure 3.21 Finding Partial Differences to Solve Subtraction Problems.

Grade 2 Outcome #8: Adding up to Four Two-Digit Numbers

As children become proficient in adding using strategies as counting on, doubles, and making tens, they should be able to apply these strategies in adding columns of up to four numbers together. For example, in adding 37, 22, 84, and 76 together, children should see that the 6 and 4 in the ones column form a 10. The 10 ones plus the 9 ones is a total of 19 ones. Ten of the ones will need to be regrouped as a ten. In the tens column, children should be able to determine that the 7 and 3 make 10 tens and the 8 and 2 make another 10 tens. These 20 tens are added to the 1 regrouped 10 to make a total of 21 tens. The 21 tens plus the 9 left-over ones makes a sum of 219 (Figure 3.22).

+ 1 (the regrouped 10)
 37
 22
 84 (4 + 6 is 10; 10 plus (7 + 2) is 19
+ 76 (in the tens column, 3 + 7 is ten and 8 + 2 is ten; that is 20; + the regrouped 1 is 21 tens)
 219

Figure 3.22 Adding Four Two-Digit Numbers Using the Making-Tens Strategy.

Grade 2 Outcome #9: Odd and Even Groups of Numbers up to 20

Concepts concerning odd and even numbers can be introduced to children using pairing activities. Once children understand the concept, they can count by twos to locate even numbers.

Sample Activity #1: Do I Have a Partner?

This is a simple activity to introduce children to the idea of an odd or even number. The teacher would place various groups of children together and give them a number card depicting the number of children in the group. When the teacher tells the children to begin, children in each group would pair up. It would be pointed out that the number in groups where each child has a partner is even, and the number in groups where someone does not have a partner is odd. These odd and even numbers should be recorded on the board in columns labeled "Odd" and "Even." The teacher could refigure the groups and do the activity as many times as desired.

Sample Activity #2

In preparation for this activity, the teacher would prepare bags of pennies or centimeter cubes, etc. (enough for one bag for every child in the class) with various numbers in each bag. The total number of pennies or other objects should be written on the front of each bag. Each child would need a recording sheet showing two columns: one labeled "Odd" and the other labeled "Even." When children receive their bag of pennies or other objects, they should be instructed to dump the objects on their desks and pair them up. If a child can make equal pairs, then the number is even. If the child has one penny or object that does not have a partner, then the number is odd. The number representing the total of pennies or objects in the bag would then be recorded in the correct column on the recording sheet. After the pennies or other objects are replaced in the bags, they should be traded until each student has had the opportunity to pair the pennies or objects in each bag.

Sample Activity #3

Materials needed for this activity include hundreds charts, writing implements, and containers of centimeter cubes, pennies, or other manipulatives for each child. Starting with the number 1, children would lay out one manipulative and try to pair it with another manipulative. Since one manipulative would not have a partner, it is an odd number. Children would place an "O" for odd in the block on the hundreds chart with the 1. Next, the children would move to the number 2, take out two manipulatives and pair them. Since the two manipulatives are partnered, 2 is an even number. Children would place an "E" in the block with the number 2. This procedure would continue for all 100 numbers or until a pattern is noticed.

Children would then color all the even numbers a specific color and all the odd numbers a different color. Children could then practice counting by odd or even numbers to 100.

Grade 2 Outcome #10: Write an Equation to Express an Even Number as a Sum of Two Equal Addends

Sample Activity

This is a simple activity that can be used to introduce adding two equal addends and expressing the sum as an even number. Materials needed for the activity include recording sheets, writing implements, and a die for each pair of children. Children would take turns rolling the die to determine the addend. Both children would then write the addend twice in an equation to determine that the sum is an even number. For example, if Partner #1 rolls a five, both children would record: $5 + 5 = 10$ (even). Children could use their hundreds charts from the previous activity to verify even sums. It would then be Partner #2's turn to roll the die.

After the activity, it would be important for the teacher to hold a discussion with the children to determine what they learned from the activity. Simply stated, when doubles are added together, the sums are even numbers.

Grade 2 Outcome #11: Add Using Arrays up to Five Columns and Rows; Write an Equation to Express the Total as a Sum of Equal Addends

Sample Activity

Children can be introduced to counting objects in arrays by providing arrays such as those in Figure 3.23. Children would count the total number of objects and then write an equation to find the sum using the addends from either the rows or columns or both.

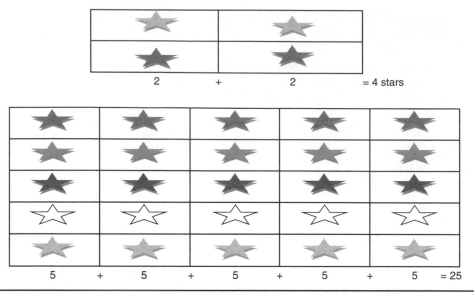

$$2 \quad + \quad 2 \qquad = 4 \text{ stars}$$

$$5 \quad + \quad 5 \quad + \quad 5 \quad + \quad 5 \quad + \quad 5 \quad = 25$$

Figure 3.23 Counting Objects in Arrays and Writing Equations to Determine Sums.

CONTENT STANDARDS FOR GRADE 3

Content standards in the NCTM document *Principles and Standards in School Mathematics* (2000) are not presented by individual grades or age levels, but are grouped in age or grade bands. The 3–5 grade band includes the following standards:

Analyze characteristics and properties of two- and three-dimensional geometric shapes and develop mathematical arguments about geometric relationships:

- identify, compare, and analyze attributes of two- and three-dimensional shapes and develop vocabulary to describe the attributes;
- classify two- and three-dimensional shapes according to their properties and develop definitions of classes of shapes such as triangles and pyramids;
- investigate, describe, and reason about the results of subdividing, combining, and transforming shapes;
- explore congruence and similarity;
- make and test conjectures about geometric properties and relationships and develop logical arguments to justify conclusions.

Specify locations and describe spatial relationships using coordinate geometry and other representational systems:

- describe location and movement using common language and geometric vocabulary;

- make and use coordinate systems to specify locations and to describe paths;
- find the distance between points along horizontal and vertical lines.

Apply transformations and use symmetry to analyze mathematical situations:

- predict and describe the results of sliding, flipping, and turning two-dimensional shapes;
- describe a motion or a series of motions that will show that two shapes are congruent;
- identify and describe line and rotational symmetry in two- and three-dimensional shapes and designs.

Use visualization, spatial reasoning, and geometric modeling to solve problems:

- build and draw geometric objects;
- create and describe mental images of objects, patterns, and paths;
- identify and build a three-dimensional object from two-dimensional representations of that object;
- identify and draw a two-dimensional representation of a three-dimensional object;
- use geometric models to solve problems in other areas of mathematics, such as number and measurement;
- recognize geometric ideas and relationships and apply them to other disciplines and to problems that arise in the classroom or in everyday life.

(www.nctm.org/standards/)

The following NCTM *Focal Points* are the recommended content emphases for mathematics in grade 3:

- Developing understandings of multiplication and division and strategies for basic multiplication facts and related divisions facts.
- Understand the meanings of multiplication and division of whole numbers through the use of representations (e.g., equal-sized groups, arrays, area models, and equal "jumps" on number lines for multiplication, and successive subtraction, partitioning, and sharing for division).
- Use properties of addition and multiplication (e.g., commutativity, associativity, and the distributive property) to multiply whole numbers and apply increasingly sophisticated strategies based on these properties to solve multiplication and division problems involving basic facts.
- Comparing a variety of solution strategies, students relate multiplication and division as inverse operations.
- Developing an understanding of fractions and fraction equivalence.

- Develop an understanding of the meanings and uses of fractions to represent parts of a whole, parts of a set, or points or distances on a number line.
- Understand that the size of a fractional part is relative to the size of the whole, and they use fractions to represent numbers that are equal to, less than, or greater than 1.
- Solve problems that involve comparing and ordering fractions by using models, benchmark fractions, or common numerators or denominators.
- Understand and use models, including the number line, to identify equivalent fractions.

(2006, p. 15)

The following grade 3 standards are listed in the *Common Core State Standards* (2010):

Grade 3 Standard #1: Represent and solve problems involving multiplication and division:
1a. Interpret products of whole numbers (e.g., 5×7 is the total number of objects in 5 groups of 7 objects.);
1b. Interpret whole-number quotients of whole numbers (e.g., interpret 56 divided by 8 as the number of objects in each share when 56 objects are partitioned equally into 8 shares);
1c. Use multiplication and division within 100 to solve word problems in situations involving equal groups, arrays, and measurement quantities;
1d. Determine the unknown whole number in a multiplication or division equation relating three whole numbers.

Grade 3 Standard #2: Understand properties of multiplication and the relationship between multiplication and division:
2a. Apply properties of operations as strategies to multiply and divide (commutative, associative, and distributive properties);
3b. Understand division as an unknown-factor problem.

Grade 3 Standard #3: Multiply and divide within 100.

Grade 3 Standard #4: Solve problems involving the four operations, and identify and explain patterns in arithmetic:
4a. Solve two-step problems using the four operations;
4b. Identify arithmetic patterns (including patterns in the additional table or multiplication table).

Grade 3 Standard #5: Use place-value understanding and properties of operations to perform multi-digit arithmetic:
5a. Use place value understanding to round whole numbers to the nearest 10 or 100;

5b. Fluently add and subtract within 1000 using strategies and algorithms based on place value, properties of operations, and/or the relationship between addition and subtraction;
5c. Multiply one-digit whole numbers by multiples of 10 in the range 10–90; e.g., 9×80.

Grade 3 Standard #6: Develop understanding of fractions as numbers:
6a. Understand a fraction 1/b as the quantity formed by 1 part when a whole is partitioned into b equal parts;
6b. Understand a fraction as a number on the number line; represent fractions on a number line diagram.

— Represent a fraction 1/b on a number line diagram by defining the interval from 0 to 1 as the whole and partitioning it into b equal parts;
— Represent a fraction a/b on a number line diagram by marking off a length 1/b from 0.

6c. Explain equivalence of fractions in special cases, and compare fractions by reasoning about their sizes:

— Understand two fractions as equivalent (equal) if they are the same size, or the same point on a number line;
— Recognize and generate simple equivalent fractions, e.g., ½ = ²/₄, and ⁴/₆ = ²/₃. Explain why fractions are equivalent;
— Express whole numbers as fractions and recognize fractions that are equivalent to wholes. Examples: express 3 in the form of 3 = ³/₁, etc;
— Compare two fractions with the same numerator or the same denominator by reasoning about their size.

(2010, pp. 23–24)

GRADE 3 OUTCOMES

Grade 3 Outcome #1: Understand Place Value to 10,000 in Various Contexts
Instructional strategies used in grade 2 are also applicable in grade 3 as children expand their understanding of place value, writing numbers using words, and writing numbers in expanded form. Children can also play games in which they are asked the value of digits within a number.

Sample Activity #1: Whole-Group Place-Value Activity
In preparation for this game, the teacher would create large numeral cards from 1 to 9. (When the children become competent in reading and writing numbers without zeroes, the zero should be added to the numerals to demonstrate how zero functions as a place holder.) Additionally, place-value signs—for ones, tens, hundreds, thousands, and ten thousands—would be created and taped on the board in the front of the classroom (Figure 3.24).

Five children would be chosen each day to choose a numeral and stand beneath one of the place-value signs. Children at their tables or desks would create five columns on a

Figure 3.24 Place-Value Signs for Place-Value Game.

piece of paper and label the place-value columns. When the five children are situated beneath the place-value signs, the teacher would ask for a volunteer from the other children to read this "big" number. Everyone in the class would repeat the number, and children at their desks or tables would write the numerals in the appropriate place-value columns. One by one, the teacher would ask the positioned children what they are "worth" depending on which sign they are beneath. For example, if the numerals under the place-value signs are "3 7 1 2 5," the teacher would state:

"Ellen, you are a 5 in the ones column; what are you worth?"
"Sam, you are a 2 in the tens column; what are you worth?"
"Lauren, you are a 1 in the hundreds column; what are you worth?"
"Tom, you are a 7 in the thousands column; what are you worth?"
"Jacob, you are a 3 in the ten thousands column; what are you worth?"

After the children state their "worth," everyone would slide to the right, and Jacob would move to the ones column. Again, the teacher would ask for a volunteer from the other children to read the new "big" number, pointing out that the numerals did not change, just the position of the numerals in the number. Children in their seats would write the new numerals in the appropriate place-value spaces.

The teacher would then ask each of the positioned children what they are "worth" now in their new position. For example:

"Jacob, you were just worth 30,000 in the ten thousands column; what are you worth now in the ones column?"
"Ellen, you were just worth 5 in the ones column; what are you worth now in the tens column?"
"Sam, you were just worth 20 in the tens column; what are you worth now in the hundreds column?"
"Lauren, you were just worth 100 in the hundreds column; what are you worth now in the thousands column?"
"Tom, you were just worth 7,000 in the thousands column; what are you worth now in the ten thousands column?"

The positioned children could be asked to move until all five "big" numbers have been created and the value of each numeral stated for each.

Extension Activities: The numbers generated from the place-value activity described above could be used in the following ways:

1. The numbers could be ordered from least to greatest or greatest to least.

2. Numbers could be compared using terminology and signs as "greater than" or "less than."
3. Numbers could be written in word form.
4. Numbers could be written in expanded form.
5. Numbers could be represented using base-ten blocks.
6. Two numbers could be added together or subtracted to find the difference.

Sample Activity #2: Can You Guess My Number?

This game could be played as a whole group or by small groups of children. Numbers could extend to 10,000. For example, the teacher or a child could state, "My thousands place is a 4, my hundreds place is a 6, my tens place is 0, and my ones place is a 2. What is my number? Children could write the numerals for the different values on paper or boards.

Grade 3 Outcome #2: Round Whole Numbers to the Nearest 10 or 100

Sample Activity

This activity could be used to help children visualize the rounding process. Using their individual hundreds chart, children would be asked to locate a number on the chart other than a number with a 5 in the ones place; e.g., 76. Children would then determine which two tens the number 76 is between on the hundreds chart – 70 and 80. Without using any rules, children should be able to see on the charts that 76 is closer to 80 than 70; thus, 76 rounds to 80. This procedure should continue with a few examples before introducing a number with a 5 in the ones place.

Children could color the fives column on their hundreds charts. Children would need to be taught that if a number has a 5 in the ones column, then that number always rounds to the higher ten. For example, the number 25 is between the 20 and 30 on the hundreds chart. Since there is a 5 in the ones place, 25 rounds to 30. At some point children would learn that when rounding to the nearest ten, the numeral in the ones place shows the way: if the numeral in the ones place is 4 or lower, the number rounds to the lower ten; if the numeral in the ones place is 5 or above, the number rounds to the higher ten.

When children are comfortable in using their hundreds charts to round whole numbers to the nearest ten, they could draw models for rounding, focusing on the number in the ones place. As an example, see Figure 3.25. Children learn to reason that 82 rounds to 80, since the numeral in the ones place is lower than 5.

Children could use booklets as described in Grade 2 Outcome #5 to develop a conceptual understanding of rounding a whole number to the nearest 100. For example, using their booklets, children could be asked to locate the number 468. They would then determine that the number 468 is between 400 and 500. Children should be able to visually see that the number 468 is closer to 500 than it is to 400, thus the number 468 rounds to 500.

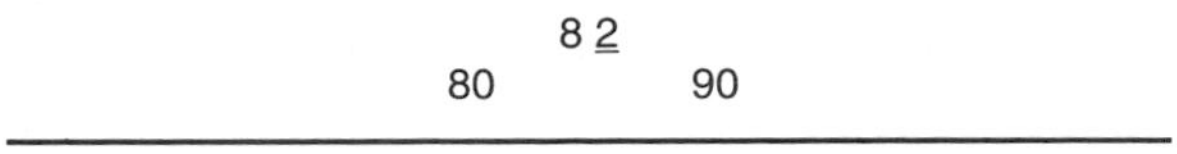

8 2
80   90

Figure 3.25 Rounding to the Nearest Ten Model.

After more examples to develop understanding, children could place a star next to spaces with 50, 150, 250, etc. in them. They would learn to focus on the tens and ones place together in determining rounding to the nearest hundred. They would learn that if the tens and ones place together is less than 50, the number rounds to the lesser hundred; if the tens and ones place together is 50 or greater, the number rounds to the greater hundred. When children are comfortable with this concept using their booklets, they could draw models.

Children learn to reason that 447 rounds to 400 since 47 (the numerals in the tens and ones places) is less than 50 (Figure 3.26).

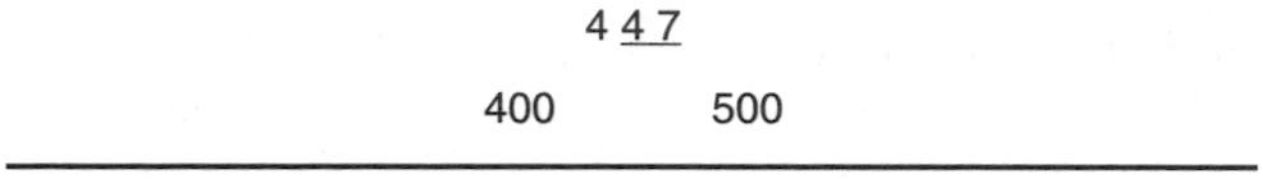

4 4 7

400   500

Figure 3.26 Rounding to the Nearest Hundred Model.

Grade 3 Outcome #3: Use Properties of Addition to Solve Problems; Add and Subtract Fluently within 1000; Use Mental Math

Strategies used to develop conceptual understanding for addition and subtracting in grade 2 can be continued in grade 3 as children become fluent in adding and subtracting within 1,000. It is important to remember that children should not be using a strategy they do not understand. If a child is having difficulty with an algorithm or procedure for addition or subtraction, the teacher needs to determine where a child's understanding breaks down and begin instruction for that child at that point. Continuing to work with a process that is not understood only leads to frustration and a possible disliking of mathematics in general.

As children develop number sense or a sense about how our base-ten number system works, they should be able to mentally compute problems that are not too complex. For example they should be able to mentally compute problems such as: 400 + 300, 600 − 300, 9,000 − 2,000, and 2,300 + 2,000.

Sample Learning Center Activity

Materials needed for this activity include checker boards, chips and a calculator. Each checker board would be prepared with stickers on each of the spaces. Each sticker would contain a problem to be solved mentally as in the examples above. Children would play the checkers game; however, in making a move or jump, a child would need to solve the problem mentally in order to stay on the space. Children could check each other's calculations or verify a disputed calculation using a calculator.

Grade 3 Outcome #4: Understanding Multiplication

Sample Activity #1

To help children understand multiplication, they should first be given large piles of objects to count. The total number of objects should be so large that it is cumbersome and time-consuming to count the objects one by one. As small groups of children are engaged in counting, the teacher could point out how time-consuming and difficult the task is to count all of the objects in the pile one by one and ask children for their ideas on how to make the task easier. Children should be guided in realizing that if they put the objects in groups of 5s or 10s, they could count the objects that way.

As groups of children determine how many groups of five or 10 objects they made, the teacher should note this on the board. For example, perhaps a group of children made groups of 10 and counted out 32 groups. The teacher would write "10 objects × 32 groups." Children could count the 32 groups by 10s to determine the total, or use a calculator. The total is not the important focus for this activity. The focus is on helping children understand the meaning of the factors in a multiplication problem.

In recounting the objects, children should be asked to form groups again, but to choose a different number of objects to place in groups. For example, a group of children could decide to form groups of seven. After grouping, there are perhaps 21 groups. The more experience children have in creating factors, the better they will understand the meaning of multiplication.

Depending on the number of objects children place in groups, they may not always be able to form a last, complete group. Teachers could use this situation to introduce the concept of a partial group. Children would need to decide what to do with a partial group of objects as they are counting the total number of objects in their pile.

Sample Activity #2

Children need experiences in working with equal groups, arrays and area models, equal groups, and making equal "jumps" along a number line as they are learning strategies to understand basic multiplication facts and identify arithmetic patterns.

Using Arrays or Area Models: In working with arrays or area models, children could use repeated addition to determine the total number of squares in the array. Eventually children would learn to multiply the number of blocks in a column by the number of blocks in a row or the number of blocks in a row by the number of blocks in a column to compute the total number of blocks in the array or area model (Figure 3.27).

Making Equal Groups: Children could count out specific numbers of objects and arrange them into equal groups. They could then record their arrangements as multiplication equations. For example 12 circles can be arranged in various group arrangements (Figure 3.28).

Equal "Jumps" on a Number Line: Children could make equal "jumps" on a number line in demonstrating multiplication equations. For example, the number line in Figure 3.29 depicts 3 × 4, or 4 jumps of three numbers each, and 3 + 3 + 3 + 3. This helps children learn to count by multiples, which prepares them to understand multiplication tables.

Multiplication Chart: A multiplication chart is a tool that children could use to help them conceptualize math facts. Going down any column, the column number multiplied by the number of the row provides the solution to a multiplication problem. For example (column 6) × (row 4) = 24. Children can practice equal "jumps" on the multiplication chart (Figure 3.30).

1	2
3	4

2 + 2 = 4 or
2 in a row x 2 in a column = 4

1	2	3
4	5	6
7	0	9

3 + 3 + 3 = 9 or
3 in a singular column x 3 in a row = 9

1	2	3	4
5	6	7	8
9	10	11	12

4 + 4 + 4 = 12 or
4 in a row x 4 in a column = 12

Figure 3.27 Arrays and Area Models.

Grade 3 Outcome #5: Strategies for Learning Basic Facts

When children understand multiplication conceptually, they are ready to begin memorizing the basic facts. They learn strategies such as multiplying a number one time or times 1. In understanding groups, children realize that if there are no groups, then the answer in the multiplication equation is zero. As children continue skip-counting by 2s, 5s, and 10s, and they should realize that, in doing so, they have been repeating the 2, 5, and 10 multiplication tables. Many children learn to multiply double numbers rather easily: 1×1, 4×4, 7×7, etc.

Oftentimes the terminology used with children can be confusing to them. For example, stating 3×4 could be confusing. Changing the terminology to "3, 4 times" or "3 groups of 4," could help clarify the meaning for children. The focus needs to be on helping children understand, not confusing them.

Once children know their 2 times tables, the 4 times table is just double the two times table. For example, $\underline{2} \times 6 = \underline{12}$, so $\underline{4} \times 6$ is going to be $\underline{24}$. This is double the two times table. Likewise, once children know their three times table, the six times table is just double the three times table ($\underline{3} \times 4 = \underline{12}$; $\underline{6} \times 4 = \underline{24}$). Once the four times table is learned, the eight times table is just double the four times table ($\underline{4} \times 6 = \underline{24}$; $\underline{8} \times 6 = \underline{48}$). The only facts left to be learned are those 7×7 and 9×9, since all the other facts have been learned in other times tables.

When children see the connection among the basic math facts, the task of memorizing these facts is not such a daunting task for many.

Sample Activities

Children need to practice the basic multiplication facts in order to memorize them. Classrooms should be stocked with a variety of different ways to practice facts so

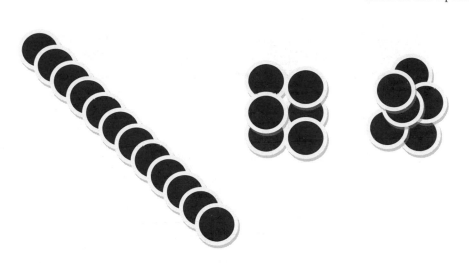

1 group of 12
12 circles x 1 group = 12 circles
12 x 1 = 12 or
1 x 12 = 12

2 groups of 6
6 circles x 2 groups = 12 circles
6 x 2 = 12 or
2 x 6 = 12

4 groups of 3
3 circles x 4 groups = 12 circles
3 x 4 = 12 or 4 x 3 = 12

3 groups of 4
4 circles x 3 groups = 12 circles
4 x 3 = 12 or 3 x 4 = 12

Figure 3.28 Making Equal Groups.

Figure 3.29 Equal "Jumps" on a Number Line.

Times (x)	1	2	3	4	5	6	7	8	9	10
1	1	2	3	4	5	6	7	8	9	10
2	2	4	6	8	10	12	14	16	18	20
3	3	6	9	12	15	18	21	24	27	30
4	4	8	12	16	20	24	28	32	36	40
5	5	10	15	20	25	30	35	40	45	50
6	6	12	18	24	30	36	42	48	54	60
7	7	14	21	28	35	42	49	56	63	70
8	8	16	24	32	40	48	56	64	72	80
9	9	18	27	36	45	54	63	72	81	90
10	10	20	30	40	50	60	70	80	90	100

Figure 3.30 Multiplication Chart.

children do not become bored with one method. For example, there are many games teachers can make or purchase that focus on practicing multiplication facts. Typically, children make multiplication flash cards and quiz each other in memorizing facts. Children can become frustrated if they are being required to practice too many multiplication facts at one time. Many children need to focus on one times table at a time as they are memorizing these facts. Children who are having difficulty in learning their facts should only practice a few new facts along with facts they already know, so as to not become overwhelmed.

Sample Game

As children become proficient in memorizing multiplication facts, they could play games with each other using the multiplication chart in Figure 3.30. One child could state a product from the chart, and the other child could try to name all the factors that result in that particular product. For example, a product of 40 can be derived by multiplying 10 × 4, 4 × 10, 8 × 5, and 5 × 8.

Grade 3 Outcome #6: Relating Multiplication Fact to Division; Multiply and Divide within 100

It would be beneficial to have children learn multiplication and division facts in fact families. For example, 36, 9, and 4 make a multiplication/division fact family. Four facts can be written from this fact family: $9 \times 4 = 36$; $4 \times 9 = 36$; 36 divided by 9 = 4; and 36 divided by 4 = 9. As children demonstrate competency in learning multiplication facts, they should begin viewing the factors and products as fact families.

Sample Learning Center Activity: Write the Facts!

Materials needed for the center include paper or recording boards, writing implements and a container of multiplication/division fact families stated as: 54, 6, 9. Children would copy the three numbers and then write the two multiplication facts and two division facts using the numbers in the fact family.

Grade 3 Outcome #7: Understand Division as an Unknown Factor

Once children understand the relationship between multiplication and division facts, they can begin to understand that equations involving division are really problems in which the unknown factor must be determined. For example, in the equation 81 divided by 9, children need to ask the question, "What number times nine will give a product of 81?" Children should be provided with experiences in which they are required to determine the unknown factor in division fact equations.

Grade 3 Outcome #8: Communicating the Meaning of Multiplication and Division Fact Problems

Sample Activity: Journal Writing

Journal writing is one way that teachers could use to determine children's understandings of the different math concepts they are learning. Children should be able to explain in their journal writing what 6×4 means outside of merely computing the product. For example, a child should be able to explain that 6×4 means there are four groups with six objects in each group or that there are six groups with four objects in each group.

Likewise, children should be able to explain that 56 divided by 8 means that 56 objects need to be partitioned equally into eight different groups.

Grade 3 Outcome #9: Use Multiplication to Solve Word Problems; Use Properties of Addition and Multiplication to Solve Problems

Teachers should try to create multiplication word problems for children that relate to real-life circumstances. For example, the following problem could be presented to children: "Roselyn is having a birthday party with her friends and relatives. After cake, everyone is going to the water park. If three cars each take five people to the water park, how many people are at Roselyn's birthday party?" The problem could be solved using multiple strategies: $5 + 5 + 5$ (repeated addition), 5×3 or 3×5 (multiplication), making representational drawings, or by using manipulatives.

Another type of problem teaches children the distributive property of multiplication. For example, children could be presented with the following problem: "Jose has 3×4 crayons, and Lola has 6×4 crayons. How many crayons do they have all together?" Children would, most likely, find the product of both sets of factors and add the products. They should be challenged to think about the answer using the distributive property. For example, both children have a number of crayons times four, so the first factors could be added for a total of nine. The nine could then be multiplied by four: $(3 + 6) \times 4$.

Grade 3 Outcome #10: Multiply One-Digit Numbers by Multiples of 10 between 10 and 90; Identify Arithmetic Patterns

There are a variety of activities that can be used to help children understand computing the product when multiplying one-digit numbers by multiples of 10. For example, children could use repeated addition and then write the addition equation and the multiplication equation.

Sample Activity

Children could make groups of 10 straws or other objects depicting the number of tens required to compute the multiples problem. For example, in computing 8×10, children would make eight groups of ten straws and then count the groups by 10s. They could write: "$10 + 10 + 10 + 10 + 10 + 10 + 10 + 10 = 80$ and $8 \times 10 = 80$."

Children could also use their fingers to depict the number of tens required to compute the multiples problem. For example, in multiplying 7×10, children would put up seven fingers and then count by 10s along their raised fingers.

Once children "see" the pattern of adding a zero to the number being multiplied by 10, they should be able to complete the equation without counting objects or fingers (Figure 3.31). They should also see the relationship of multiplying a one-digit number by 1 to multiplying a one-digit number by 10 (Figure 3.32).

1 x 10 = 10	6 x 10 = 60
2 x 10 = 20	7 x 10 = 70
3 x 10 = 30	8 x 10 = 80
4 x 10 = 40	9 x 10 = 90
5 x 10 = 50	

Figure 3.31 Multiplying a One-Digit Number by Ten.

1 x 1 = 1; 1 x 10 = 10	6 x 1 = 6; 6 x 10 = 60
2 x 1 = 2; 2 x 10 = 20	7 x 1 = 7; 7 x 10 = 70
3 x 1 = 3; 3 x 10 = 30	8 x 1 = 8; 8 x 10 = 80
4 x 1 = 4; 4 x 10 = 40	9 x 1 = 9; 9 x 10 = 90
5 x 1 = 5; 5 x 10 = 50	

Figure 3.32 Multiplying a One-Digit by One and by Ten.

Grade 3 Outcome #11: Determine the Unknown Whole Number in Multiplication and Division Equations Relating Three Whole Numbers

Sample Learning Center Activity

Materials needed for this activity include a generic board game, game markers, dice, a hundreds chart, and a container of multiplication and division equations including an unknown. Sample equations:

$8 \times ? = 40$
$6 = ?$ divided by 3
$5 \times 5 = ?$
48 divided by 6 = ?

To play the game, a child would roll a die and move that many spaces on the game board. He or she would then pull an equation from the container and find the missing factor, product, or quotient. If the unknown is determined correctly, the child would stay on the space. If the unknown is not determined correctly, the child would need to go back to the previous space. Children could use a hundreds chart or a calculator to check each other's calculations.

Grade 3 Outcome #12 Solve Multiplication and Division Problem within 100 in Situations Involving Equal Groups, Arrays, and Measurement Quantities; Use Drawings or Equations with an Unknown Number

Sample Activity

Children could create their own multiplication and division word problems. These should be developed using drawings depicting equal groups, arrays, or equal "jumps" on a number line to ensure problem accuracy. Once the problems have been created and checked for accuracy, they should be printed as note cards. Pairs of children trade note cards and solve each other's problems. Once solved, each child would check the other's calculations. As children complete one note card problem, they trade with other children.

Grade 3 Outcome #13: Solve Two-Step, Whole-Number Problems Using the Four Operations; Represent Problems Using Equations with a Letter Standing or Unknown Quantities; Assess Reasonableness of Answers

Children need practice in solving two-step problems, since they typically want to find only one solution to a problem and move on. They need to read word problems carefully and look for all the question marks. If there are two question marks in a problem, then two solutions must be determined.

Word problems that children are asked to solve should be applicable to real-life situations, so they are meaningful to the children. The following sample problem could be presented to children: "James earned $12.00 raking leaves in the neighborhood. He put $6.00 in his piggy bank. How much money did James have left? He then divided the money that was left between his two brothers and himself. How much money did James give each of his brothers?" The problem could be solved in using the following equations:

$12.00 − $6.00 = x
$12.00 − $6.00 = $6.00

This is a reasonable answer, because James put half of the $12.00 in his piggy bank. Half of $12.00 is $6.00.

$6.00 divided by 3 boys = x
$6.00 divided by 3 = $2.00
James gave each of his brothers $2.00

This answer is reasonable because $2.00 + $2.00 + $2.00 is the $6.00 James had left after putting $6.00 in his piggy bank.

Grade 3 Outcome #14: Understand a Fraction as Equal Partitions of a Whole;
Understand a Whole as the Sum of its Equal Partitions

Children need to work with visual fraction models to develop a conceptual understanding of fractions (Figure 3.33).

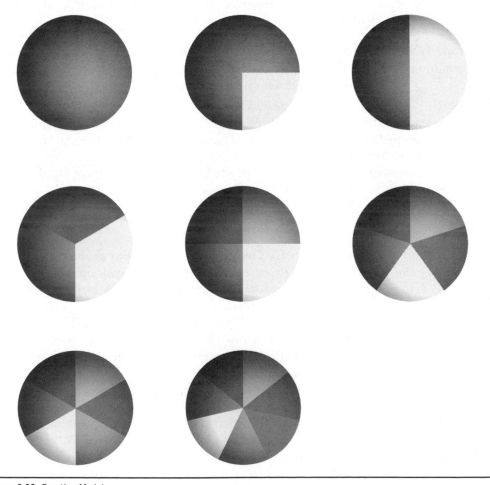

Figure 3.33 Fraction Models.

Using fraction models, teachers can have children analyze one fractional whole at a time. Children need to first learn how to state fractions as part of a whole properly and then write them. For example, in using the fourths fractional partitions, children would learn to identify each fractional partition of the whole as ¼ (one out of four partitions); two fractional pieces as ²/₄ (two out of four partitions); three fractional pieces as ¾ (three out of four partitions); and four fractional partitions as the whole (⁴/₁) or four partitions).

A common mistake children make in writing fractions is to state the denominator of a fraction as representing the number of partitions *left* instead of the number of partitions in the *whole*. For example, in writing the fraction depicting one partition of thirds, children often write "½" because they see there are two of the thirds left. The terminology used in writing fractions can help children better understand writing fractions. For example, in referring to the fraction model in Figure 3.33, the teacher could have the children identify the partition that is shaded or the partitions that are not shaded. The teacher could state, "One part out of all five parts is shaded." We write the fraction as "¹/₅" and say, "One out of five pieces is shaded." Four parts out of all five parts are unshaded. We write this fraction as "⁴/₅" and say, "Four out of five pieces are unshaded" (Figure 3.34).

Children need a lot of practice in identifying, naming, and writing fractions as equal partitions of wholes. Likewise, children need practice in realizing that the whole is created by putting all equal partitions of the whole together.

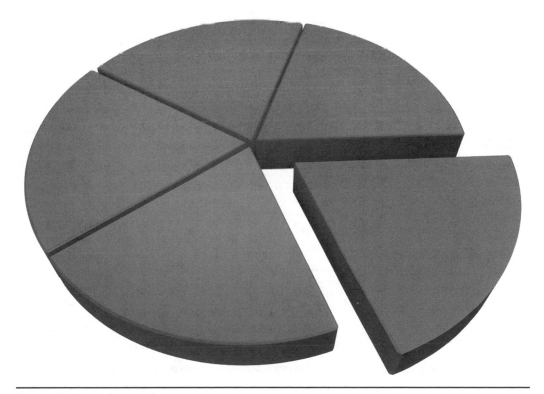

Figure 3.34 Fraction Partition Model.

Children also need to be introduced to fractional pieces as parts of a set.

Sample Activity

For this activity, children would need double-colored chips or tokens (Figure 3.35), paper, and writing implements. The teacher could demonstrate the activity using a Smart Board™ or overhead projector as children are performing the activity at their desks or tables. Children would be asked to lay out four chips, blue side up. They would then be asked to turn one chip over so the red side is up (Figure 3.36). Children would identify and write a fraction for the part of the set that is red: ¼. Children would identify and write a fraction for the part of the set that is blue: ¾.

Front   Back

Figure 3.35 Double-Colored Chips or Tokens.

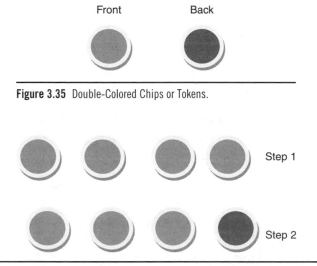

Figure 3.36 Fractional Parts of a Set.

Children should be asked to explain their thinking. For example, a child could state, "I know that the fraction is ¼ because only one chip out of all four chips is red." Another could state, "I know that the fraction is ¾ because three out of the four chips are blue.

Grade 3 Outcome #15: Represent a Fraction on a Number Line Diagram; Define the Interval from 0 to 1 as the Whole and Partition it into Equal Parts

Sample Activity

Provide children with a paper containing number line diagrams (Figure 3.37).

Have the children depict various fractions in which the numerator is 1 on the number line diagram by partitioning the line into equal parts determined by the fraction. For

0   1

Figure 3.37 Number Line Diagram.

example, the fraction ½ would be shown by partitioning the line diagram into two equal parts, and ¹/₃ would be shown by partitioning the line diagram into three equal parts (Figure 3.38).

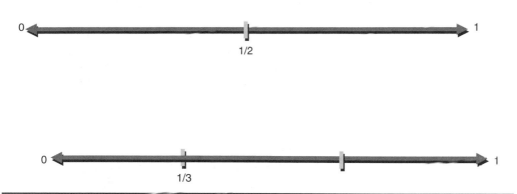

Figure 3.38 Showing Fractional Parts on a Number Line Diagram.

Grade 3 Outcome #16: Represent Fractions on a Number Line Diagram

Sample Activity

Again provide children with a paper containing number line diagrams. Children use the diagrams to depict fractions in which the numerator is greater than 1 (Figure 3.39).

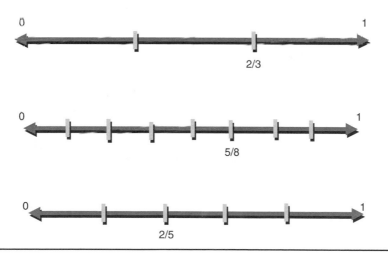

Figure 3.39 Showing Fractions on a Number Line Diagram.

Grade 3 Outcome #17: Understand Two Fractions as Equivalent or Equal if they are the Same Size or the Same Point on a Number Line

The concept of equivalent fractions is best developed by having children use visual fraction models (Figure 3.33) and by comparing fractional parts on number line diagrams.

Sample Activity #1: Are We Equal?

Materials needed for this activity include a set of visual fraction models for each pair of children to share, recording boards, and a container of fraction cards. Fraction cards should have two fractions on each for children to compare using their fraction models. The focus of the activity is for children to determine whether or not the two fractions are equal. A child's decision—yes or no—is written on the recording board. Boards are shown when all children have written a response. For example, children could be asked to compare ½ and ³/₆. Using the fraction models, children would find one of the half model and three of the sixths model. The fractions should be compared by laying one model on top of another. If the models take up the same amount of space, the fractions are equal. If one takes up more space than the other, the fractions are not equal. In this case, the fractions are equal.

Sample Learning Station Activity

Materials needed for the learning center include a set of number line diagrams depicting various fractions (see Figure 3.38 for examples), paper, and writing implements. Children using the learning station would draw two number line diagrams from the container and lay them so that one number line diagram is above the other. They would then compare the fractions on the number line diagrams to determine whether or not they were equal. Children would write the two fractions on the paper and write either "Yes" or "No" beside them to indicate whether or not they were equal.

Grade 3 Outcome #18: Compare Two Fractions with the Same Denominator or Numerator by Reasoning About Their Size and Using "Greater Than," "Less Than," and "Equal" signs; Comparisons are Only Valid When the Two Fractions Refer to the Same Whole

In order for children to compare two fractions in which the numerators are the same but the denominators are different (e.g., ³/₅ and ³/₈), children need to first realize that the more pieces that a whole is partitioned into, the smaller the pieces are going to be.

Sample Activity #1: Partitioning Equal Wholes

Mr. Bozzo's third grade children have been working on comparing fractions using visual fraction models. He wanted to transition them from using visual models to thinking about the size of fractional pieces of equal wholes. For example, he wanted them to be able to compare ³/₅ and ³/₈ using their reasoning skills about the size of the pieces. He developed the following activity to guide his students' thinking.

Mr. Bozzo handed out three strips of paper (8½ × 2 inches) to each of his children, along with a pair of scissors. Each strip of paper was a different color. The lesson proceeded as follows:

Mr. Bozzo: "Take your yellow strip of paper, fold it in half, lengthwise, open it up, and then cut along the folded line. How many pieces did you make?"
Class: "Two."

Mr. Bozzo: "Great! Now take the blue strip of paper, fold it in half twice the same way, open it up, and cut along the three folded lines. How many pieces did you make?"

Class: "Four."

Mr. Bozzo: "You are doing a great job. Now, take the red strip of paper, fold it in half four times, open it up, and cut along the seven folded lines. How many pieces did you make?"

Class: "Eight."

Mr. Bozzo: "Excellent! Now, lay out your yellow pieces, side by side. Next, lay out your blue pieces, side by side, beneath the yellow pieces. Last, lay out your red pieces, side by side, beneath the blue pieces. What do you notice?"

Greg: "If we taped the pieces together, we would have whole strips again."

Mr. Bozzo: "Yes, that is correct. What else do you notice?"

Clara: "I noticed that the strips are all the same length, but we made different-sized pieces out of them."

Mr. Bozzo: "Do you see a relationship between the number of folds you made and the size of the pieces?"

Jeff: "I see what you mean. The more folds and cuts we made, the smaller the pieces we made."

Mr. Bozzo: "That's great thinking, everyone—good job! Now, let's think about using what we have just learned in thinking about comparing fractions.

(Mr. Bozzo writes two fractions on the board: "$1/5$ and $1/8$.")"

Mr. Bozzo: "Okay, class. Let's think of these two fractions in terms of strips of paper. How many pieces would we cut a strip of paper into to make fifths?"

Class: "Five."

Mr. Bozzo: "That is correct. How many pieces would we cut a strip of paper into to make eighths?"

Class: "Eight."

Mr. Bozzo: "Which pieces would be larger?

Class: The fifths."

Mr. Bozzo: "How do you know?"

Julie: "You would need to make more cuts to make eighths, so the fifths would be larger pieces."

Mr. Bozzo: "So which fraction is larger—$1/5$ or $1/8$?

Class: $1/5$."

Mr. Bozzo: "Who thinks they can write the two fractions on the board using comparison signs? Try it, Sam."

(Sam writes "$1/5 > 1/8$.")

Mr. Bozzo: "That is correct. Let's try some more comparisons of fractions with equal numerators."

Once understanding is developed, children (as were those in Mr. Bozzo's class) would be asked to compare additional fractions with unlike denominators when the numerators are the same. For example, in comparing $2/5$ and $2/6$, children would reason that $2/5$ is larger than $2/6$ because the sixths would be smaller pieces, even though there are two of each piece in the fractions.

Sample Activity #2

In this activity, children would be asked to compare fractions with the same denominators: ⁴/₈ and ³/₈, and ⁴/₆ and ¹/₆. Using knowledge gained from the paper strip activity in *Activity 1*, children would be able to reason that all of the fractional pieces are the same size, so they are just comparing how many pieces are in each fraction.

Grade 3 Outcome #19: Expressing Whole Numbers as Fractions; Recognize Fractions that are Equivalent to Whole Numbers

Number line diagrams such as the one shown in Figure 3.40 can be used to help children understand how to write whole-number fractions. In the example, four out of four pieces is at the same point on the number line diagram as 1, so ⁴/₄ is the same as the whole (1). Likewise, the fractions ⁶/₁, ⁴/₁, ¹⁰/₁, and ³/₁ are ways of writing whole numbers as fractions. Children would reason that 6/1 is the same as 1 or the whole.

Figure 3.40 Expressing Whole Numbers as Fractions.

Sample Activity

Materials needed for this activity include two-columned papers labeled "Whole" and "Not a Whole," number line diagrams, writing implements, and a container of fraction cards. In the activity, children gain practice in representing fractions on number line diagrams, writing fractions, and deciding whether or not fractions represent a whole or one. The children would take turns drawing a fraction card from the container. All children would depict the fraction on the number line diagrams and then decide whether or not the fraction was a whole. The fraction would be written in the appropriate column.

Grade 3 Outcome #20: Recognize and Write Simple Equivalent Fractions

Children can begin exploring the concept of equivalent fractions first using the fourths and halves models and then adding the eighths models. Through hands-on exploration, children determine that ²/₄ is the same as ½ and that ⁴/₈ is the same as ½ and ²/₄. Children can then explore the relationship between the sixths and thirds models; the fifths and the tenths models.

Sample Activity

In this activity, children explore patterns as they analyze sequences of equivalent fractions. The teacher would display the following equivalent-fraction sequence on a Smart Board™, board, or overhead projector:

½ ²/₄ ³/₆ ⁴/₈ ⁵/₁₀

Children would be asked to look for numerator and denominator patterns from ½ to ⁵/₁₀. They should note that the numerator increases by one (+1) and the denominator increases by two (+2). Using this knowledge, children would determine what equivalent fraction would come next: 6/12 (5 + 1 = 6 and 10 + 2 = 12). Children could use their visual fraction models to verify equivalent fractions.

ADAPTATIONS FOR CHILDREN WITH SPECIAL NEEDS

It might be necessary to make adaptations when planning numbers and operations lessons and activities depending on the individual needs of the children in the classroom. Some adaptations for measurement activities could include:

- Breaking activities into smaller parts or reducing the number of steps
- Asking children to repeat directions
- Reviewing key words in instructions
- Using pictures and visual cues
- Providing raised or textured objects for children who are visually impaired
- Providing larger nonstandard units for children who experience difficulty in picking up smaller objects
- Positioning students who are visually and hearing impaired so they can see and hear what is going on in the classroom
- Teaching and allowing children to use multiple methods of problem solving
- Using modeling
- Using hands-on manipulatives
- Giving children sufficient time to learn and practice skills
- Making sure children understand content vocabulary
- Having children work in small groups or pairs
- Checking for understanding
- Using a variety of assessment methods.

ADAPTATIONS FOR MATHEMATICALLY PROMISING CHILDREN

Depending on the strengths of children in prekindergarten, kindergarten, and primary-aged school children, gifted children may need adaptations made to the math curriculum that challenge them. Adaptations could include ideas from the section on mathematically promising children under "Children with Special Needs" in Chapter 1 (p. 15–16).

ADAPTATIONS FOR ENGLISH LANGUAGE LEARNERS (ELL)

Adaptations for children who are learning English as their second language could include:

- Connecting concepts to a child's first language—learn important number and operation words in the child's first language to help connect the English words to the first-language words
- Reinforcing measurement vocabulary with visual cues, pictures, and gestures
- Using multicultural literature and pictures that depict various aspects of numbers and operations
- Providing objects from children's cultural backgrounds for them to count, compare, and order
- Providing picture cues on children's recording sheets to help them remember the sequence of a procedure

- Establishing what the child already knows and then moving forward from that point
- Labeling items in the classroom to enhance general vocabulary
- Instructing the children with direction words, simple numbers and commands
- Having children work in small groups and pairs.

HOME/SCHOOL CONNECTION IDEAS AND ACTIVITIES

There are numerous opportunities to engage children in numbers and operations activities in the home setting. The following ideas could be provided to parents/caregivers as ways to reinforce numbers and operation concepts at home:

- Playgrounds—count objects/equipment; count how many seconds it takes to get to various activities on the playground.
- Ball—count the number of bounces before missing; count the number of times a ball can be thrown between two or more people before it is dropped.
- In the car—count the number of dogs, cars, trucks, red cars, blue cars; count the number of cars in a train; count the seconds waiting for a traffic light.
- Money—start a savings account; count the pennies in a jar; exchange pennies for nickels, dimes, quarters, dollars; shop at the dollar store; count out change.
- General counting—the steps in a house, the number of pews in a church, the number of people in the row, the number people in a movie theater.
- Compare numbers counted.
- Count objects in storybooks.
- Educational games—card games that require keeping score and counting.
  Online resources—the National Association for the Education of Young Children (NAEYC) has an "Information for Families" website located at http://www.naeyc. org/families/; the website provides resources for families, including activities to do at home, to encourage child development.

CURRICULUM INTEGRATION

Concepts of numbers and operations are integrated into all other mathematics concept areas and found across the curriculum in all other subject areas. Number concepts are an important element in all areas of mathematics—collecting data/graphing results, counting sides/angles in geometry, measuring to find how many or how much, and measuring growth over time. Science and mathematics are closely related in regard to using numbers as children measure, collect data, and compare results. In social studies, children experience numbers regarding populations, sizes of areas, and distances between points on maps. Children also experience numbers in the stories they read and in the numbering of pages in the books they use.

NUMBERS AND OPERATIONS CONTENT VOCABULARY

Listed below is numbers and operations content vocabulary that teachers could be using in their conversations with children, depending on the age level of the children. It is of utmost importance that teachers use various means to help children learn and understand the meanings of content vocabulary words as they are learning concepts of numbers and operations.

- *Operations*
  numeral, digit
  equation
  parenthesis
  unknown
  addition, add, addends, sum, plus sign
  subtraction, subtract, difference, take away, minus sign
  multiplication, multiply, repeated addition, factors, product, arrays, area models, equal groups, horizontal, vertical, rows, columns
  division, divide, partition, groups
  regroup
- *Properties*
  commutative, associative, distributive
  die, dice
  skip-count
  order, ordering
  compare, comparison
- *Fractions*
  partitions, parts, whole
  numerator, denominator
  number line diagram
  equivalent, compare, comparison
  set
- *Place Value*
  place value, place-value mat
  ones, tens, hundreds, thousands, ten thousands
  base-ten, units, strips of ten, flats of one hundred, cubes of one thousand
  pair, even, odd
  equal, equal sign, greater than, greater-than sign, less-than sign
  order, compare

LITERATURE CONNECTIONS

Children's literature can be beneficial in developing concepts of numbers and operations in helping children relate what they are learning to the real world. The following storybooks and series books are relevant in developing the concept of measurement from prekindergarten through primary-aged schoolchildren.

There are many children's books that focus on numbers and counting; however, other children's books that do not directly focus on these concepts can also be used to support mathematics learning. Some of these include:

The Napping House by Audrey Wood and Don Wood
Harcourt Brace Jovanovich, 1984

This book offers a number of counting opportunities to support learning of number concepts.

Where the Wild Things are by Maurice Sendak

Harper & Row Publishers, 1963

Counting opportunities to support the development of number concepts are provided in this story.

Magic Tree House #7, Sunset and the Sabertooth (1996) by Mary Pope Osborne

Scholastic Inc., 1996

This book could be used for simple data gathering and graphing, as well as counting.

Cat in the Hat by T. S. Geisel and A. S. Geisel

Random House Inc., 1985

This book could be used to support language acquisition as well as mathematics outcomes. Simple vocabulary—such as one, two, and other numbers to five, big, tall, above, below, next to—can all be used to help children understand relative positioning in geometry along with basic counting in numbers.

Pearl the Cloud Fairy, part of the Rainbow Magic series by D. Meadows

Scholastic, 2004

This book can be used to support learning in estimating, counting, taking polls, and other simple mathematics concepts.

If You Take a Mouse to School by L. Numeroff

HarperCollins Publishers, 2002

This book could be used with younger children in practicing counting skills. Older children could use some of the pictures in the book to extend their work with rows, columns, and arrays.

Chicka, Chicka Boom Boom by B. Martin, Jr. and J. Archambault

Simon and Schuster Books, 1989

This book supports geometric concepts, along with opportunities to count and compare.

A House for the Hermit Crab by Eric Carle

Picture Book Studio, 1987

This book lends itself to early number and basic geometry concepts.

Jennie B. Jones and Her Big Fat Mouth by Barbara Park

Random House Publishers, 1993

Some of the story takes place in a bus. There are opportunities for children to collect graphing data and work with arrays as they arrange children on the bus.

Amber Brown Sees Red by P. Danziger

G. P. Putnam's Sons, 1977

This story offers a variety of activities from different chapters for upper grade students. These include:

Chapter 1: Estimation
Chapter 4: "How many?"-type questions
Chapter 5: Collecting data
Chapter 6: Stating and writing number in the thousands

Utterly Me, Clarice Bean by L. Child

Candlewick Press, 2002

In this book, loose connections can be made to geometry and finding the area of different places and objects. Drawing plans for table designs could be used as an extension activity from the story.

ASSESSING CHAPTER OUTCOMES

1. Compare/contrast numbers and operations standards for prekindergarten and kindergarten children.
2. Chart the development of numbers and operation concepts from prekindergarten through third grade. Does this development seem like a logical progression to you? Why or why not?
3. Create additional activities that would be developmentally appropriate for prekindergarten children in meeting numbers and operation standards; kindergarten children.
4. Create additional activities that would be developmentally appropriate for children in first, second, and third grade.
5. Choose an activity. What would you say to a parent or administrator in explaining the purpose of the activity and why it is appropriate for children in that particular age group?
6. Choose an activity and plan adaptations for a child with special needs (choose a specific disability such as hearing or visually impaired, autistic, fine motor skills impairment, etc.).
7. Choose an activity and explain how you would help an ELL student to learn this concept of measurement.
8. Choose an activity and explain how you would adapt it to challenge mathematically promising children.
9. Using information from Chapter 1 on assessing young children's development and learning, create authentic assessments for each age group to assess their knowledge of numbers and operations concepts particular to their age group.
10. Create a sequence of activities you might use to develop the skills and understanding of counting on to 120.
11. Develop a series of lesson plans that creates an understanding of place value and how to use it with first-graders.
12. Explain how to use concrete models to develop a sequence of teaching strategies leading to multiple ways to solve addition problems.
13. Show how real data from classroom surveys or other outside sources may be used in the classroom to develop practical use of the objectives in this chapter.

CHAPTER EXTENSION ACTIVITIES

1. Research additional literature that could be used with prekindergarten, kindergarten, first grade, second grade, and third grade children to help them understand numbers and operation concepts.
2. Use a concept map to identify the concepts and goals of the chapter with a short explanation of how you will use the concepts in your own classroom in the future.
3. Create a five-lesson plan for one concept in the chapter such as multiple and invented strategies to add; creating an understanding of place value; being able to read and write numbers.
4. Develop a brochure which is a tip list for parents/care givers related to the concepts and strategies found in the chapter.
5. Examine any two websites and write a paper explaining how the sites might be used in a classroom to support learning.

REFERENCES

Bahr, D. & de Garcia, L. (2009). *Elementary Math is Anything but Elementary*. Belmont, CA: Wadsworth.

Common Core State Standards Initiative: Preparing America's Students for College & Career (2010). Washington, D.C: National Governors Association Center for Best Practices/Council of Chief State School Officers.

Copley, J. V., Jones, C. & Dighe, J. (2010). *The Creative Curriculum for Preschool: Mathematics*, vol. 4. Washington, D.C.: Teaching Strategies.

National Council of Teachers of Mathematics (NCTM) (2000). *Principles and Standards of School Mathematics*. Reston, VA: Author. Accessed from http://www.nctm.org/standards/content.aspx?id=4294967312.

National Council of Teachers of Mathematics (NCTM) (2006). *Curriculum Focal Points for Prekindergarten Through Grade 8 Mathematics: A Quest for Coherence*. Reston, VA: Author.

4

PATTERNS, FUNCTIONS, AND ALGEBRAIC THINKING

CHAPTER OUTCOMES

After reading this chapter, teacher candidates will be able to:

➢ Describe the development of algebra concepts from prekindergarten through third grade.
➢ Describe algebra activities that are developmentally appropriate for prekindergarten-aged children.
➢ Describe algebra activities that are developmentally appropriate for kindergarten-aged children.
➢ Describe algebra activities that are developmentally appropriate for first through third grade children.
➢ Explain how early algebra activities lay a foundation for future, higher mathematical understanding, reasoning, and problem solving.
➢ Explain how children's literature can be used to support learning of algebra concepts.
➢ Describe the types of adaptations that could be planned for English Language Learners (ELL) and children with special needs that might help them acquire algebra concepts.
➢ Describe the types of adaptations that could be planned to challenge mathematically promising children in this content area.
➢ Explain how to involve families/caregivers in supporting the acquisition of algebra concepts at home.

OVERVIEW OF CONCEPT DEVELOPMENT

Algebraic thinking develops over time, and the concepts that contribute to algebraic thinking begin at the prekindergarten level (NCTM, 2008). Typically, one would not expect to hear the terms "functions" and "algebra" being used in prekindergarten,

kindergarten, or primary school mathematics programs; however, the term "patterning," including repeating and growing patterns, is more commonly accepted as a term appropriate for these age groups. What preservice teachers may not realize is that patterning, a frequent focus of mathematics activities involving young children, is foundational in developing pre-algebraic reasoning and concepts of function.

First, let us define the terms "pattern," "function," and "algebra" as they relate to mathematics programs for prekindergarten, kindergarten, and primary-aged school-children. Patterns can be described as repetitions, sequences, and relationships. Examples of these include a sequence of sounds or shapes, an arrangement of beads on a necklace or bracelet, the sequence of seasons in a year or the days in a week, the quantitative change in height or weight as one grows, and the relationship of one number to another in a number sequence. Once children recognize that patterns operate as rules, they are beginning to understand function (Bickart, Jablon, & Dodge, 1999). Algebra, then, for young children, emphasizes relationships and the way relationships change relative to one another (Smith, 2006).

Young children experience patterns in their daily lives in a variety of ways before formal schooling ever begins. Children love to listen to storybooks as they are read to them. Many stories follow patterns that children readily recognize. This is also true of many songs and verses that children experience at a young age. Children learn to recognize patterns in nature, events, at home or in daycare facilities, and during their play. As young children become aware of patterns, they learn to copy simple patterns made with objects and then progress to creating and extending their own patterns (Clements, 2004). Copley (2000) states, "Thinking about patterns helps children make sense of mathematics . . . working with patterns helps young children predict what will happen, talk about relationships, and see the connections between mathematical concepts and their world" (p. 83). In other words, recognizing patterns helps children view their world in a logical and predictable way.

As children progress through the primary grades in school, they "develop fluency with numbers, identify relationships, and use a variety of representations to describe and generalize patterns and solve equations" (NCTM, 2008, p. 1). In exploring number concepts involving decomposing (5 = 2 + 3 or 5 = 4 + 1), putting together, adding to, taking apart, and taking from, children are building a foundation for understanding concepts of addition and subtraction, the relationship between these two concepts, and the associative and commutative properties of operations. Likewise, as children work with equal groups and rectangular arrays, they are building a foundation for understanding multiplication and the relationship between multiplication and division (*Common Core State Standards*, 2010). An understanding of children's invented symbols and conventional symbols develops as children use words, concrete manipulatives, and drawings in writing equations (NCTM, 2006).

In *Principles and Standards for School Mathematics*, the National Council of Teachers of Mathematics (NCTM, 2000) indicates that all areas of mathematics, geometry, and data analysis in particular, are linked to algebra, and that many and varied experiences with number provide opportunities to establish a foundation in algebra. As children collect data, they can learn to use tables and graphs to represent and analyze patterns and functions they are discovering as they work with various concepts of number.

BUILDING CONCEPTS OF PATTERN, FUNCTION, AND ALGEBRA AT THE PREKINDERGARTEN LEVELS

Experiences with patterns (identifying, copying, and creating) and recognizing naturally occurring change are fundamental to pre-algebraic thinking. Even before being introduced to the term "pattern," young children have acquired the ability to recognize, copy, and perhaps create simple AB or AABB patterns. These include patterns in visual, auditory, tactile, and kinesthetic modalities. They are also aware of order or sequence in their day. For example, try skipping an element of a day's regular routine or a page in a favorite storybook, and a young child will, most likely, point out the missing piece. Young children also become aware of patterns or sequences in nature. Regardless of where one lives, children learn that certain things happen during different seasons of the year.

Teachers of young children should capitalize on the wealth of information children have informally acquired through their interactions in and observations of their world. They should then extend this knowledge base so children are able to work with more complex patterns, such as growing patterns. A typical day can afford a teacher of young children a plethora of opportunities to identify, explore, and extend students' knowledge base concerning patterns. Copley (2000) states:

> Opportunities to identify patterns occur frequently during spontaneous play episodes, routine activities, outdoor trips, literacy lessons, circle time, snack and lunch, shared reading, play with friends . . . Understanding patterns, functions, and algebra is a continual process of connecting what is noted in the real world with planned pattern discovery activities in the classroom.
>
> (pp. 83–84)

Copley, Jones, and Dighe (2010) provide recommendations for teachers as they "challenge children to identify patterns in many settings, represent those patterns auditorily and with objects, and extend those patterns in consistent ways" (p. 767). These recommendations include:

1. Identify different patterns in daily routines.
2. Encourage pattern "talk" and identification.
3. Point to numerals as you count out loud.
4. Begin with color patterns and progress to shape and size patterns.
5. Describe positional patterns (up, down, right, left, high, low, etc.).
6. Focus on the unit that is to be repeated in a pattern (have children become part of the unit by making different colored squizzley lines).
7. Use patterned stories and verses.
8. Create pattern and change books.
9. Provide opportunities to observe change.
10. Use a variety of representations for patterns.
11. Extend pattern units for at least five units in order to establish a pattern.

(2010, pp. 767–769)

Activities for prekindergarten children should involve visual, auditory, tactile, and kinesthetic patterns and include patterns typical of various cultures, especially cultures represented by the children in the classroom. All children, including children with special needs and English Language Learners (ELL), need challenging, yet attainable tasks that provide meaningful experiences reflective of their interests, individual abilities, and family culture (Pennsylvania Department of Education and Department of Public Welfare, 2007).

CONTENT STANDARDS FOR PREKINDERGARTEN

Algebra is the second content area defined in the NCTM document *Principles and Standards in School Mathematics* (2000). It is not considered a key concept in *Curriculum Focal Points for Prekindergarten through Grade 8 Mathematics: A Quest for Coherence* (NCTM, 2006) for prekindergarten children, but is identified as a "Connection to the Focal Points." This means that instruction in this content area lays a foundation for higher mathematical studies in future mathematics classrooms.

Content standards in the NCTM document *Principles and Standards in School Mathematics* (2000) are not presented by individual grades or age levels, but are grouped in age or grade bands. The first group of standards spans patterns, functions, and algebra expectations from prekindergarten through grade 2. These include:

Understand patterns, relations, and functions:

- sort, classify, and order objects by size, number, and other properties;
- recognize, describe, and extend patterns such as sequences of sounds and shapes or simple numeric patterns and translate from one representation to another;
- analyze how both repeating and growing patterns are generated.

Represent and analyze mathematical situations and structures using algebraic symbols:

- illustrate general principles and properties of operations, such as commutativity, using specific numbers;
- use concrete, pictorial, and verbal representations to develop an understanding of invented and conventional symbolic notations.

Use mathematical models to represent and understand quantitative relationships:

- model situations that involve the addition and subtraction of whole numbers, using objects, pictures, and symbols.

Analyze change in various contexts:

- describe qualitative change, such as a student's growing taller;
- describe quantitative change, such as a student's growing two inches in one year.

(http://www.nctm.org/standards/)

As a connection to the NCTM *Focal Points* (2006) for a prekindergarten program, algebra is defined as the following:

> Children recognize and duplicate simple sequential patterns (e.g., square, circle, square, circle, square, circle, etc.).
>
> (2006, p. 11)

The following are outcome examples from prekindergarten standards. Included with the examples are sample activities and other ideas that could be used in exploring pattern, function, and algebra concepts.

PREKINDERGARTEN OUTCOMES

Prekindergarten Outcome #1: Compare and Classify Objects

Sample Activity

For this whole-group activity, children will compare objects and classify them into two groups according to function. The teacher will randomly display two sets of objects (enough so that each child has an object to hold)—writing/drawing objects (crayon, pencil, tablet, eraser, marker), and objects used for eating (spoon, dish, bowl, saucer, glass). Each child, in turn, will be asked to pick up one of the objects and hold it in his or her hands. The children will be asked to look at the object carefully and then form two groups according to their object's purpose or function. Each child should be asked why he or she chose to place the object in a particular group.

Prekindergarten Outcome #2: Order Objects by Properties

Sample Activity

The focus of ordering activities is to have children begin thinking about properties of objects. This concept can be introduced in whole-group, teacher-directed settings, and then children can further explore the concept at learning stations. In teacher-directed settings it is important for the teacher to guide students to understanding by asking "Why?" and "How do you know?" questions of the children. For example, during one session, the teacher could present the children with a variety of pinecones. As a whole group, individual children could be asked to choose the smallest pinecone and place it at the beginning of the designated space. Another child would pick the next pinecone and place it next to the first pinecone. After each pick, the teacher should ask the child why he or she chose a particular pinecone for the lineup. This procedure would continue until each pinecone has been placed.

To extend any ordering activity, children could be asked to draw the arrangement of the objects on paper. In picture form, the objects should depict the arrangement produced in the activity. For the pinecone activity, children's drawings should depict pinecones progressing from the smallest to the largest on their paper (Figure 4.1).

Figure 4.1 Pinecones for Ordering by Size.

Prekindergarten Outcome #3: Sort, Classify, and Order Objects According to One Characteristic

Sample Activity

The concept of sorting, classifying, and ordering objects by one characteristic can be introduced to prekindergarten children in a whole-group setting using a variety of familiar objects. During whole-group activities, the teacher should ask children to explain how the objects are alike (comparison) and why certain objects go together (classification). Sorting could be by color, shape, size, function, etc., depending on the objects used for the activities. Introducing this concept as a whole-group activity can easily lead to further exploration at learning stations, where various materials to sort, classify, and order are provided. Examples of materials for learning station activities could include attribute blocks, connecting cubes, buttons, mini colored clothes pins, coins, articles of clothing, shells, cereal, and pebbles. As children work in learning stations, teachers should ask "How?" and "Why?" questions of the children to encourage them to explain their rationale for sorting materials as they did (Figure 4.2).

Prekindergarten Outcome #4: Sort, Classify, and Order Objects According to Two Characteristics

Sample Activity

Sorting, classifying, and ordering objects by two characteristics can be introduced in a series of whole-group activities using familiar objects. The focus of sorting materials in

Figure 4.2 Children Can Explore Sorting Buttons.

these activities, however, is using two characteristics instead of just one characteristic. The teacher could begin by sorting a selected group of objects without explaining what he or she was thinking. After watching the teacher classify and order the objects, children would be encouraged to provide an explanation as to why they thought the teacher sorted the objects this way. For example, maybe the teacher sorted yellow and blue attribute blocks by size and color. The children would perhaps note that all the yellow blocks are small and all the large blocks are blue.

Note: Sorting, classifying, and ordering objects by two characteristics should first be introduced to children in a whole-group setting using familiar objects. Teachers are able to ask questions and listen to children's responses and rationales as to why certain objects belong in certain groups, which in turn guides instruction.

Mrs. Schwin has her preschool children gathered around a circular table where she has displayed a variety of buttons for the children to view. Some of the buttons are shank style while others have holes. Each style of button is represented in two different colors: yellow and blue. The preschool children have been working on sorting objects by one characteristic. This activity creates an extension of the sorting activity in that the buttons can be sorted by type and color. Mrs. Schwin allows the children to pick up and examine several buttons before she begins the activity.

Mrs. Schwin asks, "How do you think we could sort these buttons?

Several children chime, "By color."

Mrs. Schwin allows children in turn to pick up a button and put it into a color group. After the buttons are sorted by color, Mrs. Schwin continues. She says, "Let's look at the buttons in each color group and see if we can sort them another way." She asks each child to pick up a button in the yellow group and examine it. She then asks two children to compare their yellow buttons. (One is a shank button and the other has holes.)

The two children note the difference between their two yellow buttons and explain the difference to the teacher and classmates. Mrs. Schwin then divides the children into two groups. One group of children is asked to sort the yellow buttons by type, while the other group is asked to sort the blue buttons by type. As the children are sorting the buttons, Mrs. Schwin asks the children why a certain button belongs to a particular group and why it does not belong in the other group.

As a whole group, Mrs. Schwin asks the children to summarize how the buttons were sorted today, pointing out that two characteristics of the buttons were used in the sorting activity—color and type of button.

Questions

1. What important insights did the preschool children experience through this sorting activity?
2. What might be a logical extension activity for the preschool children?

Prekindergarten Outcome #5: Recognize, Describe, and Extend Patterns
Sample Activities

Opportunities to explore patterns with young children are endless. Teachers should guide children in becoming "pattern detectives." Patterns can be recognized and identified in the clothing teachers and/or children wear, children's artwork and play, songs sung in the classroom, storybooks read to the children, materials or objects found in the classroom and outdoor environment. Through questioning, teachers should prompt students to describe the patterns they are experiencing and also ask students what would come next in the pattern, when applicable (Figures 4.3a–e).

Figure 4.3a–e Exploration in Patterns is Endless.

Teachers can model clapping and other auditory patterns, and children should be encouraged to create their own auditory patterns. These patterns can be shared with the class and duplicated by other children (Figure 4.4).

Figure 4.4 Duplicating a Pattern on a Tambourine.

Movement patterns are also important to explore. Teachers can line children up for activities in a certain pattern and ask children to identify the pattern. Another idea is to begin lining up children in a specific order and then ask the children what should come next. For example, a teacher could begin lining up children in a boy/girl, boy/girl pattern and then ask the children what type of child should come next.

CONTENT STANDARDS FOR KINDERGARTEN

As a connection to the NCTM *Focal Points* (2006), algebra in a kindergarten program is defined as:

> Children identify, duplicate, and extend simple number patterns and sequential and growing patterns (e.g., patterns made with shapes) as preparation for creating rules that describe relationship.
>
> (2006, p. 12)

The *Common Core State Standards* (2010) begin at the kindergarten level. As stated in the *Common Core State Standards* document, kindergarten children should:

> 1. Decompose numbers less than or equal to 10 in pairs by using objects or drawings and recording each.
> 2. For any number from 1 to 9, find the number that makes 10 when added to the given number.
>
> (2010, p. 11)

The content for this standard is further developed in Chapter 3 of this textbook pertaining to numbers and operations.

KINDERGARTEN OUTCOMES

It is important for kindergarten children to continue exploring and investigating different repeating patterns (AB, AB, AB, or ABB, ABB, ABB, etc.) in a variety of modalities, and also extend their exploration into growing or shrinking patterns. They should continue to identify, describe, predict, and extend patterns based on shape, size, color, sound, or number (Figures 4.5a–c).

Other ideas for identifying patterns at the kindergarten level could include games such as "I Spy," in which the teacher or a child gives a clue for a pattern he or she sees, and the other children would then try to guess which pattern the teacher or child is referring to in the clue. Children at this level could also participate in a pattern scavenger hunt.

While the focus of prekindergarten and kindergarten instruction in patterning is on identifying, duplicating, and extending patterns in various modalities, children may begin to create patterns of their own as they are playing and/or exploring materials in the classroom. The teacher, of course, should praise children for their creations and call attention to the fact that "we" can also create patterns of our own. The children's created patterns could then become topics of discussion in analyzing, duplicating, and deciding how to extend them.

Kindergarten Outcome #1: Use Concrete Objects to Show Equal or Not Equal

Kindergarten children should be given many opportunities to count equal sets of objects and use manipulatives to create sets that are equal. They could be introduced to the equal sign (=) and told that this sign means "is the same as." They would learn to make statements as "four counting bears is the same as four counting bears."

Kindergarten children also need experiences in counting and comparing sets of objects that are not equal. They could also be introduced to the not equal sign (a forward slanted line through an equal sign) and taught that this sign means "is not the same as."

Figure 4.5a–c Growing Patterns.

Figure 4.5a–c Continued.

They would learn to make statements as "four counting bears is not the same as five counting bears." These signs could be created as manipulatives, and children could place the appropriate sign between two sets of objects to indicate if they are equal or not equal.

Kindergarten Outcome #2: Determining if Sets are Equal or Not Equal

Sample Activity

For this activity, children will place sets of objects on a pan balance scale and use their comparison skills to determine if the sets are equal or not equal. Children, of course, would need to have had previous experiences using a balance scale to know how it works and what different positions of the pans on the scale mean when making comparisons. This would be a good learning station activity for children after they have had opportunities to count and compare sets of objects. The learning stations would have a set of manipulatives—connecting cubes or counting bears, for example—for the children to use, along with a pan balance scale that has already been balanced by the teacher or teacher aide. Children would also be provided with a paper containing pictures of balance scales and writing tools such as crayons, colored pencils, or regular lead pencils.

Children at the learning stations would determine how many of the manipulatives would go in each pan on the balance scale, count out the manipulatives, and place one set in each of the scale pans. Next, children would draw circles in the pans on their paper, indicating the number of the manipulatives they used in each pan of the pan balance scale. For example, perhaps the children decided to place six counting bears in one pan of the scale and 10 counting bears in the other pan. On their papers, each child would draw six circles in one pan and 10 circles in the other pan using the provided writing tools. Circles should then be numbered to connect them to the hands-on activity with the pan balance scale.

Children would then need to decide if six counting bears is the same as 10 counting bears, or if six counting bears is not the same as 10 counting bears, by looking at the scale and using their comparison skills. They would then draw either the equal sign or the not equal sign above the scale on their papers.

As the teacher circulates among the learning stations, he or she should ask the children "Why?" and "How do you know?" questions concerning the responses on their papers.

Symbols are used in algebra to express general rules about numbers, the relationship between and among numbers, and operations (Copley, 2000). The following activity is described in Copley's book, *The Young Child and Mathematics*. It provides a bridge for children in progressing from the concrete to symbolic representation.

Kindergarten Outcome #3: Equal Equations

Sample Activity

Working with a pan balance [scale] and connecting cubes (single and units made up of two, three, four, or more cubes), children get a wealth of concrete experience with the concept of an equation. For example, a child may place a two-cube unit on the left side of the scale and then one single cube on the right side. Finding the left side heavier, the child balances the scale by adding another singe cube to the right side. Now he or she has an equation.

If children do not start such play themselves, the teacher may ask, "How can I make the scale balance, Michael?"

After children have had extensive experiences balancing sets of concrete objects, the teacher can encourage them to explore various ways of representing their "equations" and at some point acquaint them with the conventional representation $2 + 2 = 4$ (Copley, 2000).

Kindergarten Outcome #4: Recreate a Simple Story Problem Using Concrete Objects or Pictures

Sample Activity

This concept could first be modeled by the teacher using a flannel board and felt manipulatives or using a Smart Board®. An example of a story could be "Today on the way to school I saw three toads jumping in the grass." The teacher would place three flannel toads on the board or project three toads on the Smart Board®: "As I was parking my car I saw another toad jumping in the grass." The teacher could ask the children how many more toads he or she should place on the flannel board or Smart Board® and then add the toad to the board and ask, "How many toads did I see on the way to school today?" It would be important for the teacher to allow children to explain how they arrived at their solution to the problem.

As an extension activity, children could use manipulatives or draw circles on whiteboards or paper to represent the toads their teacher saw on the way to school. Children would need to be provided with many more opportunities to represent a simple story problems using manipulatives or through drawing. These types of activities are foundational in understanding the process of addition. This activity could also be extended in using stories that involve "taking away" manipulatives or "crossing off" pictures to introduce the process of subtraction.

Kindergarten Outcome #5: Use Concrete Objects and Trial and Error to Represent a Number Story

For this outcome, children would use concrete manipulatives to depict terminology such as "the same," "less than," and "more than." For example, the teacher could say, "Yesterday I ate five chips with my lunch." The children would lay out five of their manipulatives to represent the five chips. "Today I'm going to eat the same number of chips that I ate yesterday. Lay out how many chips you think I'm going to eat with my lunch today." Again, it would be important for the teacher to allow the children to explain how they arrived at their solution to the problem.

Kindergarten Outcome #6: Use Concrete Objects or Pictures to Represent a Number Story That Involves a Missing Addend

Sample Activity

This concept could first be modeled by the teacher using a flannel board and felt manipulatives or a Smart Board®. An example of a story would be "We need 10 plastic spoons for snack time today." The teacher places 10 manipulatives on the felt board or projects 10 spoons on the Smart Board® to represent the plastic spoons, and says, "This is how many plastic spoons we need; however, so far I only have eight plastic spoons." The teacher would place eight manipulatives on the felt board underneath and lined up with the 10 spoons already on the board or do likewise on the Smart Board®: "How many more spoons do I need so we have 10 spoons?"

It would be important at this point to allow children to state how many more plastic spoons they think the teacher needs, why they think so, and how they arrived at the solution. The teacher could state, "Eight plastic spoons and two more plastic spoons is the same as 10 plastic spoons." The teacher could have plastic spoons ready and have two children "act out" the problem using the spoons.

CONTENT STANDARDS FOR GRADE 1

Content objectives for algebra beginning in prekindergarten and kindergarten are continued and enriched through the primary grades. Children should experience instructional methodologies that create meaning and connect what is being learned to the real world.

Algebra in *Curriculum Focal Points for Prekindergarten through Grade 8 Mathematics: A Quest for Coherence* (2006) is a key concept connected to numbers and operations in first grade. Children use a variety of hands-on models to help them develop an understanding of the concepts of "adding to" and "taking away from," as well as part-whole relationships, as they work with basic number facts. Also, as a connection to the focal points, children in first grade, through their experiences with number patterns in developing strategies for the basic number facts, learn other properties, such as commutativity, associativity, the identity property of 0 (zero) in addition, and odd and even numbers concepts (NCTM, 2006). Children use their developing understandings to solve arithmetic problems.

The *Common Core State Standards* (2010) for grade 1 emphasize the following operations and algebraic thinking standards:

- Represent and solve problems using addition and subtraction.
- Understand and apply properties of operations and the relationship between addition and subtraction.
- Add and subtract within 20.
- Work with addition and subtraction equations.

(2010, pp. 15)

The content for these standards is further developed in Chapter 3 of this textbook pertaining to numbers and operations.

GRADE 1 OUTCOMES

Models for hands-on exploration of addition and subtraction facts in grade 1 are endless. Some common models include connecting cubes, colored blocks, plastic chain links, pattern blocks, and plastic beads to string. The idea is for children to manipulate these models in developing understanding about addition and subtraction facts. As children experience number facts through hands-on exploration, they have the opportunity to learn that 2 + 3 is the same as 3 + 2 (commutative property). Children also have the opportunity to learn that the order in which numbers are added does not matter; the answer is always the same (associative property). For example, it does not matter in which order 5 + 2 + 1 are added, as the answer will always be the number 8 (Figures 4.6a–e).

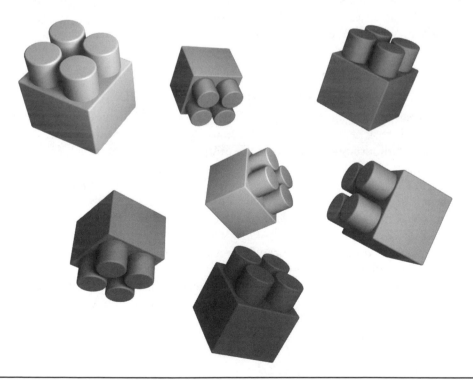

Figure 4.6a–e Examples of Manipulatives.

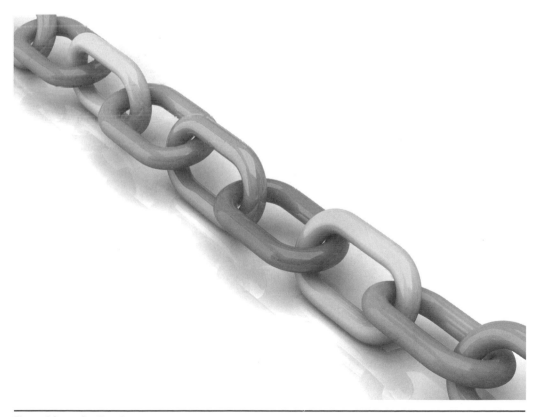

Figure 4.6a–e Continued.

Figure 4.6a–e Continued.

Grade 1 Outcomes: Illustrate General Principles and Properties of Commutativity; Use Models to Develop an Understanding of Symbolic Notations Involving Addition and Subtraction

Sample Activity

In this activity children will explore the commutative property in addition facts. Materials for the activity needed for each pair of students includes two small cups (one cup marked "Part 1"and the other "Part 2"), two different colors of centimeter cubes, a plastic bowl marked "whole" on the bottom, and recording sheets (Figures 4.7, 4.8, and 4.9).

Children can choose any math fact for the activity. For example, children could choose 6 + 2 = 8. The pair of students would put six of one color centimeter cubes in the Part 1 cup and two of the other color centimeter cubes in the Part 2 cup. In the bowl marked "whole," children would first dump the six cubes and then the two cubes into the bowl and count them. On the recording sheet they would write "6 + 2 = 8." After returning the cubes to their respective cups, the children would first dump the two cubes and then the eight cubes into the bowl and count them. On the recording sheet they would write "2 + 6 = 8." Children would continue in this manner using various addition facts. The teacher could pose the addition fact 6 + 0, and have the children use their cups and "whole" bowl to explore the identity property of 0 (zero).

Figure 4.7 Centimeter Cubes.

Figure 4.8 Cups Marked "Part 1" and "Part 2".

Figure 4.9 Bowl marked "Whole".

The activity could be extended to include a third cup, which would be marked "Part 3," and a third color of centimeter cubes. Children could practice the associative property in adding 3 + 6 + 2 by experimenting with the order in which the numbers are added together.

Hands-on exploration also affords children the opportunity to develop the understanding that numbers can be broken down in many different ways (transitivity of equality). Children learn that a number is made up of parts, thus developing the understanding of the relationship of parts to the whole. For example, in creating models of the number 7, children learn that 6 + 1 = 7, 5 + 2 = 7, 4 + 3 = 7, and 7 + 0 = 7.

Likewise, as children use models to create number facts, they learn that anything added to zero will be that number (identity property of zero in addition).

An added benefit of these activities is that children are also experiencing the relationship of the parts to the whole (4 and 3 make up the number 7). This understanding helps children with the concept of "taking away from" or subtraction. If children know that the number 7 is composed of 3 and 4, then if 3 is "taken away" or subtracted from the 7, the 4 is left. This can be illustrated using the Dixie cups, bowl, and centimeter cubes from the activity above. In using the subtraction fact $7-3 = 4$, children would first create the "whole" in the bowl, which would be 7. They would then take out the 3 (a part) and count to see what remains in the bowl (4, the other part) (Figure 4.10).

Figure 4.10 Learning Addition and Subtraction Facts.

CONTENT STANDARDS FOR GRADE 2

Algebra standards at grade 2 in *Curriculum Focal Points for Prekindergarten through Grade 8 Mathematics: A Quest for Coherence* (NCTM, 2006) include having children use patterns to "extend their knowledge of properties of numbers and operations. For example, when skip counting, they build foundations for understanding multiples and factors" (p. 14).

The *Common Core State Standards* (2010) for grade 2 emphasize the following operations and algebraic thinking standards:

> • Represent and solve problems using addition and subtraction.
> • Understand and apply properties of operations and the relationship between addition and subtraction.
> • Add and subtract within 20.
> • Work with addition and subtraction equations.
>
> (2010, p. 19)

The content for these standards is further developed in Chapter 3 of this textbook pertaining to numbers and operations.

GRADE 2 OUTCOMES

Children in grade 2 continue using the relationships and understandings they have developed concerning number facts to develop quick recall of addition facts and related subtraction facts. They also generalize methods they understand to add and subtract multi-digit whole numbers. This age group also begins building a foundation for understanding multiples and factors as they use number patterns in skip counting exercises. The hundreds chart is a versatile teaching tool in helping children discover skip-counting number patterns (Figure 4.11).

Grade 2 Outcome #1: Analyzing Patterns

Sample Activity

In this whole-group activity, children will explore number patterns on a hundreds chart. Materials needed for this activity include a laminated, class-size hundreds chart, a container of manipulatives, and an erasable marker.

The teacher can have the children sit in a circle around the container of manipulatives, which he or she then dumps on the carpet or floor in the middle of the circle. The children are told that they are going to count the manipulatives, but first they are going to put them in groups of four (or some other number). The teacher can call on several students at a time to create a group of four manipulatives. When finished, the center of the circle should be covered with groups of manipulatives.

The teacher then tells the children that they are going to count the groups one at a time and put an "X" on the number on the hundreds chart after each count, to keep

1	2	3	4	5	6	7	8	9	10
11	12	13	14	15	16	17	18	19	20
21	22	23	24	25	26	27	28	29	30
31	32	33	34	35	36	37	38	39	40
41	42	43	44	45	46	47	48	49	50
51	52	53	54	55	56	57	58	59	60
61	62	63	64	65	66	67	68	69	70
71	72	73	74	75	76	77	78	79	80
81	82	83	84	85	86	87	88	89	90
91	92	93	94	95	96	97	98	99	100

Figure 4.11 Hundreds Chart.

track of how many they have counted. The children begin with four, and a child puts an "X" on the number 4 on the hundreds chart. The next group is counted, continuing with the number 5, and then numbers 6, 7, and 8, and another child places an "X" on the number 8 on the hundreds chart. This procedure continues until at least six or seven "Xs" are on the hundreds chart.

At this point the teacher can ask the children if they can see a pattern on the hundreds chart as they are counting. If no one sees a pattern, the children can continue counting and marking "Xs" on the hundreds chart. When the children notice that they are skip-counting by fours, the procedure can be reversed. The teacher can ask the children what number they think they are going to place an "X" on next. Children can count the next group of four manipulatives to find out for sure. At some point the children can individually practice skip-counting by fours. This same procedure can be repeated for various sizes of groups of manipulatives.

Sample Activities

Calendar-related activities in first and second grade afford children the opportunity to recognize and analyze patterns. One of the first patterns that children come to recognize is the pattern of the days of the week. As calendar activities become a daily part of their classroom routine children have the opportunity to become aware of many patterns involving numbers (Figure 4.12).

Figure 4.12 Number Patterns on a Calendar.

Grade 2 Outcome #2: Work with Addition and
Subtraction Equations

Mr. Miller is teaching his students to use pictures to illustrate situations involving addition and subtraction. He is first instructing the children as a whole group before pairing them to create problems of their own.

Mr. Miller and the children had previously taken a walk to count the number of trees on the playground. They counted 11 trees altogether. Each child came to the carpeted instruction area with a whiteboard and marker. Once they were all seated Mr. Miller began.

"Today we are going to do addition and subtraction problems starting with the number of trees we counted, but instead of just using the number 11, we're going to draw pictures. What kind of a tree pictures could we draw?"

One student suggested they draw lollipop trees and another suggested a standing-up arrow for the trees (vertical arrow). The class voted to use standing up arrows to represent the trees.

Mr. Miller stated, "Let's suppose we decide that there aren't enough trees on the playground. How many more trees do you think we might need?" After some discussion it was decided that the playground could use 10 more trees. "Okay, 10 more trees it is! How can we write how many trees we have and how many more trees we want as an addition problem?"

The children stated that they needed to write "11 + 10 = 21 trees."

Mr. Miller continued: "How can we draw pictures to represent our addition problem?"

The children suggested they draw 21 arrow trees.

Mr. Miller stated, "But if we just draw 21 trees, how will we know which ones are the 11 already on the playground and the 10 more that we want to plant?"

Billy suggested they first draw 11 arrows for the ones on the playground and then draw 10 more trees underneath the 11 trees. The class thought this was a good idea, so everyone drew the trees on their whiteboards. Mr. Miller further suggested that they write the numbers 10 and 11 underneath the picture of the trees they had drawn.

Mr. Miller continued: "Let's suppose now that we decide that 21 trees are too many; there isn't enough room to play on the playground. How many trees should we dig out and give to someone else to plant?" It was decided that they could dig up 5 of the trees from the playground. Mr. Miller asked the children to write a subtraction problem to show this. The children wrote, "21 − 5 = 16 trees."

"How can we show this using our tree pictures?" The children decided they could "X" off 5 of the new trees they had planted because they would be the easiest trees to dig up. After "Xing" off 5 trees, the children counted to make sure there were 16 trees left.

Mr. Miller then paired the children and sent them to their seats to create addition and subtraction tree problems. They were reminded to use arrow tree drawings to represent their problems. Each pair will share one addition and one subtraction problem with the whole group.

Grades 1 and 2 Outcome: Change over Time

Sample Activities

There are many opportunities for children to experience change over time. One idea is to measure children's heights at various times during the school year, record heights on a chart, and then figure out how much each person has grown from the previous measurement of heights. Each child could create a chart of growth for the school year. Another idea would be to measure the growth of plants in the classroom. A class chart could be created to record the growth patterns of the various plants (Figures 4.13 and 4.14).

CONTENT STANDARDS FOR GRADE 3

Content standards in the NCTM document *Principles and Standards in School Mathematics* (2000) are not presented by individual grades or age levels, but are grouped in age or grade bands. The 3–5 grade band includes the following standards:

Figure 4.13 Measuring Height.

Figure 4.14 Measuring Plant Growth Over Time.

Understand patterns, relations, and functions:

- describe, extend, and make generalizations about geometric and numeric patterns;
- represent and analyze patterns and functions, using words, tables, and graphs.

Represent and analyze mathematical situations and structures using algebraic symbols:

- identify such properties as commutativity, associativity, and distributivity and use them to compute with whole numbers;
- represent the idea of a variable as an unknown quantity using a letter or a symbol;
- express mathematical relationships using equations.

Use mathematical models to represent and understand quantitative relationships:

- model problem situations with objects and use representations such as graphs, tables, and equations to draw conclusions.

Analyze change in various contexts:

- investigate how a change in one variable relates to a change in a second variable;
- identify and describe situations with constant or varying rates of change and compare them.

(http://www.nctm.org/standards/)

As a key concept in the *Curriculum Focal Points for Prekindergarten through Grade 8 Mathematics* (2006), children in third grade continue working with number patterns to understand the meaning of multiplication and division. They develop this understanding through the use of representations such as equal-sized groups, the number line, and arrays. As children work with these models, they can begin to recognize and analyze patterns and relationships, which can be depicted in graphs, tables, and equations.

In grade 3 the *Common Core State Standards* (2010) include:

- Represent and solve problems involving multiplication and division.
- Understand properties of multiplication and the relationship between multiplication and division.
- Multiply and divide within 100.
- Solve problems involving the four operations, and identify and explain patterns in arithmetic.

(2010, p. 23)

These *Common Core State Standards* for grade 3 are further developed in Chapter 3 of this textbook pertaining to numbers and operations.

GRADE 3 OUTCOMES

Grade 3 Outcome #1: Analyze and Represent Patterns

Sample Activity

In this activity, children will use arrays to discover multiplication-table patterns. Materials needed for the activity include graph paper and pencils.

For example, in order to understand the pattern sequence when multiplying by 3, students would first draw one vertical group of three squares on graph paper. Underneath this array students would write "3 × 1 = 3." Next, students would draw two vertical groups of six squares each, side by side, on the graph paper and write "3 × 2 = 6." This pattern of array drawing would continue until the students had drawn and written "3 × 10 = 30" or "3 × 12 = 36." In making multiplication flash cards, students could write the multiplication fact to be practiced on one side of the flash card and the picture of the array and corresponding answer on the other side of the flash card. As children practice the multiplication facts, they will have a visual representation of the facts as arrays (Figures 4.15 and 4.16).

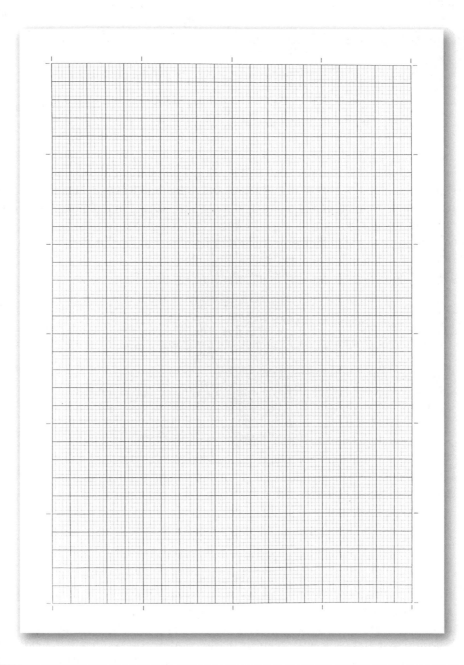

Figure 4.15 Graph Paper.

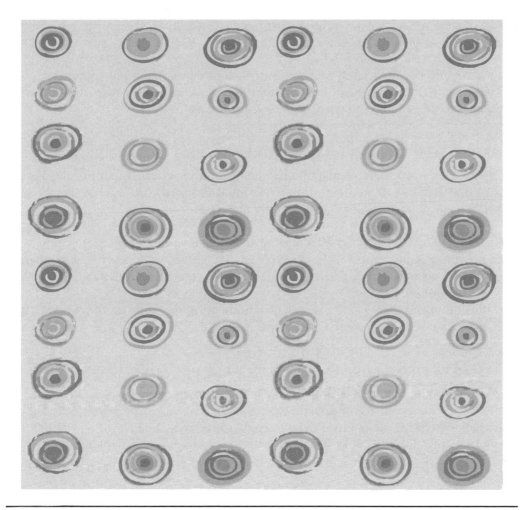

Figure 4.16 8 × 6 Array.

Children can use the same graph-paper array patterns in understanding division. For example, using the 8 × 6 = 48 array, children could practice first dividing the 48 squares into groups of eight and then groups of six. In this manner children are working with the numbers 6, 8, and 48 as a multiplication fact family, which depicts the relationship of multiplication to division.

Grade 3 Outcome #2: Use Equations to Express Mathematical Relationships

Sample Activity

The teacher could pose a problem to the children, such as: "We are on a picnic at the lake, and we see four geese each followed by five goslings. We want to know how many geese and goslings there are, but since they do not stand still long enough to be counted, we are going to write an equation representing how many geese there are in all. How can we do that?"

Students can work in pairs or groups of three to write equations to represent the problem. The teacher may want to guide students in drawing representations of the geese on paper so they can be counted. Then, students would decide how to represent the total number of geese and goslings as a math equation. A child may suggest the problem be written as: "6 + 6 + 6 + 6 = 24" or "4 + (4 × 5) = 24," the total number of geese in all. It would be important for each pair or group of children to share their equations.

There are many problems of this sort that teachers can pose to help children write equations. Also, children can pose problems for the class to solve.

ADAPTATIONS FOR CHILDREN WITH SPECIAL NEEDS

It might be necessary to make adaptations when planning pattern, function, and algebra lessons and activities depending on the individual needs of the children in the classroom. Several adaptations for activities could include:

- Breaking activities into smaller parts or reducing the number of steps
- Providing larger, raised, or textured objects for children who are visually impaired
- Providing larger manipulatives for children who experience difficulty in picking up smaller objects
- Positioning students who are visually and hearing impaired so they can see and hear what is going on in the classroom.

ADAPTATIONS FOR MATHEMATICALLY PROMISING CHILDREN

Depending on the strengths of children in prekindergarten, kindergarten, and primary-aged schoolchildren, gifted children may need adaptations made to the math curriculum that challenge them. Adaptations could include ideas from the section on mathematically promising children under "Children with Special Needs" in Chapter 1 (p. 15–16).

ADAPTATION FOR ENGLISH LANGUAGE LEARNERS (ELL)

Adaptations for children who are learning English as their second language could include:

- Connecting pattern, function, and algebra concepts to a child's first language— learn important terminology in the child's first language to help connect the English words to the first-language words
- Reinforcing vocabulary with visual cues, pictures, and gestures
- Using multicultural literature, pictures, and stories that depict various cultures, especially the cultures of the children represented in the class
- Providing objects to sort and classify, and patterns to investigate from children's cultural backgrounds
- Providing picture cues on children's recording sheets.

HOME/SCHOOL CONNECTION IDEAS AND ACTIVITIES

The following ideas could be provided to parents/caregivers as ways to reinforce pattern, function, and algebra concepts at home:

- Explore and investigate patterns at home or in surrounding areas.
- Discuss or duplicate patterns and talk about what would come next.
- Create your own patterns with household objects and toys.
- Identify patterns in daily routines.
- Read storybooks and sing songs that are arranged in patterns.
- Use vocabulary as "same," "more than," "less than," "greater," "fewer".
- Order objects at home by properties—small to large, short to tall, light to heavy.
- Sort objects at home according to one or two attributes.
- Children can discuss properties of number patterns as they practice their math facts.
- Children can participate in array hunts at home and in surrounding areas.
- Children can practice putting objects they find around their home or surrounding areas into equal groups.
- Children can create books about change (e.g., "a book about how I'm growing"). Online resources: the National Association for the Education of Young Children (NAEYC) has an "Information for Families" website located at http://www.naeyc. org/families/. The website provides resources for families, including activities to do at home, to encourage child development.

CURRICULUM INTEGRATION

There are many opportunities to integrate patterning concepts in mathematics with other content areas. Examples include patterns in storybook text and poetry, clapping patterns, and lyrics and rhythms in songs children sing. For example, in Pat Hutchins' storybook *The Doorbell Rung*, the author has created a pattern in the text that children can repeat as the story is being read to them. Patterns in nature, the environment, and art provide discovery opportunities for prekindergarten children as well as primary-aged children. Daily schedules, days of the week, and months of the year follow patterns. Connecting patterning concepts to other subject areas provides children with the opportunity to expand their perspective concerning math in the context of the real world.

PATTERNS, FUNCTIONS, AND ALGEBRA CONTENT VOCABULARY

Listed below are pattern and algebra content vocabulary that teachers could be using in their conversations with children, depending on the age level of the children. It is of utmost importance that teachers use various means to help children learn and understand the meanings of content vocabulary words as they are learning pattern and algebra concepts.

- sort, sorting, sorted
- classify, classifies, classified
- order, ordering, ordered
- pattern
  - identify a pattern
  - growing pattern
  - repeating pattern
  - extending a pattern

- ○ duplicating a pattern
- ○ number pattern
- ○ geometric pattern
- ○ auditory pattern
- objects
- properties or characteristics of objects
- symbol
- represent, representation
- associate, associative property
- skip count
- calendar
- number line
- hundreds chart
- array
- area model
- equal, not equal
- repeated addition
- equation

LITERATURE CONNECTIONS

Children's literature can be beneficial in developing concepts of pattern, function, and algebra in helping children relate what they are learning to the real world. The following storybooks and series books are relevant in developing these concepts from prekindergarten through primary-aged schoolchildren.

Storybooks

The Button Box by Margarette S. Reid

Puffin, 1995

An imaginative little boy explores the many pleasures that can be found in—and made from—his grandmother's button box.

Benny's Pennies by Pat Brisson

Dragonfly Books, 1995

This is the tale of a boy's shopping expedition, which has a cumulative refrain.

Eight Hands Round: A Patchwork Alphabet by Ann Whitford Paul and Jeanette Winter

HarperCollins, 1996

Information about pioneer life is provided through speculation about the origins of 26 quilt patterns—one for each letter of the alphabet.

No Dodos: A Counting Book of Endangered Animals by Amanda Wallwork

Scholastic Trade, 1993

The focus of this counting book is on environmental concerns of endangered animals, presenting the numbers 1 to 10 and simple identifications (e.g., 9/nine dolphins). Each page contains a patterned border.

Patterns in Peru: An Adventure in Patterning by Cindy Neuschwander and Bryan Langdo

Henry Holt & Co., 2007

The Zills twin children are visiting Peru, where their parents are studying the mysterious lost city of Quwi. The children stumble into an adventure in which they must use their understanding of patterns and sequences.

Pattern Fish by Trudy Harris

Millbrook Press, 2000

The book is written in rhyming prose and follows brightly colored cartoon fish as they inhabit a world of patterns, beginning with the simplest AB pattern and growing increasingly complex.

Pattern Bugs by Trudy Harris

Millbrook Press, 2001

This book uses repetitious rhyme. Children can find and identify repetitive patterns.

Brown Bear, Brown Bear, What Do You See? by Bill Martin, Jr. and Eric Carle

Henry Holt and Co., 1992

The pattern in this book is repeated over and over. The predictable rhyme can easily be detected.

Cookie's Week by Cindy Ward

Putnam Juvenile, 1997

Children progress through the days of the week, following a mischievous kitten's antics.

A Place for Zero: A Math Adventure by Angeline Sparagna Lopresti

Baker & Taylor, CATS, 2009

Zero learns about his additive and multiplicative identities as he searches to find his place among the other digits.

The Action of Subtraction by Brian P. Cleary

Millbrook Press, 2008

This book offers children a look at the function of subtraction in a rhyming, silly way.

The Mission of Addition by Brian P. Cleary

First Avenue Editions, 2007

Children learning about addition using silly rhymes.

Minnie's Diner: A Multiplying Menu by Dayle Ann Dodds

Candlewick, 2007

This story offers children a humorous adventure in doubles.

The Great Divide: A Mathematical Marathon by Dayle Ann Dodds

Candlewick, 2005

This rhyming story demonstrates the basic principle of division through a great race.

The Doorbell Rang by Pat Hutchins
HarperTrophy, 1989

In the story, children continually need to re-share a plate of cookies as more children ring the doorbell and come to visit. The author has created a pattern in the text that children can recite.

Book Series

Math Counts by Henry Arthur Pluckrose
Children's Press, 1995
  Pattern
  Sorting
  Shape
  Size
Math for the Real World: Early Emergent Series
The Rosen Publishing Group, Inc., 2008
  How Long Is It?: Learning to Measure with Nonstandard Units by Elizabeth Kernan
  Near and Far at the Beach: Learning Spatial Awareness Concepts by Amanda Boyd
  Which Holds More?: Learning to Compare Volume by Eliza Robbins
  Who's Short? Who's Tall: Learning to Compare Heights by Kailee Herbst

ASSESSING CHAPTER OUTCOMES

1. What types of algebra activities would not be developmentally appropriate for prekindergarten through third grade children?
2. Explain to a parent or administrator how children's early experiences with patterns and functions lay a foundation for future experiences with algebraic expressions and equations.
3. Choose an activity from the chapter, or an activity you have developed and plan adaptations for a child with special needs. (Choose a specific disability, such as hearing or visually impaired, autistic, fine motor skills impairment, etc.).
4. Choose an activity from the chapter, or an activity you have developed, and plan adaptations for gifted children.
5. Explain how you would teach vocabulary words specific to concepts of pattern, function, and algebra to an ELL child.

CHAPTER EXTENSION ACTIVITIES

1. Plan an interactive "open house" itinerary for families/caregivers that will give participators ideas of activities they can carry out at home to help children practice important algebra concepts.
2. Research additional literature, websites, and/or software programs that could be used with prekindergarten and kindergarten children to help them understand pattern, function, and algebra concepts.

REFERENCES

Bickart, T. S., Jablon, J. R. & Dodge, D. T. (1999). *Building the Primary Classroom: A Complete Guide to Teaching and Learning.* Washington, D.C.: Teaching Strategies, Inc./NH: Heinemann.

Clements, D. H. (2004). Geometric and spatial thinking in early childhood education. In D. H. Clements, J. Sarama, & A. Dibiase (Eds.), *Engaging Young Children in Mathematics* (pp. 267–298). Hillsdale, NJ: Lawrence Erlbaum Associates.

Common Core State Standards Initiative: Preparing America's Students for College & Career (2010). Washington, D.C.: National Governors Association Center for Best Practices/Council of Chief State School Officers.

Copley, J. S. (2000). *The Young Child and Mathematics*. Washington, D.C.: NAEYC.

Copley, J. S., Jones, C. & Dighe, J. (2010). *The Creative Curriculum for Preschool: Mathematics*, vol. 4. Washington, D.C.: Teaching Strategies.

National Council of Teachers of Mathematics (NCTM) (2000). *Principles and Standards of School Mathematics*. http://www.nctm.org/standards/content.aspx?id=4294967312.

National Council of Teachers of Mathematics (NCTM) (2006). *Curriculum Focal Points for Prekindergarten through Grade 8 Mathematics: A Quest for Coherence*. Reston, VA: Author.

National Council of Teachers of Mathematics (NCTM) (adopted in 2008). *Algebra: What, When, and for Whom* (A Position Statement). Reston, VA: Author.

Pennsylvania Department of Education and Department of Public Welfare (2007). *Pennsylvania Learning Standards for Early Childhood: Prekindergarten*. Harrisburg, PA: Author.

Smith, S. S. (2006). *Early Childhood Mathematics*. Boston, MA: Pearson Education, Inc.

5

GEOMETRY

CHAPTER OUTCOMES

After reading this chapter, teacher candidates will be able to:

➤ Describe the development of geometry concepts from prekindergarten through grade 3.
➤ Describe geometry activities that are developmentally appropriate for prekindergarten-aged children.
➤ Describe geometry activities that are developmentally appropriate for kindergarten-aged children.
➤ Describe geometry activities that are developmentally appropriate for first through third grade children.
➤ Create an activity-based classroom, which allows for mathematical exploration in a natural environment.
➤ Explain how early geometry activities lay a foundation for future, higher mathematical understanding, reasoning, and problem solving.
➤ Explain how children's literature can be used to support learning of geometry concepts.
➤ Describe the types of adaptations that could be planned for English Language Learners (ELL) and children with special needs that might help them acquire geometry concepts.
➤ Describe the types of adaptations that could be planned to challenge mathematically promising children in this content area.
➤ Explain how to involve families/caregivers in supporting the application of geometry concepts at home.

OVERVIEW OF CONCEPT DEVELOPMENT

Children are naturally curious, and geometric concepts should be learned through hands-on exploration. Learning environments should be active places that support exploration to capitalize on children's natural interest. According to Clements (1999), it is important for children to handle, draw, and use shapes in many different ways. They do not develop their ideas about shapes just from looking at them. The optimal environment is an enriching one filled with all different kinds, sizes, and orientations of shapes. Also, it is important, to develop age-appropriate geometry activities that help children discover shapes all around them. As children work with shapes, they learn to name, describe, discuss, move, rotate, draw, and change shapes.

A foundation in geometric concepts develops as children find shapes in their environment and describe them in their own words. As children become aware of shapes, they use them to draw pictures and create designs. They learn to distinguish plane shapes (two-dimensional) from solid (three-dimensional) shapes. Spatial reasoning begins to develop as children problem solve in deciding which shape fits in what space in puzzles, and as they experiment with shapes around them. They learn to name shapes and use position words such as "above," "below," and "next to" to describe a shape's orientation in space. Children come to understand that a shape is still that shape regardless of its size or orientation.

As children continue exploring shapes, they begin to use defining attributes to distinguish one shape from another. They experiment with combining two- and three-dimensional shapes to create other shapes, and they use these composed shapes in creating pictures and in building designs. Children gain experience in partitioning circles and rectangles into two, four, and three equal parts and use terminology to describe a part of the whole shape. For example, a part could be "half" of a circle or "a fourth" of a square. Through partitioning experiences children learn to describe a whole as two of the parts, three of the parts, or four of the parts. As they continue working with partitioning activities, they come to realize that equal parts of identical wholes are not necessarily the same shape. For example, a fourth of one of two identical rectangles partitioned lengthwise will have a different shape than a fourth of another identical rectangle partitioned widthwise.

Children in second grade learn to recognize and draw shapes that have specified attributes such as a specific number of equal faces or number of angles. Identified shapes include triangles, quadrilaterals, pentagons, hexagons, and cubes. Partitioning activities include dividing rectangles into rows and columns of equal-sized squares. Children begin to develop the concept of area as they count the number of squares in partitioned rectangles.

When children reach third grade, they calculate the perimeter of polygons. They solve mathematical problems involving perimeter in which the measurement for a side of the polygon is not given. Children use the information given to determine the length of the missing side and then calculate the perimeter. They explore rectangles that have the same area but different perimeters and rectangles that have the same perimeter but different areas. Their understanding of shapes broadens to include different categories and subcategories. They can determine which shape fits into a specific category and which does not fit into a specific category.

As children continue to develop geometric concepts, it is important for teachers to continue to plan activities that provide hands-on exploration, problem solving situations, and opportunities to develop content vocabulary and communicate mathematically.

BUILDING CONCEPTS OF GEOMETRY AT THE PREKINDERGARTEN LEVEL

Building a solid foundation in geometric concepts in children's early years is imperative for later geometric understanding. Teachers of young children should capitalize on children's natural inclination to explore and enjoy building constructions with blocks and other building materials, drawing pictures, and exploring shapes in a variety of ways. Copley, Jones, and Dighe (2010) state that "Children view objects from a variety of perspectives as a result of their constant movement" (p. 751).

The teacher's role is to be cognizant of children's explorations and amazing constructions out of blocks and other building materials and scaffold children's understanding as they explore concepts of geometry. Children should be encouraged to reflect on the activities as they are involved in their explorations. Teachers should also use and reinforce appropriate vocabulary in regard to describing shapes or in referring to the orientation of a shape in space (Copley et al., 2010).

Copley et al. (2010) have outlined various strategies teachers can employ that contribute to children's numerical understanding. These strategies include:

1. Provide opportunities for all children to use the block area.
2. Label shapes with correct names as the children use them.
3. Provide a rich variety of shapes for investigation.
4. Ask children to predict and investigate what will happen when two shapes are combined.
5. Model and describe how to make two- and three- dimensional shapes.
6. Guide children to act out stories that use positional and spatial words.
7. Begin with three-dimensional shapes before children work with paper representations of objects.
8. Provide activities that ask children to visualize and represent particular shapes.
9. Use technology to help children visualize geometric ideas.
10. Use the word "not" to introduce non-examples of specific shapes.
11. Make class maps and have children use them to find particular objects.
12. Suggest the children sketch their building plans so they can be remembered.
13. Encourage the discovery of shape attributes.
14. As children work puzzles, use words like turn, clip, or slide to explain how the pieces might fit.
15. Have children clean up by placing shapes on a shelf or in a box so they can easily fit.

(2010, pp. 751–754)

CONTENT STANDARDS FOR PREKINDERGARTEN

Geometry is the third content area defined in the NCTM document *Principles and Standards in School Mathematics* (2000). It is a key concept in *Curriculum Focal Points for Prekindergarten through Grade 8 Mathematics: A Quest for Coherence* (NCTM, 2006) at all grade levels. The *Common Core State Standards* (2010) begin at the kindergarten level, so there are no standards in this document to guide prekindergarten programs; however, geometry standards are an important focus in grade-level standards contained in the document.

Content standards in the NCTM document *Principles and Standards in School Mathematics* (NCTM, 2000) are not presented by individual grades or age levels, but are grouped in age or grade bands. The first group of standards spans geometry expectations from prekindergarten through grade 2. These include:

- Recognize, name, build, draw, compare, and sort two- and three-dimensional shapes;
- Describe attributes and parts of two- and three-dimensional shapes;
- Investigate and predict the results of putting together and taking apart two- and three-dimensional shapes;
- Describe, name, and interpret relative positions in space and apply ideas about relative position;
- Describe, name, and interpret direction and distance in navigating space and apply ideas about direction and distance;
- Find and name locations with simple relationships such as "near to" and in coordinate systems such as maps;
- Recognize and apply slides, flips, and turns;
- Recognize and create shapes that have symmetry;
- Create mental images of geometric shapes using spatial memory and spatial visualization;
- Recognize and represent shapes from different perspectives;
- Relate ideas in geometry to ideas in number and measurement;
- Recognize geometric shapes and structures in the environment and specify their location.

(http://www.nctm.org/standards/)

The following NCTM Focal Points are the recommended content emphases for mathematics in prekindergarten. It is essential that these Focal Points be addressed in contexts that promote problem solving, reasoning, communication, making connections, and designing and analyzing representations. As a key concept in the NCTM *Focal Points* (2006), geometry is defined as the following for this age group:

- Identify shapes and describe spatial relationships
- Develop spatial reasoning by working from two perspectives on space; examine the shapes of objects and inspect their relative positions
- Find shapes in their environments and describe them in their own words
- Build pictures and designs by combining two- and three-dimensional shapes, and solve such problems as deciding which piece will fit into a space in the puzzle
- Discuss the relative positions of objects with vocabulary such as "above," below," and "next to."

(2006, p. 11)

PREKINDERGARTEN OUTCOMES

Prekindergarten Outcome #1: Identify Shapes and Describe Spatial Relationships

Sample Activity #1

The focus of this activity is to give children experiences in identifying shapes in their environment. Looking around the classroom, the teacher would begin by stating, "I spy with my eye . . ." and continue to describe the shape he or she spies. The children would try to guess the shape the teacher is describing. Children can take turns being the "spy" as they become familiar with the activity.

Sample Activity #2

In this activity children use position vocabulary such as "above," "below," and "next to," as they are describing the location of a two- or three-dimensional shape. In preparation for the activity, the teacher would place two- and three-dimensional shapes around the classroom in various locations for the children to search and find. Shapes should be strategically placed so children could use the position vocabulary mentioned above. Once a shape is located, children would describe its location.

Sample Activity #3

Materials needed for this activity include a set of two-dimensional shapes the children have been identifying, a container, shape labels, and string. To begin the activity, a child would select a shape from the container. The teacher would choose a small group of children, and, using the shape as a guide, the children would position themselves to form the shape. Once the shape is made, string can be used to outline the shape for all to see. A name label for the shape would be identified, selected, and placed inside the string shape (Figures 5.1 and 5.2).

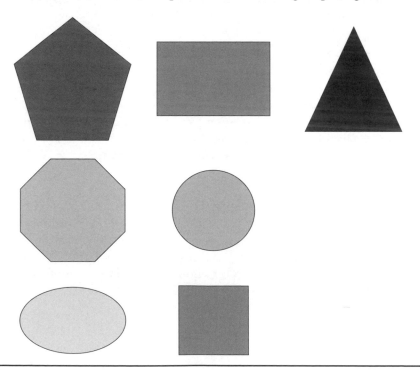

Figure 5.1 Shapes.

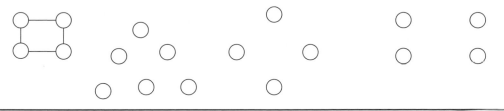

Figure 5.2 Creating Shapes Using Children.

Sample Activity #4

For this activity, the teacher would need to provide various shapes for the children to view that depict shapes of objects in the children's world. Children would be asked to look at various shapes, and using their imaginations, think of an object in the real world that has the same shape (Figure 5.3).

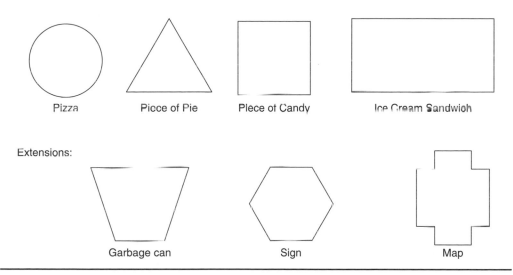

Figure 5.3 Relating Shapes to Real-Life Objects.

Sample Activity #5

For this activity, children would be "shape detectives," as they relate the shapes they have been identifying in the classroom to shapes in their real world. Children could be shape detectives in their classroom, the building where their classroom is located, and outdoors. They can also be asked to find shapes at home (Figure 5.4).

Following are ideas for centers that involve children in identifying shapes and describing spatial relationships.

Center Idea #1—Sorting

At this center, children would be asked to sort two- and three-dimensional objects as they consider the physical attributes of various shapes. Geometric shapes should be of

Figure 5.4 Shapes in the Real World.

different sizes, colors, and textures. Teachers' questions should enable children to explain why he or she has sorted shapes a certain way. Example questions could include:

How did you sort these shapes?
Why did you put these shapes in one pile and not include these shapes?

Center Idea #2—Constructing

At this center, children would be involved in constructing and manipulating three-dimensional shapes as they begin to understand spatial orientation. Manipulatives in this center could include a basic set of three-dimensional blocks, cube blocks, rectangular prisms, cones, and spheres (Figures 5.5 and 5.6).

Sample questions from teachers as children are constructing could include:

What shapes did you use to build your design?
How did you go about constructing your design?
How high do you think you are able to build a tower without it falling over?
Do you think you can add any blocks that are round in your design?
Are you able to make an object using blocks that have straight edges and flat faces?

Center Idea #3—Spatial Relationships

In this center, children explore a sense of space. Materials needed are throw-away cardboard boxes from appliance stores. Several large refrigerator and range boxes enable

Figure 5.5 Three-Dimensional Blocks.

Figure 5.6 Cones, Cubes, Cylinders, and Spheres.

children to create their own use of space. This low-cost activity can help children build spatial concepts needed to understand three-dimensional space. Sample teacher questions could include:

Why did you arrange the boxes the way you did?
Does this look like anything we see outside of school?
What is your favorite spot in the structure? Why?
If you were going to make your construction larger, what would you add to it?

Center Idea #4—Building with Clay

Children in this center would be encouraged to build shapes out of clay. Children would explore attributes of three-dimensional shapes as they build their shapes. Children could be encouraged to combine their clay shapes to design creations. Drawing materials should be available so that children can visually record on paper what they have constructed. Teachers' questions should enable children to explain their designed shapes (Figure 5.7).

Center Idea #5—Puzzles

Puzzles provide enriching problem solving opportunities as children turn and rotate pieces to fit into spaces in a puzzle. As children are placing pieces in puzzles, teachers

Figure 5.7 Building and Combining Clay Shapes.

should use transformation vocabulary such as "flip," "turn," and "slide." Children should be asked to describe what they did with a puzzle piece to have it fit in the space where it belongs. They should be encouraged to use sentences such as "I flipped the piece" or "I turned the piece so it would fit in the space" (Figure 5.8).

Real-World Connections

It would be important for prekindergarten children to explore shapes in various contexts. For example, they could go on a shape walk around the school building or outside in their play area. They could look for shapes on clothing, shoes, toys, items around their classroom, and other areas in their environment.

Figure 5.8 Puzzles.

CONTENT STANDARDS FOR KINDERGARTEN

In the NCTM *Focal Points* (2006) document, geometry for kindergarten children is described as follows:

> • Interpret the physical world with geometric ideas (e.g., shape, orientation, spatial relations) and describe it with corresponding vocabulary.
> • Identify, name, and describe a variety of shapes such as squares, triangles, circles, rectangles, (regular) hexagons, and (isosceles) trapezoids presented in a variety of ways (e.g., with different sizes or orientations), as well as such three-dimensional shapes as spheres, cubes, and cylinders.
> • Use basic shapes and spatial reasoning to model objects in their environment and to construct more complex shapes.
>
> (2006, p. 12)

The following kindergarten standards are listed in the *Common Core State Standards* (2010):

Kindergarten Standard #1: Identify and describe shapes (squares, circles, triangles, rectangles, hexagons, cubes, cylinders, and spheres):
1a. Describe shapes in the environment and describe relative positions;
1b. Recognize shapes and name correctly regardless of size or orientation;
1c. Determine whether shapes are two-dimensional or three-dimensional (flat or solids) . . .

Kindergarten Standard #2: Analyze, compare, create, and compose shapes:
2a. Analyze and compare two- and three-dimensional shapes, in different sizes and orientations, using informal language to describe their similarities, differences, parts, and other attributes;
2b. Model and draw shapes in the real world;
2c. Compose simple shapes to make other shapes or a larger more complex shape.

(2010, p. 12)

KINDERGARTEN OUTCOMES

Kindergarten Outcome #1: Describe Shapes in the Environment and the Relative Positions of These Objects; Correctly Name Shapes Regardless of Their Orientations or Overall Size

Sample Activity #1

In this activity, children will be exploring their classroom to locate familiar shapes. Each child chooses a shape from a container. Shapes could include squares, circles, triangles, and rectangles. Each child is then asked to find an object in the classroom that is the same shape as the one he or she pulled from the container and to draw a picture of it on a piece of paper. For example, a child with a circle could find and draw a picture of the clock on the wall. After each child has found and drawn their pictures, they are asked to describe the location of the shape they found. Examples of locations could include: finding a rectangle on the floor below the table; finding a circle behind the classroom door; or finding a triangle beside the window. The teacher should model location vocabulary as children are describing where they found their shapes (Figure 5.9).

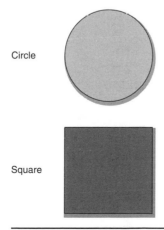

Circle

Square

Figure 5.9 Basic Shapes (continued overleaf).

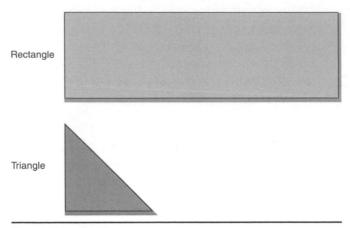

Rectangle

Triangle

Figure 5.9 Continued.

Sample Activity #2

In this activity, children move shapes in various orientations as the teacher or another child provides directions. Each child would need a set of shapes the children have been identifying. These could include some of the following: square, circle, triangle, rectangle, hexagon, cube, cone, cylinder, and sphere. The shapes would be laid out in a straight line on tables or on an area of the floor. The teacher could begin by stating, "Move the circle so it is above the square. Now move the triangle so it is next to the rectangle." Directions should include: "above," "below," "beside," "in front of," "behind," and "next to" (Figure 5.10).

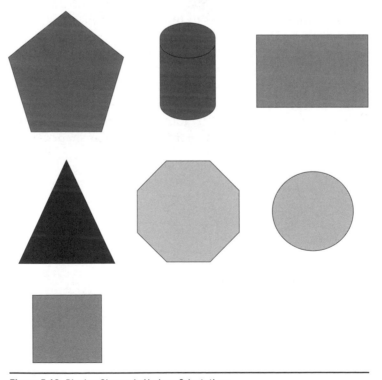

Figure 5.10 Placing Shapes in Various Orientations.

Kindergarten Outcome #2: Correctly Name Shapes Regardless of Their Orientations or Overall Sizes

Sample Activity #1

In this activity, children design circle faces, square faces, triangle faces, and rectangular faces using smaller, matching shapes. The objective of the activity is to have children recognize shapes that are the same but in various orientations. Children would be directed to use the paper shapes and paste eyes, ears, nose, hair, and a mouth on the faces. When completed, the children could give their faces names that correspond with the shapes used to create the face. For example, the square face could be Sarah Square, the circle face could be named Cory Circle, the triangle face could be named Tammy Triangle, and the rectangle could be called Reggie Rectangle (see Figures 5.11–5.14).

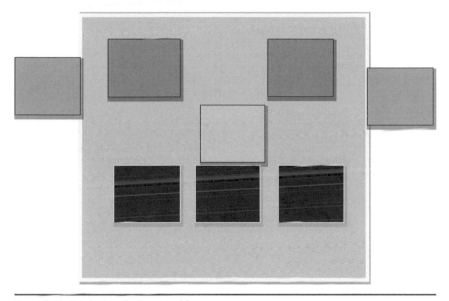

Figure 5.11 Reinforcing the Concept of Squares.

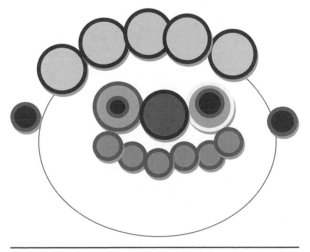

Figure 5.12 Reinforcing the Concept of Circles.

Figure 5.13 Reinforcing the Concept of Triangles.

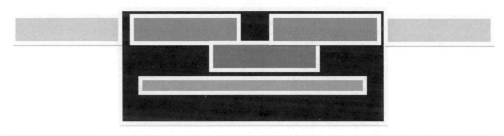

Figure 5.14 Reinforcing the Concept of Rectangles.

Sample Activity #2

Mrs. Nelson wants to help her kindergarten children understand that a shape remains the same shape regardless of its size or orientation in space. After gathering the children on the carpet in her instructional area, she holds up plastic shapes, one by one, and asks the children to identify them. Shapes include squares, circles, triangles, rectangles, and hexagons. She has also taped or placed a variety of the same shapes, in various sizes, around the classroom.

Mrs. Nelson: "Wow; you did a great job naming these shapes!"

Harry: "We know our shapes!"

Mrs. Nelson: "We sure do; I was wondering, though, about the shapes that are taped or placed around the room. I wonder what shapes they could be? Does anyone see a shape?"

Julie: "I see one on the door." (It is a square standing on a point.)

Mrs. Nelson: "Good eyes, Julie. What shape is it?"

Julie: "It is almost a star."

Mrs. Nelson: "What makes you think it is almost a star, Julie?"

Julie: "Well, stars have points like that."

Mrs. Nelson: "You are right, Julie. They do have points like that. What does someone else think?"

Bob: "It looks like a baseball diamond to me." (Other children agree.)

Mrs. Nelson: "Okay; let me turn the shape, and we'll look at it again." (She walks over to the door and turns the square so it is resting on one side.) "What does it look like now?"

Children: "It's a square!"

Mrs. Nelson: "Oh my—you mean, we turned the diamond, and now it is a square?

Children: Yes!"

Mrs. Nelson: "That is very interesting. Does someone see another shape?"

Sarah: "I see a circle on the bookshelf." (Sarah is looking at a smaller-sized circle than the one Mrs. Nelson had the children identify previously.)

Mrs. Nelson: "Well, now, wait a minute. (She holds up a larger circle.) I thought you said this was a circle."

Sarah: "It is a circle. It's just bigger."

Mrs. Nelson: "How many of you agree that the shape Sarah found is a circle?" (All raise a hand.) "I think we made a great discovery here. Both shapes are circles, even though they are different sizes."

Anthony: "I see a really big triangle on the wall behind your desk, Mrs. Nelson."

Mrs Nelson: "But I thought you all said this was a triangle" (She holds up a smaller triangle.)

June: "It doesn't matter that it's smaller; it's still a triangle."

Mrs. Nelson: "How many of you agree that these are both triangles, even though they are different sizes?" (All raise a hand.) "Well, what if I put this triangle I'm holding behind my back?"

Ben: "It's still a triangle."

(Everyone agrees.)

Mrs. Nelson: "What if I put it over my head?"

Children: "It's still a triangle!"

Mrs. Nelson: "You children are such good shape detectives. Let's see what else we can discover. Who sees another shape?"

(The activity continues as children discover other shapes in various sizes and orientations.)

Kindergarten Outcome #3: Identify Shapes as Two-Dimensional (Flat) or Three-Dimensional (Solid)

Sample Activity

For this activity, the teacher would need to collect about 20 two-dimensional and three-dimensional shapes that can be spread out on a tablecloth on the floor. The teacher would create a Venn diagram using two pieces of rope, string, or two hoola hoops. One side of the Venn diagram should be labeled with a picture of a two-dimensional shape;

the other side should be labeled with a three-dimensional object. Each child would have a turn at picking up a shape or object from the tablecloth and deciding on which side of the Venn diagram the shape or object should be placed. Children should be asked to explain their reasoning in placing a shape or object in a specific area of the Venn diagram (Figure 5.15).

Figure 5.15 Venn Diagram.

Kindergarten Outcome #4: Analyze and Compare Two- and Three-Dimensional Shapes, Describing Their Similarities and Differences (Number of Sides, Vertices/ Corners) and Other Attributes (Having Sides of Equal Length)

Sample Activity

This activity is a continuation of the two- and three-dimensional sorting activity using the Venn diagram arrangement described above. For this activity, the teacher would have a child select two shapes or objects from either side of the Venn diagram used for the sorting activity. After displaying the two shapes or objects, pairs of children should be given time to talk to each other about how the shapes or objects are alike and how they are different. After a minute or so, pairs of children should share what they noticed about the shapes or objects with the rest of the children. The teacher should guide children in analyzing attributes of the shapes or objects that they might not have noticed.

Kindergarten Outcome #5: Model Shapes in the World by Building Shapes from Components Using Sticks or Clay and Drawing Pictures

Center Idea

Materials for the center could include clay, toothpicks, pipe cleaners, snap cubes, paper, drawing implements, and a container of shapes (circle, square, rectangle, triangle, hexagons, cubes, cylinders, and spheres). Each child at the center would choose a shape from the container, look around the classroom for an object that matches the shape, and either draw the shape or recreate the shape using the materials at the center (Figure 5.16).

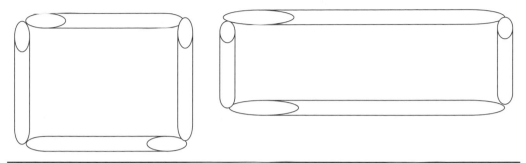

Figure 5.16 Building shapes Using Straws and Pipe Cleaners.

Kindergarten Outcome #6: Compose Simple Shapes to Form Larger Shapes
Center Idea

Materials needed at this center include sets of plastic tangrams, paper, and drawing implements. The children could use some or all of the tangram pieces to create their own, new shapes. After creating a new shape using tangram pieces, children could draw a representation of their new shapes on paper to share with the other children. As the teacher is circulating among the children, it would be important to ask the children to name the shapes they used to create the new shapes (Figure 5.17).

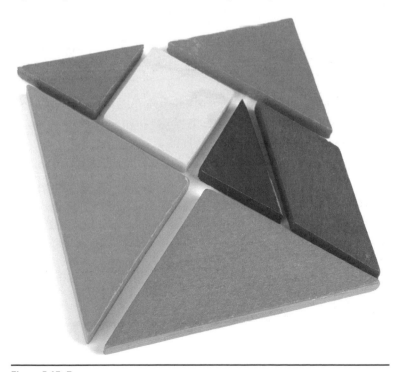

Figure 5.17 Tangrams.

Real-World Connections

It would be important for kindergarten children to explore shapes in various contexts. For example, they could go on a shape walk around the school building or outside in their play area. They could look for shapes on clothing, shoes, toys, items around their classroom, and other areas in their environment. They could look for examples of shapes that are combined to make other shapes.

CONTENT STANDARDS FOR GRADE 1

Content objectives for geometry beginning in prekindergarten and kindergarten are continued and enriched through the primary grades. Children should experience instructional methodologies that create meaning and connect what is being learned to the real world.

Geometry in *Curriculum Focal Points for Prekindergarten through Grade 8: A Quest for Coherence* (NCTM, 2006) is a key concept for first grade. Key points for geometry at the first grade level include:

> • Compose and decompose plane and solid figures . . ., thus building an understanding of part-whole relationships as well as the properties of the original and composite shapes.
> • Combine figures; recognize them from different perspectives and orientations, describe their geometric attributes and properties, and determine how they are alike.
> • Developing a background for measurement and initial understandings of such properties as congruence and symmetry.
>
> (2006, p. 13)

In the *Common Core State Standards* (2010) the geometry standard for first grade is defined as "Reason with shapes and their attributes" (p. 16). There are three defined parts under this standard for first grade children:

> a. Distinguish between defining attributes (e.g., triangles are closed and three-sided) versus non-defining attributes (color, orientation, size); build and draw shapes to possess defining attributes.
> b. Compose two- or three-dimensional shapes to create a composite shape, and compose new shapes from the composite shape.
> c. Partition circles and rectangles into two and four equal shares and describe the shares using halves, fourths, and quarters and use the phrases half of, fourth of, and quarter of.
>
> (2010, p. 16)

GRADE 1 OUTCOMES

Grade 1 Outcome #1: Distinguish Between Defining and Non-Defining Attributes of Shapes

Sample Activity #1

For this activity, children would be given pre-cut geometric shapes including rectangles, squares, trapezoids, triangles, half-circles, and quarter-circles that are all the same color. The children would be asked to sort the shapes according to attributes that define them as different from other shapes. After the sorting activity, children should be asked to describe their sorting strategies.

Sample Activity #2

This is a teacher-directed activity using the pre-cut geometric shapes from the previous sample activity. In this activity, children would be given directions as: Find all the shapes which have the round edges; three points; four corners; three sides, etc (Figure 5.18).

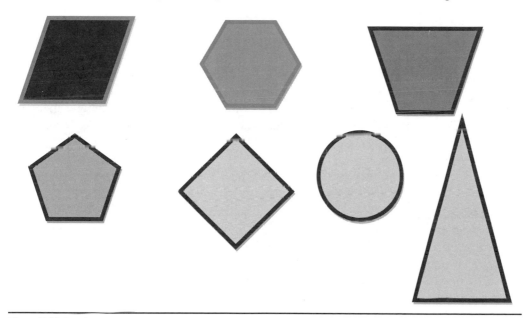

Figure 5.18 Developing an Understanding of Different Geometric Characteristics by Counting Sides, Round Edges, and Points or Corners.

Grade 1 Outcome #2: Compose Two-Dimensional Shapes

Center Idea #1

Materials at the center would include a variety of shapes in different sizes (rectangles, squares, trapezoids, triangles, half-circles, and quarter-circles), paper, and writing implements. Children using the center would be asked to use two or more shapes to create new shapes. Once a new shape is created, children would duplicate the shape by tracing it onto a piece of paper. Children at this level could be asked to write the name of the new shape on the paper beside the traced shape. Another idea would be to have ready-made labels for shapes available that children could choose from in naming the shape they created (Figure 5.19).

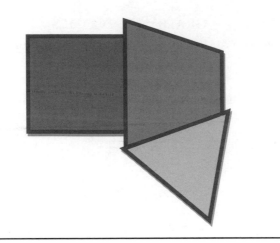

Figure 5.19 Combining Shapes to Make Complex Geometric Designs.

Center Idea #2

Materials needed at this center include geo boards, pictures of shapes, rubber bands, paper, and drawing implements. Children using the center would be asked to duplicate pictures of shapes on the geo boards and then combine shapes to make new shapes. After creating a new shape, children would draw a representation of the new shape on paper. Children could write a label for the new shape or match a ready-made label to the new shape.

Grade 1 Outcome #3: Compose Three-Dimensional Shapes

Center Idea #3

Materials needed at this center include cubes, right rectangular prisms, cones, and right circular cylinders. Children using the center would be asked to construct new shapes from those provided at the center. As children are constructing, the teacher should circulate among the children and ask children to describe the three-dimensional shapes they are using to construct the new design. As the teacher circulates among the children, it would be important to ask the children to identify the shapes being used to create the new designs (Figure 5.20).

Grade 1 Outcome #4: Partition Circles and Rectangles into Two and Four Equal Shares

Sample Activity

For this activity, the teacher would group the children according to the number of equal shares they will be creating that day with the circles and rectangles. For example, on a day when children will be partitioning circles and rectangles into halves, children would be paired. After handing out circles and rectangles, the children would be given the task of folding their shapes to create two equal shares. The circles and rectangles could be cut along the folded lines to create the equal shares. Each equal share would then be labeled "half." Next, the children would be asked to put two halves of the circle and two halves of the rectangle together to see what happens. Children should determine that the two halves made a whole circle and a whole rectangle.

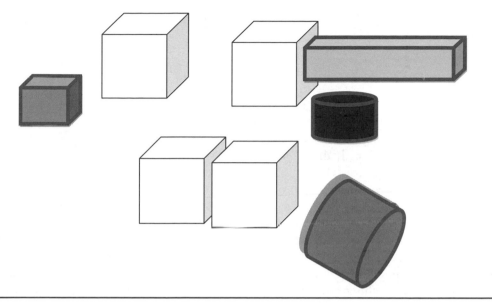

Figure 5.20 Combining 3-D Shapes.

The same procedure can be used to partition circles and rectangles into four equal shares, except that children could be placed in groups of four (Figures 5.21 and 5.22).

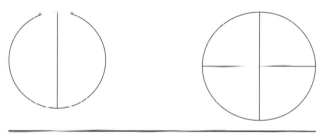

Figure 5.21 Partitioning to Make Equal Shares.

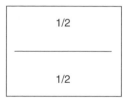

Figure 5.22 Two Equal Halves Make a Whole.

Grade 1 Outcome #5: Symmetry

Sample Activity

This activity could be used as an introduction to the concept of symmetry. Each child would be instructed to fold a piece of drawing paper in half. Children would paint a design on half of the paper and then lay the folded half of the paper on top of the painted half. When unfolded, each half should look exactly the same, or symmetrical. After this introductory activity, children could look through magazines and storybooks to find examples of symmetry.

Grade 1 Outcome #6: Congruence

Sample Activity

In preparation for this activity, the teacher would scatter two-dimensional figures or three-dimensional blocks in various sizes around the classroom. Children would be asked to choose one figure or block from a container and find another figure or block in the classroom that is exactly the same shape and size as, or congruent with, the figure or shape each child drew from the container. Children would then "prove" to the class that the two figures or two blocks are congruent.

Real-World Connections

It would be important for children in grade 1 to explore shapes in various contexts. For example, they could go on a shape walk around the school building or outside in their play area and explore the ways in which shapes are combined. They could look for shape combinations on clothing, shoes, toys, items around their classroom, and other areas in their environment. They could also explore symmetry and congruence in nature and in their school and home environments.

CONTENT STANDARDS FOR GRADE 2

Geometry is paired with measurement as a connection to the *Curriculum Focal Points* (NCTM, 2006) at second grade level. The connection reads as follows:

> Children . . . solve problems involving movement through space. By composing and decomposing two-dimensional shapes (intentionally substituting arrangements of smaller shapes or substituting larger shapes for many smaller shapes), they use geometric knowledge and spatial reasoning to develop foundations for understating area, fractions, and proportions.
>
> (2006, p. 14)

As stated in the *Common Core State Standards* document (2010), children at grade 2 should be able to "Reason with shapes and their attributes" (p. 20). The standard is further defined as:

- Recognize and draw shapes having specified attributes (triangles, quadrilaterals, pentagons, hexagons, and cubes)
- Partition a rectangle into rows and columns of same-sized squares and count to find the total number of them
- Partition circles and rectangles into two, three, or four equal shares, describing the shares using the words halves, thirds, half of, a third of, etc., and describe the whole as two halves, three thirds, four fourths. Recognize that equal shares of identical wholes need not have the same shape.

(2010, p. 20)

GRADE 2 OUTCOMES

Grade 2 Outcome #1: Movement through Space

Center Idea

Children in second grade should continue investigating the movement of geometric shapes in space. For this activity, children will be making paper bracelets. Materials needed for the activity include pattern blocks, 8-inch strips of paper (wide enough for shapes to fit on them with room to spare), and writing and coloring implements. Children using the center would choose a pattern block from the container and trace it at one end of a strip of paper. They would then turn, flip, or slide the shape into another position and trace the shape again. Before making another move, the children would label the movement as "turn," "flip," or "slide." They would continue flipping, turning, and sliding the shape until they reach the end of the strip of paper, being sure to label each move. Children could then color the shapes on the paper strip. When completed, the strip of paper could be taped end to end to create a shape-movement bracelet.

Grade 2 Outcome #2: Composing and Decomposing Shapes

Center Idea

Materials needed at the center include small triangles and rectangles along with a large triangle template and a large rectangle template. Children using the center would be asked to choose one of the large templates and the corresponding smaller shapes. The task would be to duplicate the large template by placing the smaller shapes within the large template. The children could count the smaller shapes to determine how many small triangles were required to duplicate the large shape template. This activity could be used to lay a foundation for later understanding of area (Figure 5.23).

Grade 2 Outcome #3: Recognize and Draw Shapes Having Specified Attributes (Triangles, Quadrilaterals, Pentagons, Hexagons, and Cubes)

Sample Activity

Materials for this activity could include popsicle sticks, straws, pipe cleaners, or paper strips of different lengths. As the teacher describes a shape having specified attributes, students would recreate the shape using the materials provided. For example, the teacher could ask the children to create the shape that has four equal faces and four angles. Children would use the provided materials to create a square (Figure 5.24).

Grade 2 Outcome #4: Partition a Rectangle into Rows and Columns of Same-Sized Square and Count to Find the Total Number of Them

Center Idea

Materials needed at the center include various-sized rectangles, centimeter graph paper, inch graph paper, and writing implements. Children using the center would choose a rectangle and trace it on one of the pieces of graph paper. They would then count the number of squares contained within the traced shape and write the number counted inside the rectangle.

To help children keep count of the number of squares they are counting, they could place a dot in each square as it is counted. When they get to the end of a column

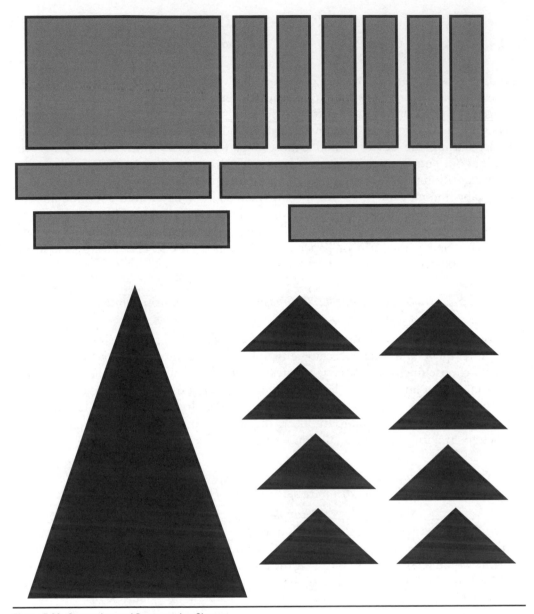

Figure 5.23 Composing and Decomposing Shapes.

or row, depending on how they are counting, they could write the number counted thus far at the end of the row or column so they do not lose track of the number as they are counting.

Children would then trace the same rectangle on the other-sized graph paper, count the number of squares in the shape, and write the number inside the rectangle. As children complete the task, they should be asked to reason why the number of squares counted in the rectangles is not the same, even though the rectangles are the same size.

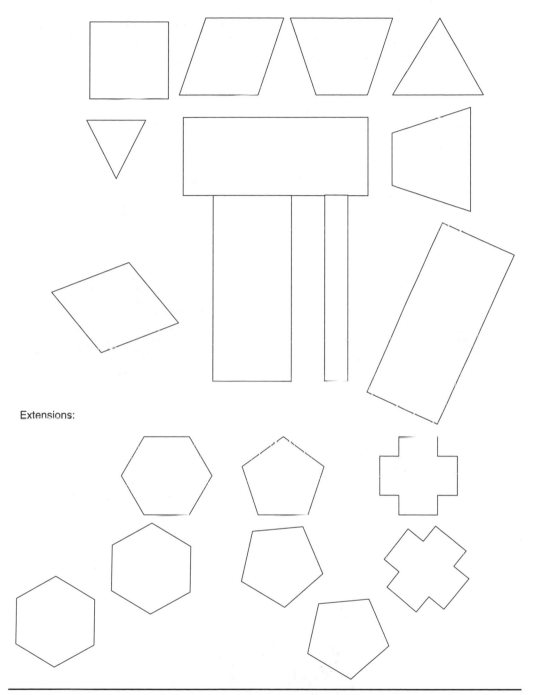

Figure 5.24 Creating Shapes with Straws.

Grade 2 Outcome #5: Partition Circles and Rectangles into Two, Three, or Four Equal Shares; Describe the Shares Using Halves, Thirds, Half of, and a Third of; Describe the Whole as Two Halves, Three Thirds, and Four Fourths

Sample Activity

Provide pairs of children with paper circles and rectangles they can fold into halves, thirds, and fourths. The children could use their imaginations to decorate the shapes to represent different foods. For example, circles could be decorated as pizzas, cookies, round cakes, or round crackers. The rectangles could be decorated as sheet cakes, candy bars, or rectangular-shaped crackers. After decorating their shapes, children would be asked to partition them into equal shares representing halves, thirds, and fourths. It would be important for children to then compose the shapes again by placing two halves together to become a whole, three thirds together to become a whole, and four fourths together to become a whole. Children should be encouraged to describe their wholes as two halves, three thirds, and four fourths (Figure 5.25).

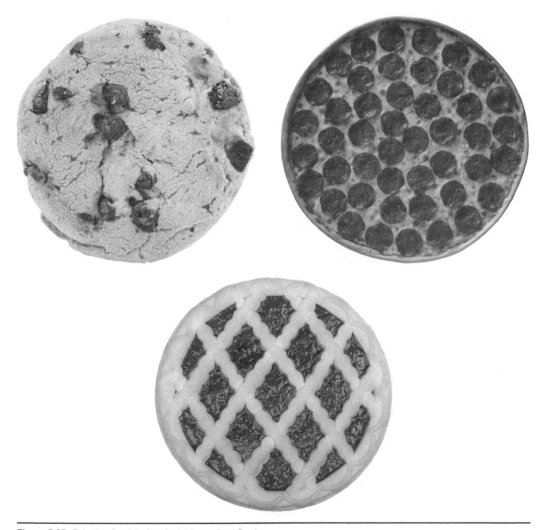

Figure 5.25 Relating Partitioning Activities to Real Food.

Grade 2 Outcome #6: Recognize that Equal Shares of Identical Wholes Need not Have the Same Shape

Sample Activity

For this paper-folding activity, each child would be provided with two identical rectangles. Taking one rectangle, the teacher would model how to fold the rectangle in half lengthwise and then in half again crosswise, forming four equal shares. Each child would take a rectangle and fold it the same way the teacher modeled, and then cut along the folded lines to create their four equal shares.

The teacher would then take another rectangle and fold it lengthwise and then lengthwise again, forming four equal shares. After the children folded their second rectangle in the same manner, they would again cut along the folded lines to create their four equal shares.

The children would be asked to lay the four equal shares from the first rectangle on top of the four equal shares from the second rectangle and compare the shape of each. The children should realize that the four equal shares from each rectangle fit together to make whole rectangles, even though the equal shares from each are not the same shape (Figures 5.26 and 5.27).

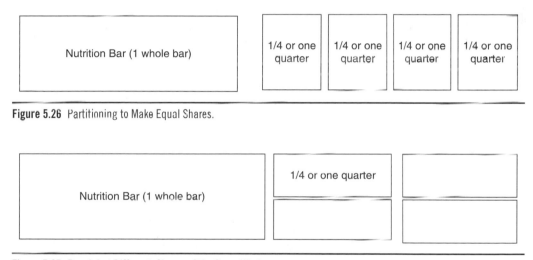

Figure 5.26 Partitioning to Make Equal Shares.

Figure 5.27 Equal, but Different, Shares of the Same Whole.

Real-World Connections

It would be important for children in grade 2 to explore geometry concepts in the context of the real world. For example, they could go on a shape walk around the school building or outside in their play area, looking for shapes in various orientations. They could look for patterns of shapes and analyze the patterns in reference to slides, flips, and turns. They could do the same with shapes on clothing, shoes, toys, items around their classroom, and other areas in their environment. They could go on a shape walk around their home environment as well, and draw pictures of what they found to share in the classroom. They could explore symmetry and congruence in nature.

CONTENT STANDARDS FOR GRADE 3

The standards identified for the 3–5 grade band in *Principles and Standards for School Mathematics* (NCTM, 2000) include the following:

- identifying, comparing, and analyzing attributes of two- and three-dimensional shapes; developing and using appropriate vocabulary to describe the attributes
- classifying two- and three-dimensional shapes according to their attributes and properties; developing definitions of categories of shapes
- subdividing shapes, combining shapes, and transforming shapes
- exploring similarity and congruence of shapes
- making and testing conjectures about properties of shapes and relationships.
  (http://www.nctm.org/standards/)

Geometry is a key Focal Point at the grade 3 level in the *Curriculum Focal Points* (NCTM, 2006) and includes:

- Describe, analyze, and compare, and classify two-dimensional shapes by their sides and angles and connect these attributes to definitions of shapes
- Investigate, describe, and reason about decomposing, combining, and transforming polygons to make other polygons
- Understand attributes and properties of two-dimensional space and the use of attributes and properties in solving problems, including applications involving congruence and symmetry.
  (2006, p. 15)

Common Core State Standards (2010) at the grade 3 level include:

Grade 3 Standard #1: Geometric measurement: understand concepts of area and relate area to multiplication and to addition:
1a. Recognize area as an attribute of plane figures and understand concepts of area measurement;
1b. Measure areas by counting unit squares;
1c. Relate area to the operations of multiplication and addition.

Grade 3 Standard #2: Geometric measurement: recognize perimeter as an attribute of plane figures and distinguish between linear and area measures:
2a. Find the area of a rectangle with whole-number side lengths by tiling it; compare the area to multiplying the side lengths; solve real-world problems;
2b. Use area models to represent the distributive property in mathematical reasoning;
2c. Recognize area as additive by adding non-overlapping parts; apply this technique to solve real-world problems.

Grade 3 Standard #3: Reason with shapes and their attributes:
3a. Understand that shapes in different categories may share attributes;
3b. Partition shapes into parts with equal areas. Express the area of each part as a unit fraction of the whole.

(2010, pp. 25–26)

GRADE 3 OUTCOMES

Grade 3 Outcome #1: Geometric Measurements of Area and Perimeter

Sample Activity #1

For this activity, children will measure the perimeter and the area of their desks. Using pre-cut, uniform paper squares, children would be asked to estimate how many squares it will take to cover their desk tops. After estimating, children could cover their desks with squares, making sure not to overlap the squares, and determine the number of squares needed to cover the area of the desks. They would be asked to use the same procedure in determining the perimeter of their desks.

After completing the activity, children would decide what the difference is between the two different types of measurement and write an explanation in their math journals. This should lead to a class discussion (Figure 5.28).

Figure 5.28 Using Paper Squares to Find Area and Perimeter.

Sample Activity #2

Have children sort the following real-life scenarios into categories of perimeter or area:

Painting the walls of a room
Putting up a fence in the back yard
Covering a garden with mulch
Putting a border around the outside of a garden to keep out bunnies
Framing a picture
Replacing the carpet in your bedroom
Pouring concrete for your new patio
Painting a model car
Pin striping the outside edge of the car
Putting a border around a doll house
Purchasing a new quilt for your bed.

Sample Activity #3

For this activity, children will trace different-sized rectangles and squares on centimeter grid paper and count the squares on the grid paper to determine the area and perimeter of each shape. Using the two measurements, children determine the difference between the shape's area and its perimeter (Figure 5.29).

Figure 5.29 Building Understanding of the Differences between Area and Perimeter.

Sample Activity #4

Children could be paired for this activity. Provide each pair of children with several samples of rectangles and squares drawn on grid paper. Ask them to count the number of squares to determine the area of the shapes. Make the point that this is a time-consuming, cumbersome task and ask the children if there might be a shorter way to calculate the area of the shapes using either addition or multiplication. After listing children's ideas on the board, have them use repeated addition and multiplication to determine the areas of the shapes (e.g., $2 + 2 + 2 = 6$ squares; $2 \times 3 = 6$ squares) (Figure 5.30).

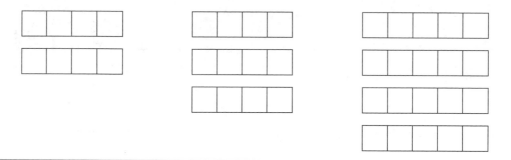

Figure 5.30 Using Repeated Addition and Multiplication to Calculate Area.

Sample Activity #5

In this activity, pairs of children will use real 3-inch or 4-inch square tiles to determine the area of taped-off sections of the classroom floor. The tiles could also be used to determine the perimeter of the same areas.

Sample Activity #6

The objective of this activity is to have children use distributive property reasoning in determining the area of a rectangle. Using inch-sized grid paper, children would be asked to draw specific-sized rectangles. For example, they might be asked to draw a rectangle that is three squares tall and six squares long. After drawing the rectangle, the children would count the squares to determine the area of the rectangle to be 18 squares.

They would then be instructed to partition the six squares of length into two groups of three squares by drawing a line on the rectangle. The sides of the rectangle would now be three squares tall (3) and three squares plus three squares in length (3 + 3). In determining the area of the partitioned rectangle, children would determine that three squares times three squares (3 × 3 = 9 squares) plus three squares times three squares (3 × 3 = 9 squares) is the same area—18 squares (9 squares + 9 squares)—as they previously counted. Consequently, multiplying three squares tall times the three squares + three squares of length—3 × (3 + 3)—would also give an area of 18 squares. As children develop an understanding of the distributive property, they could create their own rectangles on the grid paper and determine the area using this reasoning (Figure 5.31).

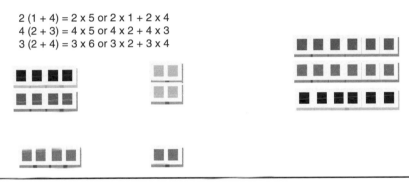

2 (1 + 4) = 2 x 5 or 2 x 1 + 2 x 4
4 (2 + 3) = 4 x 5 or 4 x 2 + 4 x 3
3 (2 + 4) = 3 x 6 or 3 x 2 + 3 x 4

Figure 5.31 Building the Foundation for Properties in Mathematics.

Grade 3 Outcome #2: Geometric Measurement: Recognize Perimeter as an Attribute of Plane Figures and Distinguish Between Linear and Area Measures

Sample Activity #1

In this activity children will find the perimeter and area of a pretend, fenced-in area of a yard or field. Questions to ask children:

Where do we see fences: ball fields, playgrounds, back yards, gardens, etc.?
How would we figure out how much fencing to purchase to fence in an area of a yard or field?

At this point, pairs of children would pretend they are fencing in an area of a yard or field. They would need to determine the length and width of the area they wish to fence in and then calculate the perimeter of the area. They could also calculate the area of the fenced-in space. Children could explore the perimeter and area of various dimensions of pretend fenced-in spaces.

Sample Activity #2

This activity is an extension of the fenced-in activity described above. In this activity, children would determine the perimeter of an area on centimeter grid paper when only given the length of one or two sides of the shape. For example, children could be asked to create a square fenced-in space in which a side is 12 squares in length; a rectangular fenced-in space in which the length is 9 squares and the width is 15 squares. After drawing the required shape, the children would be able to calculate the perimeter of each.

Sample Activity #3

In this activity, children will be comparing rectangles that have the same perimeter but different areas. The activity would begin by having the children draw the following rectangles on centimeter grid paper: a 6 squares × 4 squares rectangle, and a 2 square × 12 squares rectangle. After drawing the rectangles, the children would calculate the area and perimeter of each. Through discussion, they should determine that, although the area of each rectangle is 14 squares, the perimeter of each rectangle is quite different—20 squares and 28 squares, respectively. For further exploration of this standard, children could be given the task of drawing their own rectangles that have the same perimeters but different areas (Figure 5.32).

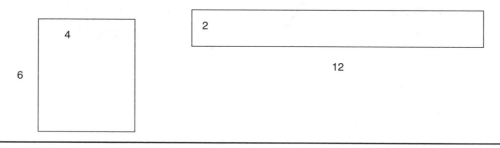

Figure 5.32 Same Areas; Different Perimeters.

Grade 3 Outcome #3: Reason with Shapes and Their Attributes; Understand that Shapes in Different Categories May Share Attributes

Sample Activity #1

Children should engage in sorting activities that require them to consider a specific attribute of shapes. For example, children could sort shapes that have four sides (rectangles, squares, trapezoids) from shapes that do not have four sides (triangles, hexagons); and quadrilaterals (rhombuses, rectangles, and squares) from shapes that are not quadrilaterals (triangles and hexagons). These types of sorting activities could help children understand that shapes in different categories (rhombuses, rectangles) may share attributes (quadrilaterals).

Sample Activity #2

Children would be given a variety of triangles (equilateral triangles, right triangles, isosceles triangles, and scalene triangles) to sort for this activity. The objective is for the children to sort the triangles by attributes and come to the understanding that, even though all the shapes can be categorized as triangles, they do not all share the same attributes (Figure 5.33).

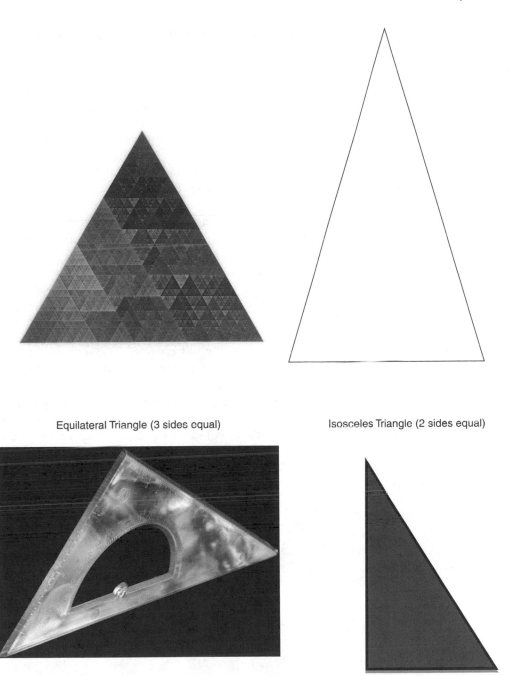

Equilateral Triangle (3 sides equal)

Isosceles Triangle (2 sides equal)

Scalene Triangle (no sides equal)

Right Triangle

Figure 5.33 Triangles.

Grade 3 Outcome #4: Partition or Decompose into Parts with Equal Areas and Describe the Portion as a Fractional Part

Sample Activity

Materials needed for this activity include centimeter grid paper, writing implements, and scissors. To begin the activity, children would be asked to draw specific-sized rectangles on the grid paper. For example, children could be asked to draw three 12 x 12 square rectangles on the grid paper. After drawing the rectangles, children would calculate the area of each square. After cutting out the squares, children would be asked to fold one square in half lengthwise and calculate the area of each half of the square. Each half would be labeled "1/2." The combined areas of each half would be compared to the area of the whole square.

Children would fold the third rectangle in half and then fold each half in half again to make fourths. The fourths would be labeled "1/4." They would determine the area of each fourth of the rectangle and compare the combined areas of the fourths to the area of the other rectangles.

Grade 3 Outcome #5: Symmetry

Sample Activity

For this paper-folding activity, small groups of children would need to be supplied with several copies of a variety of figures. Figures that cannot be folded to show symmetry should be included along with figures that do have lines of symmetry. Children would experiment in folding the figures in determining lines of symmetry. Lines of symmetry for a figure should be numbered and recorded on a chart. When children have completed the activity, they would share and compare their data (Figure 5.34).

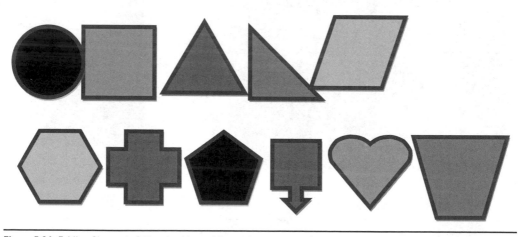

Figure 5.34 Folding Shapes to Determine Lines of Symmetry.

Grade 3 Outcome #6: Congruence

Sample Activity

For this activity, children would make a tracing of a shape in the classroom and then cut it out. All tracings would be placed in a container. Each child would then be handed a tracing from the box. The child's task would be to find the shape in the classroom that is exactly the same as, or congruent with, the tracing from the container. Children would be asked to prove that the tracing and shape in the classroom were congruent.

Real-World Connections

It would be important for children in grade 3 to explore geometry concepts in the context of the real world. They could compute the area of perimeter of various areas in their school or home environment. They could also look for examples of symmetry and congruence in the real world.

ADAPTATIONS FOR CHILDREN WITH SPECIAL NEEDS

Although children may not be formally identified as having special needs until a specific grade level, most teachers can identify children who process information slower or differently from other children. Rather than list specific activities to promote learning for children with special needs, it is more beneficial to identify specific techniques to use that might help children with special needs to learn more efficiently and productively, thus adapting the instruction of activities being planned for all the children. These techniques include (based on Van de Walle, 2007):

- Give children who process information slower more time to answer questions or to complete tasks.
- Use more repetition of activities and events to attain the same understanding of concepts.
- Group children of different abilities together so they can learn from each other.
- Use technology and other hands-on activities to stimulate interest and maintain focus.
- Make real-life connections to the material children are learning.
- Model concepts in various ways.
- Incorporate extra practice for children who process information slower or differently.
- Provide visuals to aid in understanding.
- Ask students to vocalize their understanding.
- Ask students to repeat the directions for the task at hand.
- Use flash cards to develop long term memory reinforcement of vocabulary.
- Use priority classroom seating for children who need to be near the teacher or assistant.
- Structure activities clearly.
- Use hand motions and facial expressions to clue students of intended behavior or task completion.
- Establish clear routines for the children.
- Face the students when talking to them and speak clearly and deliberately.

- Avoid overly complex visuals but scaffold to more complex things.
- Use external equipment as necessary: computers, hearing aids, large print books, microphones and speakers, etc.
- Keep work areas clutter free.
- Emphasize students' strengths: use body movements, manipulatives, kinesthetics.
- Allow one person to speak at a time.

ADAPTATIONS FOR MATHEMATICALLY PROMISING CHILDREN

Depending on the strengths of children in prekindergarten, kindergarten, and primary-aged schoolchildren, gifted children may need adaptations made to the math curriculum that challenge them. Adaptations could include ideas from the section on mathematically promising children under "Children with Special Needs" in Chapter 1 (p. 15,16).

ADAPTATIONS FOR ENGLISH LANGUAGE LEARNERS (ELL)

Adaptations for children who are learning English as their second language could include:

- Connecting geometric concepts to a child's first language—learn important terminology in the child's first language to help connect the English words to the first-language words
- Reinforcing vocabulary with visual cues, pictures, and gestures
- Using multicultural literature, pictures, and stories that depict various cultures, especially the cultures of the children represented in the class
- Providing objects to sort and classify and patterns to investigate from children's cultural backgrounds
- Providing picture cues on children's recording sheets to help them remember what to do.

HOME/SCHOOL CONNECTION IDEAS AND ACTIVITIES

Through interactions with their children, parents and child care providers can enhance the learning of geometric concepts. Here are a few examples which you can use as a guide to help your parents support the learning of geometric concepts.

1. Identifying shapes: As children are playing with toys, draw their attention to shapes on the toys or the shape of the toy itself. (Supports identifying shapes)
2. Comparing shapes: What shape is Sponge Bob? How is Sponge Bob different from _____? (Supports shape attribute identification)
3. When cleaning up after a meal, ask the child what size container might hold the leftovers? (Supports the concept of space)
4. Use directional words such as "next to," "above," "behind," etc. (Supports spatial orientation development and spatial mapping)

5. Identify shapes on clothing. (Enhances pattern development and shape definition and recognition)
6. Baking, building, etc. Estimations: Do you think this board is long enough? Do you think all the cookies will fit in this jar? How many jelly beans do you think are in this bag? (Supports the concept of space)
7. Outside play-jungle gym (Spatial relationships; what body parts will fit in what space; spatial mapping)
8. Museums: What shapes do you see in that animal, bird, picture, and airplane?

Interactions with children can be enhanced by equipping the home environment with materials that can support mathematical learning. These materials can include:

- Different types of block and plastic containers of different shapes and sizes (supports development of size and space concepts)
- Clay (building and constructing three-dimensional shapes)
- Lincoln logs, erector sets, and Lego (spatial orientation and connections)
- Puzzles (logical thinking; movement of shapes in space)

CURRICULUM INTEGRATION

Look around our world and there are shapes everywhere. They are a part of our environment; however, because we encounter shapes so frequently, we have a tendency to take them for granted. Children encounter shapes in science—animals have shapes, plant parts have shapes, planets and stars have shapes. Children also encounter shapes in social studies—land masses have shapes, waterways, seas, and oceans have shapes. As children read, write, and speak, they use spatial and position words. Concepts of geometry are a natural part of children's lives; we as teachers just need to help them make the connections.

GEOMETRY CONTENT VOCABULARY

Listed below is geometry content vocabulary that teachers could be using in their conversations with children, depending on the age level of the children. It is of utmost importance that teachers use various means to help children learn and understand the meanings of the content vocabulary words as they are learning concepts of geometry.

- *Basic Two-Dimensional Shape Names*
  square, rectangle, circle, triangle, hexagon, pentagon, trapezoid, half circles, quarter circles
- *Category Words*
  quadrilateral, polygon
- *Directional Words*
  above, below, next to, over, under, beside
- two-dimensional, flat
- plane figure
- three-dimensional, solid

- *Three-Dimensional Shape Names*
  cube, cylinder, right rectangular prism, sphere, cone
- orientation
- composing and decomposing
- congruence
- symmetry
- properties and attributes
- partition; section
- components
- analyze
- distinguish
- compare

  - same
  - different

- whole
- halves; half of
- fourths, quarters; fourth of, quarter of
- thirds; third of
- equal share
- angles
- flat sides
- rows
- columns
- area, area measure
- perimeter, perimeter measurement
- linear measurement
- length
- addition, additive
- multiplication
- distributive property
- tiling
- fractional part.

LITERATURE CONNECTIONS

Children's literature can be beneficial in developing concepts of geometry. The following storybooks are relevant in developing these concepts from prekindergarten through primary-aged schoolchildren.

Nine-in-One Grr! Grr! by Blia Xiong

Children's Book Press, 1989

When reading this book to the children, use location questions such as: What animal is above the tiger in this picture? Are the monkeys above or below the tiger? What animal is next to the bunny? Which is larger—the bunny or the tiger? Hint: It would be helpful to have scanned pictures of the story or some large screen display to add to the story reading.

Shapes, Shapes, Shapes by Tana Hoban

Greenwillow Books, 1986

Cubes, Cones, Cylinders and Spheres by Tana Hoban

Greenwillow Books, 2000

These books by Tana Hoban depict various shapes in the context of the real world.

Mouse Shapes by Ellen Stoll Walsh

Harcourt Children's Books, 2007

Three mice hide under different brightly colored shapes as they run from a cat.

Rectangles by Jennifer Burke

Children's Press, 2000

This book can be used to introduce rectangles. Children can examine the different pictures and determine how the rectangles are alike.

The Light in the Attic: Poems and Drawings: Poems and Drawings by Shel Silverstein

HarperCollins Children's Books, 1981

Various poems in this collection can be used to enrich the curriculum as a literature connection to the rectangles and other shapes. The poem "Shapes," on page 77, and the drawing accompanying the poem, can be used as an introduction to a hands-on activity requiring children to paste shapes on paper to make pictures.

Color Zoo by Lois Ehlert

J. B. Lippincott, 1989

This book provides opportunities for children to compare and contrast various shapes. The last page in the book depicts animals made from different shapes. The book could be used as an introduction to various art activities.

Mutherpieces: The Art of Problem Solving by Greg Tang

Scholastic Press, 2003

This book provides a number of opportunities to introduce shapes to children. Poems in the book such as "Star Power," "Hot Spots," "Go Fish," "Mind's Eye," "Time Warp," "Drip Dry," and "Soup's Up" can be used in connecting the concept of round to circles. The poem "Square Deal" can be used in making a connection to squares.

The Greedy Triangle by Marilyn Burns

Scholastic Inc., 1994

In this story, the shape shifter turns a triangle into various types of shapes as the triangle decides he does not want to be who he is.

The Napping House by Audrey Wood and Don Wood

Harcourt Brace Jovanovich Publishers, 2009

This story can be used to support the understanding of basic shapes. Children can discover various shapes within the napping house.

The Very Busy Spider by Eric Carle

Philomel Books, 1984

The book lends itself well to basic geometry concepts. Pictures in the book can be used to support concepts of round, straight, and pointed. Circles, rectangles, and triangles are abundant in the pictures and can be used to springboard to a basic lesson in geometric shapes. For the more advance student, some of the spider webs show more complex shapes. In addition to the geometric shapes, the placement of the spider in the web can be used to begin to describe relative space.

Froggy Gets Dressed by Jonathan London

Puffin Storytime, 2007

The book offers numerous examples of basic shapes.

ASSESSING CHAPTER OUTCOMES

1. What types of geometry activities would not be developmentally appropriate for prekindergarten through third grade children?
2. Explain to a parent or administrator how children's early experiences with concepts of geometry lay a foundation for future experiences in geometry.
3. Choose an activity from the chapter or an activity you have developed, and plan adaptations for a child with special needs. (Choose a specific disability, such as hearing or visually impaired, autistic, fine motor skills impairment, etc.)
4. Choose an activity from the chapter or an activity you have developed, and plan adaptations for mathematically promising children.
5. Explain how you would teach vocabulary words specific to concepts of geometry to an ELL child.

CHAPTER EXTENSION ACTIVITIES

1. Design a word wall of geometric terms for a specific age group. Identify three strategies you would use to reinforcement for the words on the wall.
2. Design your early childhood classroom to support geometry development. Include learning stations, computer programs, and anything you believe will lead to the understanding of geometry concepts for the young child.
3. Create a brochure for one age group—prekindergarten through grade 3—and identify and describe specific mathematics activities parents could do with their children to help them develop concepts of geometry.
4. Research additional literature, websites, and/or software programs that could be used with prekindergarten and kindergarten children to help them understand geometry concepts.

REFERENCES

Clements, D. (1999). The geometric world of young children. *Early Childhood Day*, October.
Common Core State Standards Initiative: Preparing America's Students for College & Career (2010). Washington, D.C: National Governors Association Center for Best Practices/Council of Chief State School Officers.

Copley, J. V., Jones, C. & Dighe, J. (2010). *The Creative Curriculum for Preschool: Mathematics*, vol. 4. Washington, D.C.: Teaching Strategies.

National Council of Teachers of Mathematics (NCTM) (2000). *Principles and Standards of School Mathematics*. http://www.nctm.org/standards/content.aspx?id=4294967312.

National Council of Teachers of Mathematics (NCTM) (2006). *Curriculum Focal Points for Prekindergarten through Grade 8 Mathematics: A Quest for Coherence*. Reston, VA: Author.

Van de Walle, J. A. (2007). *Elementary and Middle School Mathematics: Teaching Developmentally*. Upper Saddle River, NJ: Pearson.

.

6

MEASUREMENT

CHAPTER OUTCOMES

After reading this chapter teacher candidates will be able to:

➤ Describe the development of measurement concepts from prekindergarten through third grade.
➤ Describe measurement activities that are developmentally appropriate for prekindergarten-aged children.
➤ Describe measurement activities that are developmentally appropriate for kindergarten-aged children.
➤ Describe measurement activities that are developmentally appropriate for children in the primary grades (grade 1 through grade 3) in school.
➤ Explain how children's literature can be used to support learning of measurement concepts.
➤ Describe the types of adaptations that could be planned for English Language Learners (ELL) and children with special needs that might help them acquire measurement concepts.
➤ Describe the types of adaptations that could be planned to challenge mathematically promising children in this content area.
➤ Explain how to involve families/caregivers in supporting the acquisition of measurement concepts at home.
➤ Explain how to assess children's learning of measurement concepts at different age levels.

OVERVIEW OF CONCEPT DEVELOPMENT

Prekindergarten children learn informal yet important information about measurement from their everyday experiences and interactions with adults and other children. Listening to children's conversations with others, or engaging in conversation with a prekindergarten or kindergarten child, it is not uncommon to hear or to use terminology such as "same or different;" "more or less;" "older or younger;" "faster or slower;" and "smaller or bigger." It is important in prekindergarten and kindergarten programs to capitalize on what children can do and to nurture early measurement concept development, knowing that children's experiential backgrounds are varied in their exposure to measurement concepts and the level of understanding of measurement terminology they use. It is the responsibility of prekindergarten and kindergarten teachers to take children where they are in their conceptual understanding when they enter these programs and move each child forward in developing measurement concepts. Copley (2010) states, "Young children construct measurement concepts over an extended period of time, and their process can be quite complex" (p. 119). It is important to remember that children are aware of the attributes of length, weight, capacity, and time; however, they need to learn to reason about these attributes and how to measure them accurately (Clements, 2003).

The concept of measurement begins as children apply terminology of "same/different" and "more/less" as they make direct comparisons on the basis of attributes of objects that can be measured, such as length and weight or mass. They progress to comparing and ordering up to three objects by length, and are able to compare the length of two objects in relationship to a third object. For example, if object A is smaller than object B, and object C is larger than object B, then object C is also larger than object A (concept of transitivity). When children first begin measuring length, they begin by lining up or iterating nonstandard units (paper clips, clothes pins, pencils, etc.) end to end. Through measuring experiences children learn the importance of measuring with a standard unit (inches, centimeters, etc.). They begin estimating and measuring using standard units of measure, problem solve by adding and subtracting within 100 by using drawings or equations, and represent measurements in picture graphs or bar graphs.

As children gain experience in measuring, they develop an understanding of the relationship between the size of the unit and the number of units used in a particular measurement. For example, in measuring the same length, a smaller unit of measure (e.g. centimeter cubes) will produce a larger number of total units than a larger unit of measure (e.g. inch cubes). Working with linear measurements also strengthens children's understanding of fractions as they confront measuring tasks that require the use of a partial unit. Children in third grade measure lengths using rulers that are marked with halves and fourths of an inch and depict measurement data in picture graphs and bar graphs. They learn concepts of area and perimeter, distinguishing between area and linear measurements. In working with the concept of area, they learn how this measurement is related to repeated addition and multiplication. They estimate and measure liquid volumes and masses of objects using standard units including grams, kilograms, and liters and solve one-step problems involving these measurements.

In learning concepts of time, children need to first be exposed to different types of clocks, learn about the parts of clocks, and then learn how clocks work. Children begin learning to tell time to the hour and half-hour using digital and analog clocks. They then progress to telling time to the nearest five minutes and using A.M. and P.M. when thinking about how a day is partitioned. By third grade, children are telling time to the minute, estimating time and calculating intervals of time.

Children begin thinking about money by recognizing coins and then counting money. They learn to use the cent sign (¢) and dollar sign ($) correctly and solve money problems using dollar bills, quarters, dimes, nickels, and pennies.

The importance of measurement concepts is outlined in the following statement by the National Council of Teachers of Mathematics (NCTM):

> Measurement is one of the most widely used applications of mathematics. It bridges two main areas of school mathematics—geometry and number. Measurement activities can simultaneously teach important everyday skills, strengthen students' knowledge of other important topics in mathematics, and develop measurement concepts and processes that will be formalized and expanded in later years. Teaching that builds on students' intuitive understandings and informal experiences with measurement helps them to understand the attributes to be measured as well as what it means to measure.
>
> (NCTM, 2000, p. 103)

Copley, Jones, and Dighe (2010) provide recommendations for teachers as children explore, but not master, concepts of measurement in preschool settings. These include:

1. Provide many standard measuring tools for children to use
2. Model measuring behaviors frequently
3. Talk about what you are doing as you measure
4. Encourage measurement problem solving activities (e.g. comparing weights & distances)
5. Take advantage of daily experiences to discuss measurement concepts
6. Use estimation vocabulary such as about, close to, and almost.

(pp. 760–761)

BUILDING CONCEPTS OF MEASUREMENT AT THE PREKINDERGARTEN LEVEL

Prekindergarten children use their senses to construct knowledge about measurement concepts through daily observations and interactions with real objects and events. Critical thinking and problem solving skills are acquired by involving children in developmentally and age-appropriate, hands-on, feeling-on, and mind-on experiences. This age group of children needs opportunities to actively engage with many different types of enticing objects they can hold, touch, and maneuver in a stimulating environment that fosters investigation and makes direct connections to the children's immediate world (Davis & Keller, 2009). All children, including children with special needs and English Language Learners (ELL), need challenging, yet attainable tasks that provide meaningful experiences reflective of their interests, individual abilities, and family culture.

CONTENT STANDARDS FOR PREKINDERGARTEN

Measurement is the fourth content area defined in the NCTM document *Principles and Standards in School Mathematics* (2000) and a key concept identified in *Curriculum*

Focal Points for Prekindergarten through Grade 8 Mathematics: A Quest for Coherence (NCTM, 2006) for prekindergarten children

Content standards in the NCTM document *Principles and Standards in School Mathematics* (2000) are not presented by individual grades or age levels, but are grouped in age or grade bands. The first group of standards spans measurement expectations from prekindergarten through grade 2. These include:

Understand measurable attributes of objects and the units, systems, and processes of measurement:

- recognize the attributes of length, volume, weight, area, and time;
- compare and order objects according to these attributes;
- understand how to measure using nonstandard and standard units;
- select an appropriate unit and tool for the attribute being measured.

Apply appropriate techniques, tools, and formulas to determine measurements:

- measure with multiple copies of units of the same size, such as paper clips laid end to end;
- use repetition of a single unit to measure something larger than the unit, for instance, measuring the length of a room with a single meter stick;
- use tools to measure;
- develop common referents for measures to make comparisons and estimates.

(http://www.nctm.org/standards/)

As a curriculum focal point for prekindergarten children, measurement is defined as "Identifying measurable attributes and comparing objects by using these attributes" (NCTM, 2006, p. 11). This definition is directly related to the objectives for measurement in the content standards; however, in the curriculum *Focal Points* document, specific guidelines for each standard are provided. It is recommended that a prekindergarten program emphasize the following:

- Identifying objects as "same or different," and then "more or less" on the basis of attributes the children can measure.
- Identifying measurable attributes such as length and weight.
- Solving problems using attributes by making direct comparisons.

(2006, p. 11)

The *Common Core State Standards* (2010) document begins at the kindergarten level, so there are no identified standards for prekindergarten. Geo (2003), however, has identified the following measurement attributes that may develop through play:

- Comparing magnitudes (e.g. whose is bigger) by directly matching objects
- Comparing quantities (e.g. who has more) by counting objects

- Estimating magnitudes or quantities without directly measuring or counting objects.

PREKINDERGARTEN OUTCOMES

Figure 6.1 Prekindergarten Children Explore Concepts of Length and Height Through Their Own Drawings.

Prekindergarten Outcome #1: Identify Objects as Same/Different and More/Less Based on Attributes Children Can Measure

Sample Activity

For this activity, children will explore the concept of length by "measuring" various objects using nonstandard measurement items available in their environment (Figure 6.1).

After instruction time focused on "how" to measure, children can explore this concept in a learning center, where the objects to be measured and the nonstandard unit of measure are provided. The nonstandard units for measuring could be blocks, paper clips, pennies, or any other groups of items that are plentiful in the classroom. As children explore this concept at the center, the teacher or teacher aides should engage children in conversations that include terminology such as "same/different," "more/less," and "longer/shorter" (Figure 6.2).

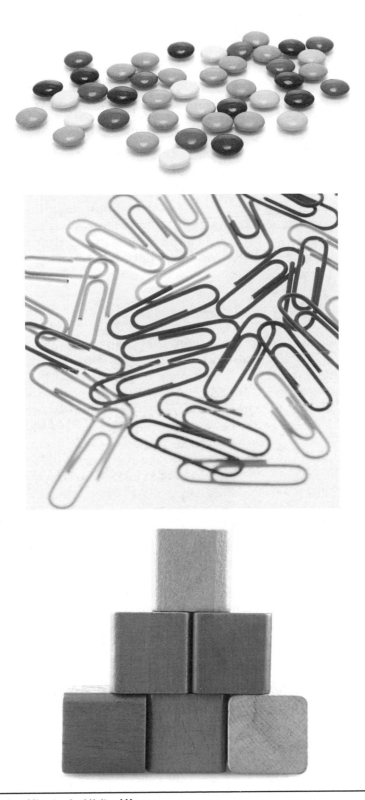

Figure 6.2 Examples of Nonstandard Units of Measure.

Prekindergarten Outcome #2: Identify Measurable Attributes Such as Length

Note: Measuring with nonstandard units is an important first step in helping children develop a conceptual knowledge of measurement. It also provides a good rationale for a standard unit. Nonstandard units make it easier for children to focus on the attribute being measured, and the size of the numbers in these early measurement activities can be kept at a reasonable number (Van de Walle, 2004).

McKenna's teacher has modeled how to measure objects with nonstandard units with the prekindergarten children. She has used various objects as nonstandard units of measure including connecting cubes, paper clips, and counting bears. The children have generated a list of objects that could be used as measuring units. The list is displayed in the front of the room, with pictures of each item beside the word that says the item, so the children can "read" the list. Terminology such as "more or less," "longer or shorter," and "same or different" has been reinforced with the children.

Today the children are going to work at various centers in groups of four with the assistance of a teacher's aide or the teacher. At McKenna's group the children are going to use popsicle sticks to measure and compare sets of two lines on the floor that the teacher has created with masking tape. There are four sets of paired lines. Each child is given a turn to measure a set of lines. After the popsicle sticks are laid along the two lines, the teacher or teacher's aide engages the four children in a conversation, comparing the two lines using the appropriate vocabulary.

When it is McKenna's turn, she takes one popsicle stick at a time and meticulously lays them end to end as the teacher had modeled with other units of measure. When McKenna is finished, the teacher asks the children, "Would we say that the two lines are the same or different?" The four children exclaim that the lines are different. McKenna points to a line, stating that the line is longer than the other one. She continues by stating that the longer line has five popsicle sticks and the shorter line has three popsicle sticks. The teacher then asks the children, "Which is more: five or three?" The children chime that five is more than three.

Questions to Ponder
1. Consider McKenna's statements and responses. What important measurement concepts has she learned?
2. What might be a logical extension activity for McKenna?

Prekindergarten Outcome #3: Identify Measuring Tools and Their Uses
(Clocks for Telling Time; Thermometers for Telling Temperature)
Sample Activity

The mathematical classroom environment should include various measurement tools that children can touch, handle, and use. Measuring tools could include clocks, thermometers, timers, stopwatches, measuring cups and measuring spoons, a height chart, and various types of scales.

Prekindergarten Outcome #4: Use Standard Measuring Items to
Explore Measurement (Inches, Yardsticks, Measuring Tape, Height Chart,
Scales, Balance Scales, Cups, Measuring Spoons)

Sample Activity

In this activity, children will explore the concept of weight and compare the weight of various objects using a balance scale.

During instruction time, children will be introduced to and learn how to use a balance scale. Through exploration with the teacher children will "figure out" what the terms "same," "more than," and "less than" mean in reference to using a balance scale. The concept of measuring using a balance scale could be compared to children using a seesaw. Situations derived from children's experiences in playing on a seesaw would make a real-world connection to the balance scale activity (Figure 6.3).

Figure 6.3 Making Real-World Connections.

Sample Learning Center Activity

A balance scale and various pieces of fruit (three, perhaps) would be provided at the learning center. Children explore the mass of the fruit in terms of weighing the same or one piece of fruit weighing more or less than another. The teacher would engage students in conversation using the appropriate terminology. As an extension activity, children could be asked to order the fruit from the lightest to the heaviest.

Prekindergarten Outcome #5: Use Measuring Cups and Measuring Spoons (Cooking Activities)

Learning Center Activity

Measuring cups, measuring spoons, and various containers could be provided in a learning center for children to explore how many cups or spoonfuls of something (rice, sand, buttons, and paper clips) would fit into various containers (Figure 6.4).

Figure 6.4 Children Exploring Concepts of Measurement.

Prekindergarten Outcome #6: Interact with Play Money, Price Tags and a Cash Register

Learning Center Activity

A learning center could include play money, items that have attached price tags, and a toy cash register. At the prekindergarten level, children would simply be exposed to these items and the idea of using money to purchase these items through play.

Prekindergarten Outcome #7: Passage of Time; Sequence of Events

Sample Activities

Teachers can talk about daily routines, sequence of events, morning and night, the calendar, and terminology that include such terms as "yesterday," "today," and "tomorrow" (Figure 6.5). Copley et al. (2010) state:

> Many daily experiences lead to discussions about measurement concepts, particularly time. Almost every day, children ask and teachers answer questions like these: "How much choice time is left?; How much longer until outdoor time?; When is snack time?; Is it time for clean-up?" They are also perfect opportunities to introduce a timer. Using a timer allows children to see time passing and, when used along with comparative words to describe time, children begin to develop an understanding of time measurement.
>
> (2010, p. 761)

Figure 6.5 Circle or Meeting Times Provide an Opportunity to Discuss Measurement Concepts Such as Sequence of Events, Morning/Night, Seasons, Calendar, Daily Routine, and Measurement Terminology.

CONTENT STANDARDS FOR KINDERGARTEN

Measurement concepts developed in prekindergarten are extended through measurement experiences in kindergarten. It continues to be important for children to hear and use spatial and position words that represent various aspects of time. Morning meetings are good times to talk about the day's schedule, events that happened in the past, events that will happen in the future, day and night, and seasons of the year. References to the clock and calendar should be part of daily conversations. While children are still measuring using nonstandard units, they are transitioning into identifying and using standard tools and units of measurement. They are experimenting with various attributes of objects and comparing these objects according to different attributes.

Measurement for kindergarten children under the *Curriculum Focal Points* (NCTM, 2006) is defined as ordering objects by measurable attributes. This includes:

- Using measurable attributes, such as length or weight, to solve problems by comparing and order objects.
- Compare lengths of two objects both directly (comparing them to each other) and indirectly (comparing both with a third object).

(2006, p. 12)

The *Common Core State Standards* (2010) for kindergarten include the following standards:

Kindergarten Standard #1: Describe and compare measurable attributes
1a. Describe measurable attributes of objects, such as length or weight. Describe several measurable attributes of a single object.
1b. Directly compare two objects with a measurable attribute in common, to see which object has "more of"/"less of" the attribute, and describe the difference.

Kindergarten Standard #2: Classify objects and count the number of objects in each category.

(2010, p. 12)

KINDERGARTEN OUTCOMES

Kindergarten Outcome #1: Tools for Measuring

During instruction time, children will be viewing various measuring tools and discussing the use of each in determining a measurement (measuring cup, measuring spoon, timer, stopwatch, clock, balance scale, weight scale, calendar, and ruler). The teacher will then show the children an object, such as a stuffed animal. After discussing what the term "height" means, the children will be asked to identify the tool that would be most appropriate in finding height. The teacher will also engage the children in a discussion of mass/weight and the appropriate tool(s) to determine this measurement. A distinction should be made between using a scale to find a number for weight and using a balance scale for determining "weighs the same," "weighs more than," or "weighs less than" in comparing objects.

Kindergarten Outcome #2: Compare Two or Three Classroom Objects Using Characteristics as Length, Height, and Weight; Investigate Ways to Measure the Various Attributes of Objects

Sample Activity

In this activity children will be comparing two different mini-sized pumpkins using attributes of height and weight (Figure 6.6).

Figure 6.6 Pumpkins.

Learning Center Activity

Items in the learning center could be a weight scale (if appropriate for the size of the pumpkins), a balance scale, a ruler, pencils and paper for recording data, and two pumpkins. Children will use the measuring tools to determine the height and mass/weight of their pumpkins. Measuring the height of the pumpkins could be compared to measuring the height of the children on a growth chart. Paper could be taped on a section of the wall. Children could stand their pumpkins against the wall and mark the height of each pumpkin on the paper.

As the teacher circulates among the children, he or she would encourage them to engage in appropriate comparing terminology in referring to the measurements of their pumpkins. Note: Pumpkins should vary enough in size so that comparing height and weight of both is easy for children to discern.

Kindergarten Outcome #3: Estimate the Length of and Measure Objects Using the Same Nonstandard Unit of Measure

Sample Activity

In this activity, children will measure their own body length using a nonstandard unit (Figure 6.7).

Previous to this activity, the teacher and/or teacher aide will have traced each child's body on butcher-block-type paper and labeled each tracing with the child's name. Using a ruler, a beginning and ending line for measuring purposes should be drawn at the top of the head and the bottom of the feet on each tracing.

Figure 6.7 Measuring Height by a Nonstandard Unit of Measure.

During instruction time, the teacher, with the help of the children, will demonstrate how to measure the length of an object such as the table top by laying a nonstandard unit such as connecting cubes across the table top end to end and snapping them together. After laying out five connecting cubes to see how far they extend across the table top, the teacher will stop and do a "talk aloud" involving the children in which he or she thinks out loud in determining how many connecting cubes it might take to measure the length of the table top. The teacher, again with help from the children, will think about how many groups of five connecting cubes will be needed to reach the end of the table top. The teacher then proceeds to measure the table top using connecting cubes. After counting, the teacher and children compare the estimate with the actual number of cubes needed to measure the table top.

The children will be told that they are going to estimate and then measure the length of their body (or one arm or one leg) on their body tracing using connecting cubes. Again, a reference of five connecting cubes snapped together can be used as a visual in making the estimate. The teacher will demonstrate where to begin and end measuring by using a body tracing as an example. Body tracings will be handed out to the children, along with containers of connecting cubes. Children will lay connecting cubes together to determine their body length (or whatever length the teacher decides is appropriate to use). Children will be encouraged to make an estimate before completing the measuring activity and to record the estimate.

After counting the connecting cubes, children will record their measurements and compare this number to their estimates. These individual measurements can be used to compare the children's body lengths.

Body tracings can be used for multiple measuring activities. For example, children could measure their body length using a different nonstandard unit, such as blocks or multiple tracings of their foot. These measurement activities afford many opportunities for making comparisons.

Kindergarten Outcome #4: Compare the Measurement of Different Classroom Objects and Use Comparison Vocabulary to Describe How the Objects are Related (Length, Height)

Sample Activity

Elizabeth's teacher has provided a box of paper clips at a measuring center, along with a container holding classroom items to be measured and compared using the paper clips as the unit of measure. Elizabeth opens the box of paper clips and then empties the container of items on the table. Picking up one item at a time, she examines each one before placing it on the table. When the three objects are on the table, there is a block from the block center, a paintbrush from the art center, and a shoe from the dress-up center.

Elizabeth begins the measuring activity by laying paper clips, end to end, across the top of the block. Leaving these paper clips on top of the block, she takes more paper clips from the box and attempts to lay them end to end on top of the paintbrush; however, the paper clips fall off. The teacher walks by the measuring center and suggests to Elizabeth that there might be another way to measure the length of the paintbrush without laying the paper clips on top of the brush. She guides Elizabeth in figuring out that the paper clips can still be laid end to end, but they can be laid beside the paintbrush instead of on top of the paintbrush. Elizabeth completes this task and moves on to the shoe. Again Elizabeth tries to lay the paper clips end to end on top of the shoe, but when some of the paper clips fall inside the shoe, she resorts to laying the paper clips end to end alongside of the shoe, as she did with the paintbrush.

At the direction of the teacher, Elizabeth begins to count the paper clips used in measuring each of the items. Elizabeth counts and records 3 paper clips for the block, 6 paper clips for the paintbrush, and 10 paper clips for the shoe. Upon showing her paper to the teacher, Elizabeth and her teacher use terminology such as "length," "more than," "less than," "greater," and "least" in referring to the objects. Elizabeth's teacher then asks her to line up the objects from the least to the greatest in length. Elizabeth does so without difficulty or hesitation.

Questions to Ponder

1. What has Elizabeth learned about measuring the length of an object from this activity?
2. Since Elizabeth was successful in measuring the three items with paper clips and ordering them from the least to the greatest in length, what might be a logical extension activity for Elizabeth?

Kindergarten Outcome #5: Select Appropriate Tools for Measuring Specific Attributes (Clock, Scale, Measuring Spoon)

Sample Lesson Plan

Children use their knowledge of measurement and measurement tools in this game-like activity.

Measurement Tools Lesson Plan

Resources

Me and the Measure of Things by Joan Sweeny

Objective

In pairs, and given a specific measurement situation, children will choose the correct measuring tool for the situation.

Standards

NCTM-S.MSR.P–2.4.1.1	recognize the attributes of length, volume, weight, area, and time
NCTM-S.MSR.P–2.4.1.4	select an appropriate unit and tool for the attribute being measured

Materials

Storybook: *Me and the Measure of Things* by Joan Sweeny

Various measuring tools, including a measuring cup, measuring spoons, clock, weight scale, balance scale, ruler, yard stick, tape measure, timer, stopwatch, calendar, gallon container, apple, orange; shopping bag to hold measuring tools.

Large piece of blue paper cut in the shape of a pond or large container to hold fish cards.

Stick and string with a magnet on the end to be used as a fishing pole.

Make the situation cards (see below) on paper that is cut in the shape of a fish. Attach a paper clip to each fish, so the fish can be picked up by the magnet on the fishing pole.

Situation Cards

1. I want to see how far I can run in one minute. Which measurement tool will I use?
2. I want to know how much water is in this container [show the gallon container]. Which measuring tool would be the best to use to find out?
3. I want to know which is heavier, the orange or the apple. Which tool could I use to find out?
4. I want to know what day of the week March 2nd falls on. Which tool can I use to find this information?
5. Mom told me to add a tiny amount of water to my pet gerbil's water dish. Which tool would be the best one to use to do this?
6. Dad told me I need to be in bed by 8 o'clock P.M. Which tool would I use to know when it is time for bed?
7. The cupcakes I made need to bake for 20 minutes. Which tool could I use to know when to take the cupcakes out of the oven?
8. I want to know how much weight I gained this past year. Which tool would I use to find out how much weight I gained?
9. I want to measure the length of my arm. Which tools could I use?
10. I want to measure how tall I am. Which measuring tool could I use to find out this information?

Additional situation cards can be created following the examples above.

Introduction/Motivation

This activity begins by reading *Me and the Measure of Things* by Joan Sweeny. After reading the storybook to the children, names can be drawn randomly for students to pull one measuring item at a time from the shopping bag. The measuring tool should be identified, followed by a brief discussion of how the tool is used in the real world. Have the children sit in a circle, with the measuring tools displayed in the middle of the circle.

Procedure

In pairs, children hold the fishing rod and catch a paper fish. The teacher reads the situation to the pair of children, and the two children decide which tool works best for the situation. The other children give the pair a thumbs-up or thumbs-down if they agree or disagree with the pair's decision.

Adaptations

It will be necessary to have adult supervision for the measurement activity to insure that all children understand the directions and how to play the game properly.

Student Evaluation

Children will be informally assessed during the measuring tool activity to determine their ability to choose the best measuring tool for the given situation.

Safety

Safety precautions and behavior expectations will need to be discussed before the activity begins. Children will need to be careful to not poke themselves or others with the fishing rod.

CONTENT STANDARDS FOR GRADE 1

Content objectives for measurement beginning in prekindergarten and kindergarten are continued and enriched with learning experiences that create meaning and connect what is being learned to the real world.

Measurement in *Curriculum Focal Points for Prekindergarten through Grade 8 Mathematics: A Quest for Coherence* (NCTM, 2006) is not identified as a key focus in first grade; however, it is identified in the "connections to the Focal Points" section of the document for grade 1. As a connection to the Focal Points, children in first grade are involved in the following:

> • Solve problems involving measurement and data.
> • Work with units of measurement by laying them end to end and then counting the units in counting by tens and ones.
> • Represent data from measurement activities in graphs.
>
> (2006, p. 13)

The *Common Core State Standards* (2010) at the first grade level also include:

> **Grade 1 Standard #1:** Measure lengths indirectly and by iterating length units:
> **1a.** Order three objects by length; compare the lengths of two objects indirectly by using a third object;
> **1b.** Express the length of an object as a whole number of length units, by laying multiple copies of a shorter object (the length unit) end to end; understand that the length measurement of an object is the number of same-size units that span it with no gaps or overlaps.
>
> **Grade 1 Standard #2:** Tell and write time in hours and half-hours using analog and digital clocks.
>
> **Grade 1 Standard #3:** Organize, represent and interpret data with up to three categories; ask and answer questions about the total number of data points, how many in each category, and how many more or less in one category than in another.
>
> (2010, p. 16)

GRADE 1 OUTCOMES

Grade 1 Outcome #1: Work with Units of Measure

Sample Activity

In this activity, children will measure the length of a desk or width of their table using four different units of measure—paper inch worms, centimeter cubes, pennies, and large paper clips.

Working in pairs, children will be given enough of each unit of measure to extend the units across the entire length of a desk or width of their table, end to end. They will also be given a recording sheet showing a picture of each unit of measure with a line next to it. Using one unit at a time, children will lay the units end to end until the entire length or width has been covered. Children will be encouraged to group the units of measure by tens (and ones, if there are any units that do not fit into a group of ten), in order to count them. The number of units recorded is written on the line next to the picture of the unit on the recording sheet. When all measurements have been completed, children can graph their data.

Grade 1 Outcome #2: Compare and Order Lengths

Sample Activity

For this activity, the teacher or aide will need to prepare beforehand paper lunch-sized bags containing three objects for pairs of children to order by length. Bags should be numbered, and each should contain a different set of objects. There should be enough bags for the number of pairs of children in the classroom. Recording sheets also need to be prepared. Spaces on the recording sheet should be numbered from one to however many bags have been prepared. Next to each number should be spaces marked "shortest," "middle-sized," and "longest."

For the activity, pairs of children will take the objects out of the bag and order them from the shortest to the longest by length. On a recording sheet, children will draw pictures of the objects under the labeled spaces and next to the number on the sheet that corresponds with the number on the bag of objects. As pairs of children finish with one bag, they can trade bags with other pairs of students until each pair has ordered objects from five different bags.

When the activity is completed, and as a whole group, each pair of children (one at a time) will remove the objects from a bag and order them from the smallest to the largest for everyone to see. Children can compare these ordered objects to what they drew on their papers.

Grade 1 Outcome #3: Tell Time to the Hour and Half-Hour on Digital and Analog Clocks

Sample Activity

For this activity, children will show a specific time on an analog clock and write the digital time. The children will each need an analog clock and an individual whiteboard, marker, and eraser.

For this activity, the storybook *What's the Time, Mr. Wolf?*, by Annie Kubler, will be read to the children. As a specific time is mentioned in the book, the teacher will stop and have the children show the time on their analog clocks. Children will also write the digital time on their whiteboards. After all the children have written the time, the teacher can call on a volunteer to write the time on the classroom chalkboard or whiteboard. Each child can check his or her written time with the one written on the classroom board (Figure 6.8).

Figure 6.8 Learning to Tell Time.

CONTENT STANDARDS FOR GRADE 2

For children in grade 2, measurement becomes a key focus in the *Curriculum Focal Points* (2006) document. *Common Core State Standards* (2010) at second grade are aligned with the curriculum Focal Points, with the addition of telling time and counting money. Measurement for grade 2 includes the following concepts:

> • Partitioning, transitivity, iteration of units.
> • Measure using standard units of measure (inch and centimeter).
> • Inverse relationship between the size of a unit and the number of units used in measuring a particular object.
>
> (2006, p. 14)

Common Core State Standards (2010) for grade 2 include:

Grade 2 Standard #1: Measure and estimate lengths in standard units:
1a. Measure the length of an object by selecting and using appropriate tools such as rulers, yardsticks, meter sticks, and measuring tapes;
1b. Measure the length of an object twice, using length units of different lengths; describe how the two measurements relate to the size of the unit chosen;
1c. Estimate lengths using units of inches, feet, centimeters, and meters;
1d. Measure to determine how much longer one object is than another; express the length difference in terms of a standard length unit.

Grade 2 Standard #2: Relate addition and subtraction to length.

Grade 2 Standard #3: Work with time and money:
3a. Tell and write time from analog and digital clocks to the nearest five minutes, using A.M. and P.M.;
3b. Solve word problems involving dollar bills, quarters, dimes, nickels, and pennies, using dollar and cent signs appropriately.

Grade 2 Standard #4: Represent and interpret data:
4a. Generate measurement data to the nearest whole unit by measuring lengths of several objects or by making repeated measurements of the same object;
4b. Draw a picture graph and a bar graph to represent a data set with up to four categories. Solve simple put-together, take-apart, and compare problems using information presented in a bar graph.

(2010, p. 20)

GRADE 2 OUTCOMES

Grade 2 Outcome #1: Partitioning (Dividing an Object, Such as a Candy Bar, into Equal Parts or Pieces)

Sample Activity

The objective of this exercise is for children to be engaged in sharing activities that involve dividing something into equal parts in order to share equally. After the teacher gives the children a problem to solve, the children can volunteer other problems.

For example, the teacher could pose a sharing problem stating that there are four candy bars and three children. If the candy is shared equally among the three children, how much candy will each child get? It is important to note here that there will probably be multiple solutions to the sharing problem. Children might suggest that each child gets a whole candy bar and one of three pieces from the fourth candy bar. Another child might suggest that all the candy bars could be cut into three equal pieces and then each child would receive one out of three pieces from each candy bar (Figure 6.9).

Grade 2 Outcome #2: Transitivity in Comparing Objects

Sample Activity

Situations involving transitivity in comparing objects are limitless. Once children become aware of the pattern in comparing objects, they too can create these comparisons. For example, using proportioned blocks shown in Figure 6.10, children could state that,

Figure 6.9 Candy Bars to Share.

Figure 6.10 Exploring Height Relationships.

since the red block is longer than a blue block and the blue block is longer than the white block, the red block is also longer than the white block.

If children have access to sets of proportioned rods or blocks, they can explore the relationship of one rod or block to another in the same manner. Children could use the rods or blocks to create their own comparison problems for a partner to solve.

Balance scales also offer opportunities for children to compare weights of various objects in exploring transitivity comparison problems.

Grade 2 Outcome #3: Iteration of Units

Children, in working with various measurement tools, begin to understand that these tools are iterations of equal units. For example, children begin to understand that the iteration of an inch makes up a foot ruler or a yard stick.

Sample Activity

For this activity children will create their own foot rulers by taping twelve paper inch worms together along a poster board strip. Completed inch-worm rulers should then be compared to a standard inch ruler. An extension of this activity could be to have three children lay their inch-worm rulers end to end and compare this length to a yard stick

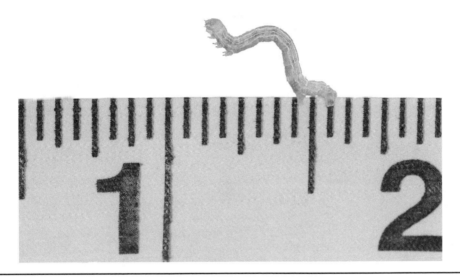

Figure 6.11 Inch-Worm Measure.

(Figure 6.11). A storybook that nicely accompanies this activity is *Inch by Inch* by Leo Lionni.

Grade 2 Outcome #4: Inverse Relationship between the Size of a Unit and the Number of Units Used in Measuring a Particular Object; Measure the Length of an Object Twice, Using Length Units of Different Lengths; Describe How the Two Measurements Relate to the Size of the Unit Chosen

Sample Activity

After reading the storybook *Measuring Penny* by Loreen Leedy, children will be given a large picture of a dog with a long tail and a recording sheet labeled with the words "inches" and "centimeters." The objective of the activity is for pairs of children to measure the dog's tail using each of the two different units of measure. They will record the number of each unit used on the recording sheet and then graph the data. A conversation should follow the graphing of the data during which children come to understand the relationship of the size of the unit of measure to the number of units used to measure the length of the tail (Figure 6.12).

Figure 6.12 Dogs' Tails.

Grade 2 Outcome #5: Measure the Length of Objects Using Appropriate Tools (Rulers, Yardsticks, Meter Sticks, and Measuring Tapes)

Children need to participate in measuring experiences in which they can explore using different measurement tools to determine length. After they explore length measurement with different tools, they should engage in conversations about the most efficient use of various tools to measure different objects. They need to experience this for themselves so it makes sense to them.

Sample Learning Center Activity

Materials needed for this learning center include various measuring tools (several rulers, yardsticks, meter sticks, and measuring tapes), a tissue-sized box containing strips of paper, each listing an object from around the room to measure, pencils, and recording sheets. The objects students measure should range from small to large in length. Larger-length objects to measure could include long strips of paper that represent the length of a car, van, or even a bus. These could be displayed in an easy access area for students to retrieve, lay out on the floor, and measure.

Children at this center begin by examining the various measurement tools. One student at a time then reaches in the box and pulls out a strip of paper containing the name of an object to be measured. The children find the object and measure its length using all four measuring tools. As a small group, they decide which tool was the most efficient in measuring the object's length. On their recording sheets, students write the name of the object, its length, and the tool most efficiently used to determine the length.

Grade 2 Outcome #6: Estimate Lengths Using Units of Inches, Feet, Centimeters, and Meters

Sample Learning Center Activity

Materials for this learning center includes various measuring tools—inch rulers, centimeter rulers, and meter sticks—a tissue-sized box containing strips of paper, each listing an object from around the room to measure, a game-type spinner with sections marked inches, centimeters, feet, and meters, and pencils and recording sheets.

As a team, and taking turns, a child at the learning center would pull a strip of paper from the object box and then spin the spinner. For example, from the object box, a child could have pulled a strip of paper listing "desk top." In spinning the spinner, the spinner hand rests on "centimeters." After examining the size of a centimeter on the centimeter rulers, each child would then make a written estimate on his or her recording sheet as to how long he or she thinks the desk top is in centimeters. After all the estimates are recorded, the child who pulled out the "desk top" strip and whose spinner landed on "centimeters" would measure the desk top using the centimeter ruler(s). All children would also record the actual measurement of the desk top in centimeters on their recording sheets. Children should discuss the accuracy of their estimates along with the reasoning behind their individual estimates. For example, in discussing the reasoning behind an estimate, a child may have determined that a centimeter was about as wide as one of his or her fingers, and then tried to determine how many fingers wide the desk top was in making this estimate.

Grade 2 Outcome #7: Determining How Much Longer One Object is than Another, Expressing the Length Difference in Terms of a Standard Length Unit

Sample Extension Activity

For this extension activity, children could take the measurement recording sheets from the previous two activities explained above and find the difference in length between two objects whose measurements were determined using the same standard unit of measure.

Grade 2 Outcome #8: Use Analog and Digital Clocks to Tell Time to the Nearest Five Minutes; Use A.M. and P.M.

Sample Activity #1

This is a Bingo-type activity. Children will be given blank Bingo cards and a list of various digital times (written to the nearest five minutes) to choose from and to copy randomly in the Bingo card spaces. There should be more digital times than are spaces on the card.

Beforehand, the teacher will have prepared cards with a different digital time written on each one. When all cards have been completed and space markers have been distributed, the game is ready to begin. The teacher pulls a digital time card randomly from the stack of cards and reads the time. Children search for the time and cover the space with a marker if they chose to copy that time in a Bingo space. The way in which "Bingo" can be achieved can be determined before the start of each new game (Figure 6.13).

Figure 6.13 Blank Bingo Card.

Sample Activity #2: Children Will Think about Their Daily Routines in Terms of A.M. and P.M.

For this activity, for each child the teacher will have created and copied a paper strip template for a 24-hour "clock," beginning and ending with midnight and with designations of A.M. and P.M. Strips should be at least 3 inches wide, allowing space for children to write activities under the various times on the "clock" strip.

Strips should be cut apart and taped together to make a continuous 24-hour "clock." When the "clock" is completed, children can write activities for the various times during a typical school day. For example, after taping the "clock" together, a child might write "sleeping" under the hours on the strip that he or she is in bed sleeping. The child might write "get up" under the time he or she usually wakes up to get ready for school.

As an extension activity, children could be given an additional "clock" strip template to complete at home for one of the weekend days (Figure 6.14).

12 A.M. Midnight	1 A.M.	2 A.M.	3 A.M.	4 A.M.	5 A.M.	6 A.M.
7 A.M.	8 A.M.	9 A.M.	10 A.M.	11 A.M.	12 P.M. Noon	1 P.M.
2 P.M.	3 P.M.	4 P.M.	5 P.M.	6 P.M.	7 P.M	8 P.M.
9 P.M.	10 P.M.	11 P.M.	12 A.M. Midnight			

Figure 6.14 24-Hour Clock Template.

Grade 2 Outcome #9: Work with Units of Measure—Time

Sample Activity: Children Practice Counting Money

In preparation for this activity, the teacher or teacher aide would place paper bills and coins in closeable, plastic baggies using play money. There should be enough baggies of money for each pair of children in the classroom.

Each pair of children is given a baggie of money. Taking turns, one of the children will give his or her partner some of the money to count. The amount counted is verified by the child who gave his or her partner the money to count. If there is a discrepancy, both children count the money together. This procedure can continue until the teacher tells the children it is time to put the money back in the baggies.

CONTENT STANDARDS FOR GRADE 3

In *Principles and Standards for School Mathematics* (NCTM, 2000), the grades 3–5 band for measurement includes the following:

Understand measurable attributes of objects and the units, systems, and processes of measurement:

- understand such attributes as length, area, weight, volume, and size of angle and select the appropriate type of unit for measuring each attribute;
- understand the need for measuring with standard units and become familiar with standard units in the customary and metric systems;
- carry out simple unit conversions, such as from centimeters to meters, within a system of measurement;
- understand that measurements are approximations and how differences in units affect precision;
- explore what happens to measurements of a two-dimensional shape such as its perimeter and area when the shape is changed in some way.

Apply appropriate techniques, tools, and formulas to determine measurements:

- develop strategies for estimating the perimeters, areas, and volumes of irregular shapes;
- select and apply appropriate standard units and tools to measure length, area, volume, weight, time, temperature, and the size of angles;
- select and use benchmarks to estimate measurements;
- develop, understand, and use formulas to find the area of rectangles and related triangles and parallelograms;
- develop strategies to determine the surface areas and volumes of rectangular solids.

(http://www.nctm.org/standards/)

Measurement for grade 3 is identified in *Curriculum Focal Points* (2006) as a connection to the Focal Points. Measurement connections in third grade include:

- Linear measurement that includes fractional parts of linear units;
- Perimeter and problems involving perimeter.

(2006, p.15)

Measurement standards for third grade in the *Common Core State Standards* (2010) can be summarized as:

- Tell time to the nearest minute.
- Measure time intervals in minutes.
- Solve problems involving addition and subtraction of time intervals in minutes.
- Estimate and measure liquid volumes using liters.
- Estimate and measure masses of objects using grams and kilograms.
- Solve one-step word problems involving masses and volume.

Common Core State Standards (2010) for grade 3 include:

Grade 3 Standard #1: Solve problems involving measurement and estimation of intervals of time, liquid volumes, and masses of objects:
1a. Tell and write time to the nearest minute and measure time intervals in minutes. Solve word problems involving addition and subtraction of time intervals in minutes;
1b. Measure and estimate liquid volumes and masses of objects using standard units of grams (g), kilograms (kg), and liters (l). Add, subtract, multiply, and divide to solve one-step problems.

Grade 3 Standard #2: Represent and interpret data:
2a. Draw a scaled picture graph and a scaled bar graph to represent a data set with several categories. Solve one- and two- step "how many more" and "how many less" problems using the information presented in scaled graphs;
2b. Generate measurement data by measuring lengths using rulers marked with halves and fourths of an inch. Show the data by making a line plot.

Grade 3 Standard #3: Understand concepts of area and relate area to multiplication and to addition:
3a. Recognize area as an attribute of plane figures and understand concepts of area measurement;
3b. Measure areas by counting unit squares;
3c. Relate area to the operations of multiplication and addition.

Grade 3 Standard #4: Recognize perimeter as an attribute of plane figures and distinguish between linear and area measurements; solve real-world mathematical problems involving perimeters of polygons.

(2010, pp 24–25)

GRADE 3 OUTCOMES
Grade 3 Outcome #1: Confront Problems in Linear Measurement
Sample Activity

In order to create meaning in confronting fractions in linear measurement activities, children will begin slowly using the concept of 1/2 of a unit of measure and then 1/4 and 3/4 of the unit of measure. Children should already be familiar with the relationship of paper inch worms to an inch on a standard inch ruler.

For this activity, children will each be given twelve paper inch worms. They will be asked to fold each paper inch worm in half. Children will be asked to lay out enough inch worms to measure 3½ inches. Children should lay out three whole inch worms and one inch worm folder in half and then write the mixed number on a sheet of paper. After laying out various measurements using the inch worms and half-inch worms, children can measure various objects that measure to exactly several whole inch worms and a half of an inch worm.

When the children demonstrate an understanding of half of a unit, they can then fold their paper inch worms into fourths and continue the same pattern of laying out inch worms and then measuring to exactly a few whole inch worms and a fourth of an inch worm. This might best be accomplished by measuring pre-drawn lines. The "wholes and a fourth" activity could extend into 3/4 using the same inch worms. The same activity can continue with additional paper inch worms showing lines to fold the worms into thirds.

At some point children can begin using standard inch rules that have inches sectioned off in fourths and thirds.

Grade 3 Outcome #2: Select Appropriate Units and Strategies for Measuring Perimeter

Children require many experiences with perimeter so that the concept becomes meaningful to them.

Sample Activity

For this activity, children will need a set of tangrams large enough for them to handle comfortably and that can easily be measured with a centimeter or inch ruler.

After reading *Grandfather Tang's Story*, by Ann Tompert, children can experiment with their set of tangrams in creating the tangram figures from the storybook. Children can then choose their favorite figure and measure the perimeter of the figure. They can create other figures and measure the perimeter of the new figures. The perimeters of each figure measured can be graphed and the data compared (Figure 6.15).

Figure 6.15 Tangrams.

Grade 3 Outcome #3: Solve Problems Involving Measurement and Estimation of Intervals of Time, Liquid Volumes, and Masses of Objects

Sample Activity #1

For this activity, children will use a "benchmark" measurement to estimate volume.

Various containers that will hold water are needed for this activity, along with a screw-cap liter container for each pair of children. Each liter container needs to be filled with water and the cap tightly secured.

To begin the activity, an empty container is displayed for the children to see. Each pair of children looks at their liter of water and, using it as a "benchmark" measurement, decides on an estimate of how many liters of water it is going to take to fill the displayed empty container. Children record their estimates. Calling on one pair of children at a time, the teacher asks them to empty their liter of water into the empty container until it is filled. Tally marks can be used to record the actual number of liters needed to fill the container. Children can check their estimates with the actual number of liters used. They should share how they arrived at their estimates.

If most of the liter bottles have not been emptied into the container, another empty container can be presented and the same procedure followed. If the empty container was large and required most liter bottles of water to be emptied into it, the liter bottles will need to be refilled before continuing with another container (Figure 6.16).

Figure 6.16 Pouring from a Liter Bottle.

Sample Activity #2

For this activity, children will use a "benchmark" measurement to estimate masses of objects. Needed for this activity are a box of small paper clips, a balance scale, and various small objects to measure.

Working in a small group, one at a time children hold a paper clip in one hand and one of the small objects in the other hand. Each child will then estimate how many paper clips he or she thinks will be needed to equal the mass of the small object. Estimates are recorded.

Using the balance scale, children place the small object on one side and, taking turns, put enough paper clips on the other side of the balance scale until the sides are even or balanced. After counting the number of paper clips required, each child compares his or her estimate with the actual number of paper clips used.

This first estimation activity can also serve as an additional benchmark measurement in estimating the mass of the second small object. For example, if the scale was balanced for the first object using 35 paper clips, and the second object is lighter than the first one, children can use this information in making an estimate of how many paper clips are going to be needed to balance the scale for the second object. This procedure can continue for as many objects as each group has to measure (Figure 6.17).

At the conclusion of the activity, students should share the various ways in which they arrived at their estimations.

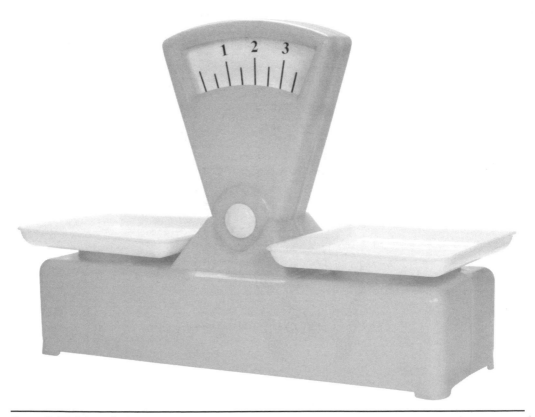

Figure 6.17 Balance Scale.

Sample Activity #3: Children Measure Time Intervals in
Minutes Within the Same Hour

This activity is introduced with the reading of the storybook *Clocks and More Clocks* by Pat Hutchins. The storybook deals with the difference in time from one clock to another in minutes. Children will need individual analog clocks for the activity.

After reading and discussing the story, children can be given various word problems that require them to add or subtract minutes on analog clocks. Word problems should be interesting to the children and actually use their names in the wording of the problems. For example, the teacher could say, "Show 3:05 on your clock. [Pause as children show the time.] In three minutes, Jason [or another child's name] is going to sneeze. What time will Jason sneeze?" Children move the minute hand on their clocks ahead three minutes and write the time, "3:08." The teacher can point out to the children that this is a time addition problem and ask the children why. The teacher should guide the children in deciding that 5 minutes plus 3 minutes is 8 minutes.

As the activity continues, the children can both add and subtract minutes from a beginning time. Children can also contribute word problems to be solved by the group in this activity.

Grade 3 Outcome #4: Geometric Measurement: Understand Concepts of Area and Relate Area to Multiplication and to Addition; Geometric Measurement, Distinguish Between Linear and Area Measures

Sample Activity

Children will measure squares and rectangles to determine the area of each shape in three different ways.

This activity should be used after the children have been introduced to the concept of multiplication and arrays, and understand the relationship between multiplication and repeated addition.

Working in pairs, children will be asked to draw one square and one rectangle on graph paper and count the squares to determine the area of each shape. Next, the children will be asked to count the number of squares along both the width and length of their shapes and, using calculators, multiply the length times the width of each shape to determine the area of each shape as well. Children should be asked to compare this calculation with the number of counted squares for each of their shapes and discuss why the numbers are the same. If the numbers are not the same, children need to discuss the reason why this happened. Last, the children will be asked to determine the area of each of their shapes using repeated addition in two different ways (adding columns and then adding rows).

A whole-group discussion should follow the activity to discuss the findings as children worked through the activity.

ADAPTATIONS FOR CHILDREN WITH SPECIAL NEEDS

It might be necessary to make adaptations when planning measurement lessons and activities depending on the individual needs of the children in the classroom. Several adaptations for measurement activities could include:

- Breaking activities into smaller parts or reducing the number of steps
- Using pictures and visual cues
- Providing raised or textured objects for children who are visually impaired
- Providing larger nonstandard units for children who experience difficulty in picking up smaller objects
- Positioning students who are visually and hearing impaired so they can see and hear what is going on in the classroom
- Having larger clocks available for children to use
- Asking children to repeat directions
- Reviewing key words in instructions
- Teaching and allowing children to use multiple methods of problem solving
- Using modeling
- Using hands-on manipulatives
- Giving children sufficient time to learn and practice skills
- Making sure children understand content vocabulary
- Having children work in small groups or pairs
- Checking for understanding
- Using a variety of assessment methods

ADAPTATIONS FOR MATHEMATICALLY PROMISING CHILDREN

Depending on the strengths of children in prekindergarten, kindergarten, and primary-aged schoolchildren, gifted children may need adaptations made to the math curriculum that challenge them. Adaptations could include ideas from the section on mathematically promising children under "Children with Special Needs" in Chapter 1 (p. 15, 16).

ADAPTATION FOR ENGLISH LANGUAGE LEARNERS (ELL)

Adaptations for children who are learning English as their second language could include:

- Connecting measurement concepts to a child's first language—learn important measurement words in the child's first language to help connect the English words to the first-language words
- Reinforcing measurement vocabulary with visual cues, pictures, and gestures
- Using multicultural literature and pictures that depict various aspects of measurement
- Providing objects from children's cultural backgrounds for them to measure, compare, and order
- Providing picture cues on children's recording sheets to help them remember the sequence of a procedure
- Providing picture cues with measurement terms (word wall).
- Establishing what the child already knows and then move forward from that point
- Labeling items in the classroom to enhance general vocabulary
- Instructing the children with direction words, simple numbers and commands
- Having children work in small groups and pairs.

HOME/SCHOOL CONNECTION IDEAS AND ACTIVITIES

The following ideas could be provided to parents/caregivers as ways to reinforce measurement concepts at home:

1. Estimate and then measure the number of steps to get from one location to another in the home/apartment or between two locations outdoors.
2. Talk aloud using common measurements around the house, in traveling, or in a store.
3. Model measuring and talk about what you are doing and why.
4. Use spatial and position vocabulary such as "under," "over," "near," "far".
5. Compare attributes of household items using measurement vocabulary such as "more/less," "longer/shorter," "bigger/smaller," "heavier/lighter".
6. Order objects by an attribute such as length, height, or weight.
7. Use household items to measure objects at home (e.g., utensils, clothes pins, safety pins).
8. Use measuring tools in play areas such as cups and measuring spoons.

The National Association for the Education of Young Children (NAEYC) has an "Information for Families" website located at http://www.naeyc.org/families/. The website provides resources for families, including activities to do at home, to encourage child development.

CURRICULUM INTEGRATION

There are many opportunities to integrate measurement concepts with other content areas. Examples include concepts of morning and night, seasons of the year, measuring growth of plants, animals, and children, size and weight comparisons, seriation (e.g., ordering from smallest to largest), and the passing of time. For example, in science class, as children are studying various ecosystems, they could measure out the lengths of various creatures that inhabit the ecosystem on paper, the classroom floor, or even the playground, and then compare their measurements. Another example would be to compare temperature, rainfall, and snowfall in different parts of the state, country, or world. In social studies class, children could compare sizes of states, populations of various states, lengths of rivers, and volumes of lakes. Many children's stories could also be used to introduce measuring activities. For example, *Counting on Frank*, by Rod Clement, could be used to introduce activities involving volume. The young boy in the story is interested in calculating the volume of just about anything. He sometimes uses his dog, Frank, as the unit of measurement.

MEASUREMENT CONTENT VOCABULARY

Listed below is measurement content vocabulary that teachers could be using in their conversations with children, depending on the age level of the children. It is of utmost importance that teachers use various means to help children learn and understand the meanings of content vocabulary words as they are learning measurement concepts.

- *Positional Words*
  under, over, above, below, beneath
- *Comparison Words*
  same/different, more/less, less than/greater than, shorter/longer, bigger/smaller, few, fewer
- *Money Words*
  penny, nickel, dime, quarter, bills
- *Time Words*
  clock, analog, digital, A.M., P.M.
  yesterday, today, tomorrow
  routine, sequence, schedule
  elapsed time/passing of time
  day, night
  season, year
- *Measure*
- *Unit*
  standard units—inch, yard, centimeter, meter, liter, gram, kilogram
  nonstandard unit
  half fourth
- estimate/about/close to/almost
- scale/balance scale
- length
- height
- weight/mass
- volume
- connect, connecting
- compare, comparison
- divide, dividing
- fraction
- end to end (iterate)
- attribute, characteristic

LITERATURE CONNECTIONS

Children's literature can be beneficial in developing concepts of measurement in helping children relate what they are learning to the real world. The following storybooks and series books are relevant in developing the concept of measurement from prekindergarten through primary-aged schoolchildren.

How Big is a Foot by Rolf Myller
Random House Children's Books, 1991
An apprentice is thrown in jail because the bed he made for the Queen is too small.

Inch by Inch by Leo Lionni
HarperCollins Publishers, 1995

A clever inch worm measures a robin's tail, a flamingo's neck, a toucan's beak, a heron's legs, and a nightingale's song to keep from being eaten.

Inch Worm and a Half by Elinor J. Pinczes

Houghton Mifflin, 2001

An inch worm sets out to measure the vegetables in her garden. The author introduces $1/2$, $1/4$, and $1/3$ as the inch worm continues to measure the vegetables.

Me and the Measure of Things by Joan Sweeny

Random House Children's Books, 2002

The author introduces young readers to units of measure. Illustrations teach children the differences between wet and dry measurements, weight, size, and length. All information is conveyed in a unique kid's-eye perspective.

Measurement by Sara Pistoia

The Child's World, Inc., 2006

Simple text describes the basic units of measurement and how to use tools to help measure objects.

More, Fewer, Less by Tana Hoban

Greenwillow Books, 1998

Photographs illustrate groupings of objects in larger and smaller numbers.

Over the River and Through the Woods: Early Reader by Sheila Higginson

Disney Press, 2007

Readers, along with the Mickey Mouse Clubhouse gang, set out to visit Goldilocks and the Three Bears by using simple maps. They learn important words and spatial concepts by following arrows and clues including "over," "under," "around" and "through."

Who Sank the Boat? by Pamela Allen

Coward-McCann, 1982

Animals attempt to balance their weight in a boat that unfortunately sinks! This book is an introduction to weight and balance.

How Many Bugs in a Box? by David A. Carter

Simon & Schuster, 1988

This pop-up book offers an introduction to the concept of capacity. Each box holds a specific number of bugs.

Guess How Much I Love You? by Sam McBratney

Candlewick, 1994

Hares jump and run various length measurements to express their love for one another.

Just a Little Bit More by Ann Tompert

Houghton Mifflin, 1993

Children can make several possible measurement discoveries as they read about and view mouse and elephant playing on a seesaw.

Tracks in the Sand by Loreen Leedy

Bantam Doubleday, 1993

This story features time measurement vocabulary such as "night," "day," "season," "and years."

A Time for Playing: A How Animals Live Book by Ron Hirschi

Cobblehill, 1994

Children experience measurement concepts as change in time, seasons, and temperature in this photograph book of animals at play.

Measuring Penny by Loreen Leedy

Henry Holt and Co., 1997

Lisa's homework assignment is to use her imagination to measure as many ways as she can using standard and nonstandard units of measure. She chooses her Boston terrier, Penny, and finds many interesting ways to measure.

Grandfather Tang's Story by Ann Tompert

Crown Publishers, 1990

Tompert spins a tale focused on two shape-changing fox fairies by using tangrams, a traditional visual aid employed by Chinese storytellers. The seven tangram pieces are used to create the characters in the story.

Counting on Frank by Rod Clement

Houghton Mifflin School, 1994

The young boy in the story is interested in calculating the volume of just about anything. He sometimes uses his dog, Frank, as the unit of measurement.

What's the Time, Mr. Wolf? by Annie Kubler

Child's Play International, Ltd., 2003

Mr. Wolf is always hungry, regardless of the time of day. The book shows analog clocks and digital time on each page.

Telling Time: How to Tell Time on Digital and Analog Clocks by Jules Older

Charlesbridges Publishing, 2000

Children learn how to tell analog time and digital time.

The Clock Struck One by Trudy Harris

Millbrook Pr Trade, 2009

This book involves comical animal antics with each striking of the hour.

Clocks and More Clocks by Pat Hutchins

Aladdin, 1994

Why do all of Mr. Higgins' clocks show a different time?

Telling Time with Big Mama Cat by Dan Harper
HMH Books, 1998
Big Mama Cat needs to tell time to stay on her busy daily schedule.

Book Series
MathStart Books by Stuart J. Murphy (Levels 1–3)
HarperTrophy

Give Me Half!, 1996 (2)
A young boy and girl learn to share by cutting things in half.

Just Enough Carrots, 1997 (1)
In this story little rabbit and his mother walk through a grocery store and compare the number of carrots, peanuts, and worms they have in their grocery cart to other grocery carts. Measurement terminology as "more," "fewer," and "the same" are emphasized.

The Best Bug Parade, 1996 (1)
Relative size is emphasized in this storybook as insects march in a parade.

Mighty Mattie, 2004 (1)
In preparation for her fifth birthday celebration, Madeline picks up her toys and compares their weight.

Bigger, Better, Best, 2002 (2)
Siblings Jeff and Jenny argue over who has the biggest or best of something.

Super Sand Castle Saturday, 1998 (2)
Three friends compete on the beach to see who can build the biggest, deepest, and longest parts of their respective sandcastles. Trouble brews as the friends measure parts of their castles using different nonstandard units.

A House for Birdie, 2004 (1)
As Birdie looks for a house that is just right for him, children are introduced to the concept of capacity.

Game Time!, 2000 (3)
As the soccer teams play, the scoreboard counts down on each page. The analog clock at the refreshment stand shows the analog time.

Let's Measure Series by Mary Elizabeth Salzmann
ABDO Publishing, 2008
What in the World is a Cup?
What in the World is an Inch?
What in the World is a Foot?
What in the World is an Ounce?
What in the World is a Pound?

Math—Early Emergent Series
Rosen Publishing Group, Inc., 2008
How Long Is It? Learning to Measure with Nonstandard Units by Elizabeth Kernan

Near and Far at the Beach: Learning Spatial Awareness Concepts by Amanda Boyd
Which Holds More? Learning to Compare Volume by Eliza Robbins
Who's Short? Who's Tall? Learning to Compare Heights by Kailee Herbst

ASSESSING CHAPTER OUTCOMES

1. Compare and contrast measurement standards for prekindergarten and kindergarten children.
2. Chart the development of measurement concepts from prekindergarten through third grade. Does this development seem like a logical progression to you? Why or why not?
3. Create additional activities that would be developmentally appropriate for prekindergarten children in meeting measurement standards; kindergarten children.
4. Create additional activities that would be developmentally appropriate for children in first grade; second grade; third grade.
5. Choose an activity. What would you say to a parent or administrator in explaining the purpose of the activity and why it is appropriate for children in that particular age group?
6. Choose an activity and plan adaptations for a child with special needs. (Choose a specific disability, such as hearing or visually impaired, autistic, fine motor skills impairment, etc.)
7. Choose an activity and explain how you would help an ELL student learn this concept of measurement.
8. Choose an activity and explain how you would adapt it to challenge mathematically promising children.
9. Using information from Chapter 1 on assessing young children's development and learning, create authentic assessments for each age group to assess their knowledge of measurement concepts particular to their age group.

CHAPTER EXTENSION ACTIVITIES

1. Develop additional activities to share with families/caregivers that reinforce concepts of measurement at home.
2. Research additional literature that could be used with prekindergarten, kindergarten, first grade, second grade, and third grade children to help them understand measurement concepts.
3. Search online for alternative ways to assess young children's development and learning.

REFERENCES

Common Core State Standards Initiative: Preparing America's Students for College & Career (2010). Washington, D.C.: National Governors Association Center for Best Practices/Council of Chief State School Officers.

Clements, D. H. (2003, September). *Good Beginnings in Mathematics: Linking a National Vision to State Action.* New York: Carnegie Corporation.

Copley, J. V. (2010). *The Young Child and Mathematics* (2nd ed.). Reston, VA: National Association for the Education of Young Children.

Copley, J. V., Jones, C. & Dighe, J. (2010). *The Creative Curriculum for Preschool: Mathematics*, vol. 4. Washington, D.C.: Teaching Strategies.

Davis, G. S. & Keller, J. D. (2009). *Exploring Science and Mathematics in a Child's World*. Columbus, OH: Pearson Merrill Prentice Hall.

Geo, K.-H. (2003). What children's play tells us about mathematics. *Young Children* 58(1), 28–33.

National Council of Teachers of Mathematics (NCTM) (2000). *Principles and Standards of School Mathematics*. http://www.nctm.org/standards/content.aspx?id=4294967312.

National Council of Teachers of Mathematics (NCTM) (2006). *Curriculum Focal Points for Prekindergarten through Grade 8 Mathematics: A Quest for Coherence*. Reston, VA: Author.

Van de Walle, J. A. (2004). *Elementary and Middle School Mathematics: Teaching Developmentally* (5th ed.). New York, NY: Pearson.

7

DATA ANALYSIS AND PROBABILITY

CHAPTER OUTCOMES

After reading this chapter, teacher candidates will be able to:

➤ Describe the development of data analysis concepts from prekindergarten through third grade.
➤ Describe the development of probability concepts from prekindergarten through third grade.
➤ Describe data analysis and probability activities that are developmentally appropriate for prekindergarten-aged and kindergarten-aged children.
➤ Describe data analysis and probability activities that are developmentally appropriate for first grade to third grade children.
➤ Explain how early data analysis and probability activities lay a foundation for future, higher mathematical understanding, reasoning, and problem solving.
➤ Explain how children's literature can be used to support learning of data analysis and probability concepts.
➤ Describe the types of adaptations that could be planned for English Language Learners (ELL) and children with special needs that might help them acquire data analysis and probability concepts.
➤ Describe the types of adaptations that could be planned to challenge mathematically promising children in this content area.
➤ Explain how to involve families/caregivers in supporting the acquisition of data analysis and probability concepts at home.

OVERVIEW OF CONCEPT DEVELOPMENT

Informal activities requiring children to compare, classify, and count objects provide the building blocks for understanding and analyzing data. Informal sorting activities are foundational to the process of learning to organize data into various categories. As children ask questions, they learn that not all answers can be given immediately, that data needs to be collected in order to discover the answers. Through guidance by their teachers and caretakers, children learn that the main purpose for gathering data is to answer some of their "I wonder" questions.

It is not uncommon to see teacher-made charts and graphs displayed on the walls in many prekindergarten, kindergarten, and primary classrooms. These can include charts of the daily schedule and helpers for the week, as well as charts and graphs depicting information the children have collected about themselves. For example, one chart or graph may depict the number of children who have a specific hair or eye color. Copley, Jones, and Dighe (2010) state that "these are important tools for data analysis, and, if used appropriately, can facilitate children's mathematical understanding" (p. 772).

Data analysis for young children includes sorting and classifying objects, representing data using objects, pictures, and graphs, and describing data using vocabulary appropriate for a specific age group of children (Copley et al., 2010). Children begin by sorting objects such as those related to geometry and measurement. These include size, length, number or quantity, orientation, number of sides, number of vertices, color, etc. At first they sort and classify according to one attribute. Later, they sort and classify up to three or four attributes or categories. Children count the number of objects in various categories or data they collected and learn to represent this data in the form of picture or bar graphs. Using the data in the graph, they first answer questions of "how many" and solve more/less problems. They solve simple comparison problems as well as putting together and taking apart problems. Children progress into drawing scaled picture and bar graphs (e.g., 1 block = 5 children), and they represent measurement-of-length data on a line plot including measurements to ¼ and ½. They learn to analyze frequency tables, bar graphs, picture graphs and line plots and solve one- and two-step problems from information on the graphs or line plot (*Common Core State Standards*, 2010; NCTM, 2006).

Copley et al. (2010) present recommendations for a teacher's role in helping children develop an understanding of data analysis, including:

1. Use classroom routines to represent data (e.g., attendance; lunch choices; bus/car riders, etc.)
2. Encourage children to organize objects by using their own rules as they naturally sort
3. Model for the children by purposely describing collections in more than one way
4. Ask children to line up in classification groups (e.g., children wearing red line up first; children wearing yellow line up next, etc.)
5. Use two groups to organize data rather than sorting into many groups
6. Use paper of the same size when collecting data for children to draw/write their choice; these can easily be put into rows or columns to create bar graphs
7. Demonstrate a sorting/classification activity and have children "guess" the describing words for the formed groups
8. Label graphs using symbols students understand to represent data (e.g.,color words can be matched with that color crayon).

(pp. 774–776)

Probability is an expression concerning the likelihood that something will happen. Probability for young children, of course, will not be expressed as percentages; however, they can learn to use terminology in responding to events and phenomena in real-world situations that is foundational in future work with probability.

Concerning data analysis and probability, the National Council of Teachers of Mathematics (NCTM), in *Principles and Standards for School Mathematics* (2000), states:

> the processes used in reasoning about data and statistics will serve students well in work and in life. Some things children learn in school seem to them predetermined and rule bound. In studying data and statistics, they can also learn that solutions to some problems depend on assumptions and have some degree of uncertainty. The kind of reasoning used in probability and statistics is not always intuitive, and so students will not necessarily develop it if it is not included in the curriculum . . .
>
> A subject in its own right, probability is connected to other areas of mathematics, especially number and geometry. Ideas from probability serve as a foundation to the collection, description, and interpretation of data.
>
> (pp. 48, 50)

BUILDING CONCEPTS OF DATA ANALYSIS AND PROBABILITY AT THE PREKINDERGARTEN LEVEL

Children are inquisitive by nature. They are great at wondering and asking all sorts of questions. It is this natural nature of children that becomes the foundation for collecting and analyzing data. Young children are data gatherers, and their questions are the major source of data.

Prekindergarten children's experiences with collecting data have most likely been informal and on the basis of "I'm curious to know." Teachers, capitalizing on kindergarten children's natural curiosity, should formally extend instruction to include guiding children in learning how to display gathered information in various ways and in interpreting what the information is telling them.

Activities for prekindergarten should involve visual, auditory, tactile, and kinesthetic patterns and include patterns typical of various cultures, especially cultures represented by the children in the classroom. All children, including children with special needs and English Language Learners (ELL), need challenging yet attainable tasks that provide meaningful experiences reflective of their interests, individual abilities, and family culture (Pennsylvania Department of Education and Department of Public Welfare, 2007).

CONTENT STANDARDS FOR PREKINDERGARTEN

Data Analysis and Probability is the fifth content area defined in the NCTM document *Principles and Standards for School Mathematics* (2000). It is not considered a key concept in *Curriculum Focal Points for Prekindergarten through Grade 8 Mathematics: A Quest for Coherence* (NCTM, 2006) for prekindergarten children, but data analysis is identified as a "Connection to the Focal Points." This means that instruction in this content area lays a foundation for higher mathematical studies in future mathematics classrooms. The *Common Core State Standards* (2010) begin at the kindergarten level, so there are no standards in this document for prekindergarten children.

Content standards in the NCTM document *Principles and Standards for School Mathematics* (2000) are not presented by individual grades or age levels, but are grouped in age or grade bands. The first group of standards spans data analysis and probability expectations from prekindergarten through grade 2. These include:

Formulate questions that can be addressed with data and collect, organize, and display relevant data to answer them:

- pose questions and gather data about themselves and their surroundings;
- sort and classify objects according to their attributes and organize data about the objects;
- represent data using concrete objects, pictures, and graphs.

Select and use appropriate statistical methods to analyze data:

- describe parts of the data and the set of data as a whole to determine what the data show.

Develop and evaluate inferences and predictions that are based on data:

- discuss events related to students' experiences as likely or unlikely.
  (http://www.nctm.org/standards/)

As a connection to the NCTM *Focal Points* (2006) for a prekindergarten program, data analysis is defined as the following:

Children learn the foundations of data analysis by using objects' attributes that they have identified in relation to geometry and measurement (e.g., size, quantity, orientation, number of sides or vertices, color) for various purposes, such as describing, sorting, or comparing.

(2006, p. 11)

PREKINDERGARTEN OUTCOMES
Prekindergarten Outcome #1: Sort, Classify, and Organize Data
Sample Activities

There are many different ways teachers can engage children in sorting, classifying, and organizing activities. There are commercially produced manipulatives that can be purchased with easily identified characteristics. These include attribute blocks (various colored shapes) and many different types of counters. Teachers can also collect household objects such as buttons, multicolored clothes pins, different types of clothes pins, lids, bottle caps, and various containers, to name just a few. Children could also sort, classify, and organize commercially produced pictures or pictures from catalogues and magazines. Cleaning-up daily routines often require children to sort toys, counters, or other manipulatives into their proper containers and then place these objects where they belong in the classroom. Teachers can expand on these routines by labeling containers, shelves, or drawers so that children experience labeling as they are working with sorting, classifying, and organizing concepts.

Sample Learning Station Activities

At learning stations, children will sort, classify, and organize objects according to one characteristic. After various whole-group sorting, classifying, and organizing activities, children can explore this concept in stations where the objects/pictures to be sorted are provided. For example, at one station, children could be sorting plastic animals or pictures of animals using the characteristic of legs. Once children are told the characteristic they are using to sort the animals, they should be given the opportunity to explore and sort them according to their own criteria. The children may decide to sort the plastic animals/ pictures by the number of legs—two- or four-legged animals. They might also choose to sort the plastic animals/pictures by long legs and short legs or long, medium and short legs. If there are animals/animal pictures that include creatures of the sea or ocean, children will most likely decide that their criteria for sorting is having legs and not having legs.

As the teacher circulates among the stations, it is important that he or she questions the children as to the reasoning behind their decision to sort the plastic animals or pictures as they did. The question "Is there another way you could sort the animals by looking at legs?" could also be posed. This expands children's thinking, in looking at the pictures from multiple perspectives.

Prekindergarten Outcome #2: Organize Data about Objects

Sample Activity

For this whole-group activity, the children will be presented with a pile of multi-type, multicolored buttons to sort (Figure 7.1). There should be enough buttons so that there is

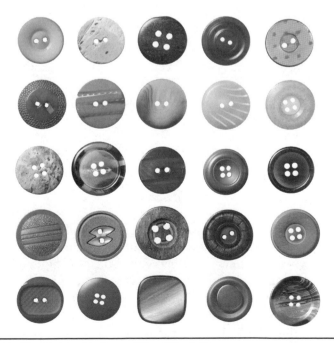

Figure 7.1 Buttons Provide a Variety of Sorting and Classifying Options.

one button for each child. The teacher asks the children for different ways the buttons could be sorted and then records these on the board. After a sorting choice is made, each child will be given a button to sort according to the sorting criteria. After the buttons are sorted, they can be lined up either vertically or horizontally, keeping the buttons in their assigned groups. The teacher then asks the children to count the number of buttons in each group. Questions should include the terms "more," "less," or "the same," where applicable.

The same pile of buttons could be sorted in different ways, following the same procedure.

Prekindergarten Outcome #3: Explain the Likelihood of an Event

The school day may present many opportunities for the teacher to discuss probability concepts with children in using terms as "likely," "not likely," "certain," "maybe," and "impossible." For this activity, children will predict the likelihood of rain for a particular day.

Sample Activity

Children oftentimes pose questions about the weather, particular, of course, to the part of the country in which they live. It would not be unlike a child to pose the question, "I wonder if it is going to rain today." Children could be guided in determining the likelihood of rain in several ways. They could begin their investigation by looking at the sky, determining if there are clouds in the sky. If there are clouds, they could identify the types of clouds that are present by comparing what they see with pictures of clouds that are displayed in the classroom. The teacher could also read/show the weather report for the day from the newspaper or go to weather.com for the day's weather report. Both the newspaper and information through the Internet most likely show picture information the children could "read." After investigating, children could decide on the terminology that is most appropriate for there being rain today.

CONTENT STANDARDS FOR KINDERGARTEN

As a connection to the NCTM *Focal Points* (2006), data analysis in a kindergarten program is defined as:

Children sort objects and use one or more attributes to solve problems. For example, they might sort solids that roll easily from those that do not. Or they might collect data and use counting to answer such questions as, "What is our favorite snack?" They re-sort objects by using new attributes (e.g., after sorting solids according to which ones roll, they might re-sort the solids according to which ones stack easily).

(2006, p. 12)

Common Core State Standards (2010) in this content area call for kindergarten children to be able to classify objects and count the number of objects in categories (p. 10). There are no formal standards addressing probability at the kindergarten level. Probability at this level is focused on the informal judgments children make through their life experiences (NCTM, 2000).

KINDERGARTEN OUTCOMES

Data gathering and analysis activities for kindergarten children should be an extension of what children have been experiencing in prekindergarten programs. It is important to remember, however, that not all children will have attended prekindergarten programs. Most likely, it will be necessary to continue sorting, classifying, and organizing activities with kindergarten children along with opportunities to gather, display, and discuss information.

Davis and Keller (2009) state that "Young children should be introduced to charting early in their education so that they come to think of it as a model and tool for capturing and displaying information that is important to them" (p. 70). Young children need to be involved in numerous opportunities to collect and display information so this becomes a natural process as they progress through their education.

Graphing Ideas

To help make graphing of information meaningful to young children, it is important to begin at a foundational level. Children can begin lining up real objects they have sorted and classified (as in the previous prekindergarten activity). They would progress to using pictures and then color in spaces or glue squared pieces of paper onto charts to depict the information they have collected (Charlesworth & Lind, 2007).

Following are outcome examples from kindergarten standards. Included with the examples are sample activities and other ideas that could be used in exploring data collection concepts.

Kindergarten Outcome #1: Gather Data about Self and/or the Environment

It is important that data collection be centered on questions children naturally express. The sample activity below indicates a method of collecting data for "wondering" questions children might pose.

Sample Activity: Children Will Vote for their Favorite Color

This activity requires preparation time by the teacher before the children vote on their favorite color. The teacher needs to prepare a large graph on butcher-block paper showing columns of squares. A different-colored circle needs to be placed at the bottom of each column along with the color word.

On the day children are voting on their favorite color, they will be given a small sticky note which has their name written on it. One by one, children place their sticky note on a square in the column above the circle that indicates their favorite color.

After all the children have voted, it is important for the teacher to guide children in a discussion as to what the information tells them. Since the squares in the columns are lined up equally, children should be able to look at the graph, count each column, and state which color was the favorite of most children by determining the column that is the highest or contains the most sticky-type notes. Equally, they should be able to state which color was chosen least as the favorite color. If the same number of children chooses two or more colors as their favorite, and the children do not state this, the teacher should ask some probing questions to determine this. If no response is indicated, the teacher needs to introduce the concept of the same amount.

Voting Ideas

There are various ways to involve children in voting to collect data. One of the simplest ways to make a "Yes" or "No" vote is to provide two bags: one marked "Yes" and the other marked "No." Children could drop a counter or other object into the bag to indicate their vote.

Children could also stand or sit in designated spots that would indicate their vote. This method of voting could have been applied in the above "favorite color" activity. Colored circles could have been hung at different places in the classroom or placed at different places on the floor. Children would vote by standing under their favorite-colored circle or standing or sitting on the floor in the same manner. Although the data would not be in graphic form, the teacher would still be able to engage the children in a discussion as to what the result of the vote told them.

Kindergarten Outcome #2: Gather, Organize and Display Data on a Bar Graph or Picture Graph

Sample Lesson Plan

An extension of prekindergarten outcomes for kindergarten children would be to involve them in gathering data and learning how to display their data on a chart or graph. The following sample lesson plan could be used as an appropriate activity for kindergarten children.

M&M Sorting, Classifying, and Graphing Lesson Plan

Resources
The *M&M's Counting Book* (2002) by Barbara Barbieri McGrath

Objectives
At the conclusion of the lesson individual students will be able to:

1. Sort & classify M&M's by color
2. Organize sorted M&M's on a bar graph
3. Answer comparison questions about their bar graph

Standard
NCTM.K.4.1.5.9   collect, organize, represent, analyze, and interpret data

Materials
one individual-sized bag of M&M's for each child
napkins (one per child)
bar graph titled "M&M Colors"
pencils
scissors (one pair per child)

Introduction/Motivation
This activity begins by reading *The M&M's Counting Book* (2002) by Barbara Barbieri McGrath, a counting book, to the children. After reading the book, each child will be given an individual-sized bag of M&M's (Figure 7.2, p. 231). The teacher asks, "What colors do M&M's come in?" The children will be able to look at their individual bags

and see what colors are represented on the bags. The teacher writes the color words on the whiteboard or chalk board and places a colored circle by each word to indicate the color. The teacher continues, "Did anyone ever count to see how many of each color is in a bag of M&M's?" After responses, the teacher informs the children that they are each going to be able to open their bags of M&M's and then sort them into colors.

Procedure

After the book is read to the children, they will each go to their individual workspace or table space, cut the top off their bag of M&M's and begin sorting their M&M's by color on a napkin. Next, the children will be given a pre-made bar graph on which to line up their M&M's. The bars on the graph should be divided into squares in which the children can place individual M&M's. Each column on the bar graph should be labeled with a color word or circles colored to depict the M&M colors. After the M&M's are properly placed on the bar graph, the children will be instructed to count the number of each color of M&M's they have and write the number underneath the color word or colored circle.

The teacher asks, "I wonder, does everyone have the same number of each color of M&M's?" Individual children can share the number of M&M's they have of different colors.

The teacher continues, "With your pencil, I want you to circle the number for the M&M's you have the most of on your bar graph." (Teacher waits for children to accomplish this.) "Now, draw a square around the number for the M&M's you have the least of on your bar graph." (Again, teacher waits for children to accomplish this.) "Does anyone have the same number of M&M's for any colors on your bar graph?" (Teacher waits for children to respond.) "Put triangles around the numbers for the M&M's you have that are the same on your bar graph." At this point some children may not have any numbers that are the same. Also, some "same as" numbers could be the numbers that have already been identified as the most or least M&M's. For these cases, the teacher could have the children put triangles underneath the circles or squares.

"Now, you are going to color in the squares where your M&M's are sitting with the crayon of the same color as the M&M's. You may take one M&M off of a square at a time, eat it, and color the square. If you don't want to eat your M&M's you may put one M&M at a time back in the bag. Be sure to color in one square before you take another M&M off of another square."

When the graphs are completed, the teacher can collect them to look at, before sending them home with the children.

Adaptations

It will be necessary to have adult supervision for the sorting, classifying, and graphing activity. Individual children need to be assisted as needed. It might be necessary to provide a child who is experiencing fine motor control difficulties with larger pieces of colored candy.

Student Evaluation

Children will be informally assessed during the activity as to their ability to sort, classify, and graph the M&M's. They will also be assessed as to their understanding of comparison terms.

Safety

Safety precautions and behavior expectations will need to be discussed before children begin the activity. It is necessary to monitor children as they use scissors.

Before using chocolate or any type of food in a classroom activity, it is important to check children's health records for allergies.

Figure 7.2 M&M's.

Opportunities to involve kindergarten children in collecting and displaying information are endless. Again, it is important to focus data collection and graphing/charting activities on questions posed by children as well as having the teacher pose "I wonder" questions relating the children in the classroom. Answer questions based on information on graphs or charts.

As children are involved in classroom activities in which they collect and chart or graph information, it is important for teachers to question children on what the information is telling them. Asking questions about collected information takes children full circle in the process of asking a question, collecting and charting or graphing the information, and finally in answering the question that started the process.

As can be seen from the scenario outlined, a question was posed (and refined), information was gathered, information was displayed and analyzed, and a question was answered.

Ms. Kernan read her kindergarten children *Green Eggs and Ham* by Dr. Seuss (1960), followed by a discussion on the different-colored foods the children liked to eat. One student in the classroom, Lizzy, wondered aloud in asking, "I wonder which color people like to eat best?" Ms. Kernan focused on Lizzy's question and continued, "Well, we can't ask everybody, but we can certainly ask everyone in our classroom." The kindergarten children thought this was a great idea and started calling out their favorite color of food to eat. Ms. Kernan quieted the children and told them that they would conduct an experiment the next day.

After some preparation and help from a teacher's aide, Ms. Kernan presented the children with four different and unconventional colors of pudding—red, blue, green, and yellow. She had prepared vanilla pudding, to which she added food coloring to make each tasting selection. Each child was given four individual taste cups, one of each color of pudding, and a plastic spoon. The children were told to taste each color of pudding and then decide which one tasted the best, but they were told to keep their favorite a secret and not say it out loud for anyone else to hear.

Ms. Kernan had prepared a horizontal chart listing the four different colors of pudding on which the children would record their choices using colored circles to correspond to the pudding colors. Each child would choose the colored circle that matched his or her favorite color of pudding and tape the circle in the row designated for that color.

After the tasting was completed and each child had taped a circle to the graph, Ms. Kernan asked the children to look at the circles to find the answers to the following questions:

1. Which color of pudding did the children like the best? (red)
2. Which color of pudding did the children like least? (blue)
3. Are there any colors of pudding that the same number of children chose as their favorite? (no)
4. What do you think might happen if we asked the other kindergarten class to vote on their favorite color of pudding? (They would pick red.)
5. So, Lizzy, what is the answer to your question? (We picked red.)

Questions to ponder:
1. What would be a good extension of the pudding tasting activity for the kindergarten children?
2. How could this activity be extended to make a home connection?

Kindergarten Outcome #3: State and Explain the Likelihood of an Event using the Terms "Likely," "Unlikely," "Certain," or "Impossible"

Children in kindergarten need to continue to think about happenings or events in terms of the probability or likelihood of something occurring.

Sample Activity

In this activity, children will determine the likelihood of an event from a storybook happening in real life.

Fairytales and other literature can provide a foundation for children in thinking about the likelihood of a happening or event occurring. For example, after reading *Jack and the Beanstalk*, children could plant bean seeds and discuss the likelihood of one or more of their beanstalks growing the way Jack's beanstalk grew in the story (Figure 7.3).

Figure 7.3 *Jack and the Beanstalk.*

Children often hear clichés such as "It's raining cats and dogs." Again, children could discuss the likelihood of it ever raining cats and dogs. One storybook that could be read to the children to begin a discussion about the likelihood of weather events actually happening is *Cloudy with a Chance of Meatballs* (1982) by Judi Barrett (Figure 7.4).

Figure 7.4 Raining Cats and Dogs.

CONTENT STANDARDS FOR GRADE 1

Content objectives for data analysis and probability beginning in prekindergarten and kindergarten. They are continued in the primary grades and enriched with learning experiences that create meaning and connect what is being learned to the real world.

In *Curriculum Focal Points for Prekindergarten through Grade 8 Mathematics: A Quest for Coherence* (NCTM, 2006), data analysis is considered as a connection to the Focal Points. As a connection in grade 1, "Children strengthen their sense of number by solving problems involving measurement and data . . . Representing measurements and discrete data in picture and bar graphs." (p. 13)

The *Common Core State Standards* (2010) state that children in grade 1 should organize, represent, and interpret data with up to three categories; ask and answer questions about the total number of data points, how many in each category, and how many more or less are in one category than in another (p. 16).

GRADE 1 OUTCOMES

Grade 1 Outcome #1: Organize, Represent, and Interpret Data with up to Three Categories

Sample Activity

For this whole-group activity, children will be presented with multi-sized, multicolored triangles, rectangles, and pentagons. Children could be asked to sort the shapes by the number of sides or the number of vertices on the shapes. Once the shapes are sorted, they can be lined up on pre-made, numbered graphs, either horizontally or vertically, and counted. Children should be guided in seeing that the number of shapes they counted in each category is the same as the number on the graph along the top line of the last shape. The shapes can then be removed, one row or column at a time, and the spaces on the graph can be colored in to represent the number of shapes that were in each row or column. To provide the children with experience in thinking about how the data is organized, the teacher can guide the children in deciding how the x-axis and y-axis should be labeled.

Once the graph is labeled, children can be asked about the information they can determine from the graph. Most likely, children will notice that there is more of one category than another or that there are two or categories with the same number in them. Children should then be asked comparison questions concerning the data in the graph. For example, in comparing two categories, the children should be asked "How many more?" and "How many less?" questions.

CONTENT STANDARDS FOR GRADE 2

Data analysis and probability is not considered a key point or a connection to the focal points at grade 2. However, children would continue data analysis activities as for grade 1.

The *Common Core State Standards* (2010) state that second grade children should:

Draw a picture graph and a bar graph (with a single-unit scale to represent a data set) with up to four categories. Solve simple put-together, take-apart, and compare problems using information presented in a bar graph.

(2010, p. 20)

It is a good idea for teachers to use student-generated questions to gather information for graphing. Children can graph the same data they collect both in a picture graph and a bar graph and compare the data in both forms. Children can discuss which type of graph best represents the data they collected.

GRADE 2 OUTCOMES

Grade 2 Outcome #1: Displaying Data in a Picture Graph and Bar Graph

Sample Activity

After reading the storybook *The Door Bell Rang* (1989) by Pat Hutchins, Mr. Kerr decided to "go" with the "teachable moment".

After recess, Mr. Kerr read his second grade students *The Door Bell Rang* by Pat Hutchins. He had prepared paper cookie manipulatives and planned on using the content of the storybook later that day as an introduction to a math lesson on dividing a given set into parts. After Mr. Kerr finished reading the story, Tim raised his hand and stated, "I wonder what kind of cookies kids in our class like as their favorite cookies?" Taking advantage of this "teachable moment," Mr. Kerr stated, "That is a great question, Tim. We can find out the answer to your 'I wonder' question."

Upon polling the children for choices of cookies, the following were chosen to be part of the survey: chocolate chip cookies, sandwich-type cookies, peanut butter cookies, and chocolate cookies. Mr. Kerr than gave each child a sticky note, on which they were asked to draw a picture of their favorite cookie from the determined choices. While the children were drawing their cookies, Mr. Kerr drew a graph on the board that would be used to construct a horizontal picture graph.

When the children had completed their cookie drawings, Mr. Kerr called three children at a time to the board to place their drawings in the graph. When the graph was completed, Mr. Kerr discussed with the children how the graph should be labeled and then had them count the number of cookies in each row. He then asked the children to get into their math groups and write questions about the data in the graph. The types of questions he wanted to illicit from the children included:

- Questions about the total number of cookies for each type of cookie;
- Comparison questions concerning the number of cookies in each category, including "How many more/less" (taking-apart questions) of one type of cookie than another type of cookie;
- Combining questions (e.g., How many children chose chocolate chip and peanut butter cookies combined?).

When the groups of students had completed their questions, Mr. Kerr called on one group at a time to ask one question concerning the data from the picture graph. As a question was asked, Mr. Kerr asked groups to check-mark the question on their papers if they asked the same question, so that questions would not be duplicated. When the groups finished with their questions, Mr. Kerr also asked questions that the children had not asked but that he thought were important for them to consider.

Finally, Mr. Kerr asked each student to construct a bar graph using the same information they had collected about cookie choices.

Questions to Ponder
1. What do you think about Mr. Kerr's decision concerning this "teachable moment?"
2. What would you have done if this situation occurred after you read the story to the children?

Grade 2 children are involved in the same types of probability activities with the addition of applying the terms "likely" and "unlikely" in discussing the probability of events happening. There are numerous opportunities for teachers to help children develop thinking skills in predicting whether an event is likely or unlikely to happen.

Grade 2 Outcome #2: Deciding if an Event is Likely or Unlikely to Happen
Sample Activity
The teacher can display a newspaper picture of a five-day forecast for the local area. Analyzing the content of a day's picture (clouds, sun, raindrops), children can decide if it is likely or unlikely that it will rain that particular day (Figure 7.5).

Sample Activity Extension
Raindrops in a forecast picture are most likely accompanied by a percentage of chance of rain. Children can begin thinking about the chance of rain, percentage-wise, in the following way. The teacher can display 10 circles, each representing 10 percent. Children learn, with practice, that the fewer circles needed to represent the percentage of chance of rain, the less likely it is to rain that day. Conversely, they learn that the more circles needed to represent the percentage of chance of rain, the more likely it is to rain that day. They also learn that, with five circles or 50 percent, either can happen—rain or not rain.

Figure 7.5 Weather Forecast Chart.

CONTENT STANDARDS FOR GRADE 3

In *Principles and Standards for School Mathematics* (NCTM, 2000) the 3–5 grade band for data analysis and probability includes the following:

Formulate questions that can be addressed with data and collect, organize, and display relevant data to answer them:

- design investigations to address a question and consider how data-collection methods affect the nature of the data set;
- collect data using observations, surveys, and experiments;
- represent data using tables and graphs such as line plots, bar graphs, and line graphs;
- recognize the differences in representing categorical and numerical data.

Select and use appropriate statistical methods to analyze data:

- describe the shape and important features of a set of data and compare related data sets, with an emphasis on how the data are distributed;
- use measures of center, focusing on the median, and understand what each does and does not indicate about the data set;
- compare different representations of the same data and evaluate how well each representation shows important aspects of the data.

Develop and evaluate inferences and predictions that are based on data:

- propose and justify conclusions and predictions that are based on data and design studies to further investigate the conclusions or predictions.

Understand and apply basic concepts of probability:

- describe events as likely or unlikely and discuss the degree of likelihood using such words as certain, equally likely, and impossible;
- predict the probability of outcomes of simple experiments and test the predictions;
- understand that the measure of the likelihood of an event can be represented by a number from 0 to 1.

(http://www.nctm.org/standards/)

In *Curriculum Focal Points for Prekindergarten through Grade 8 Mathematics: A Quest for Coherence* (NCTM, 2006), data analysis is designated as a connection to the Focal Points at the grade 3 level. At this level, children learn to analyze different forms in which data is represented—frequency tables, line plots, bar graphs, and picture graphs.

In the *Common Core State Standards* (2010), grade 3 students should be able to:

Draw a scaled picture graph and a scaled bar graph to represent a data set with several categories. Solve one- and two-step "how many more" and "how many less" problems using information presented in scaled bar graphs. *For example, draw a bar graph in which each square in the bar graph might represent 5 pets* (p. 25).

(2010, p. 25)

GRADE 3 OUTCOMES

Grade 3 Outcome #1: Design investigations and Consider the Data-Collection Method

Sample Activities

Children at this age should design investigations to survey information about themselves. Once children understand the surveying process, surveying questions should be derived from the children's curiosity to know something about themselves. Surveying topics are numerous and could include:

- How much time do you spend watching television in a week?
- How much time to you spend using a home computer in a week?
- How much time do you spend playing outside after school in a week?

Once children decide on the question for their survey, they need to decide how they are going to collect the data. For the types of survey questions listed above, children would first need to collect their data on charts, before totaling the data and then graphing the results.

Children in third grade might be interested in voting for their favorite ice-cream flavor, type of food, or favorite game to play at home after school. They might also be interested in collecting data on the number of children who live in various types of housing or the number of pockets they have on their clothing on any given day. Once this type of question is posed, children need to decide on a method of collecting the data. There are numerous options available for collecting data. These could include:

- Making a list of options and voting using tally marks
- Labeling containers with options and having children vote by placing their names in a container depicting their choice.

Grade 3 Outcome #2: Represent Data in Various Forms—Tables, Line Plots, Bar Graphs, Line Graphs, Picture Graphs; Compare and Evaluate Representations of the Same Data (Similarities and Differences)

Sample Graph Forms

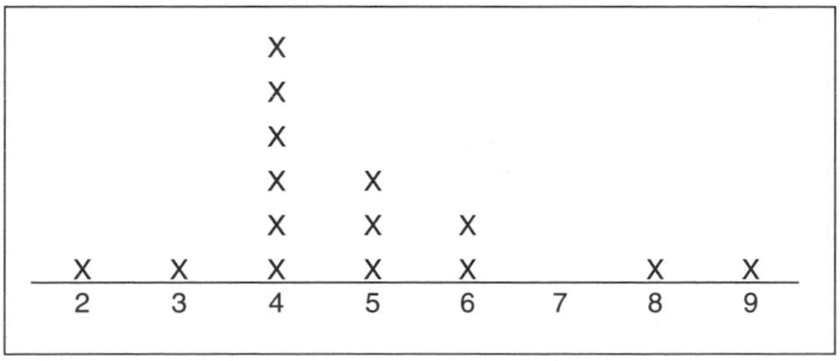

Figure 7.6 Line Plot.

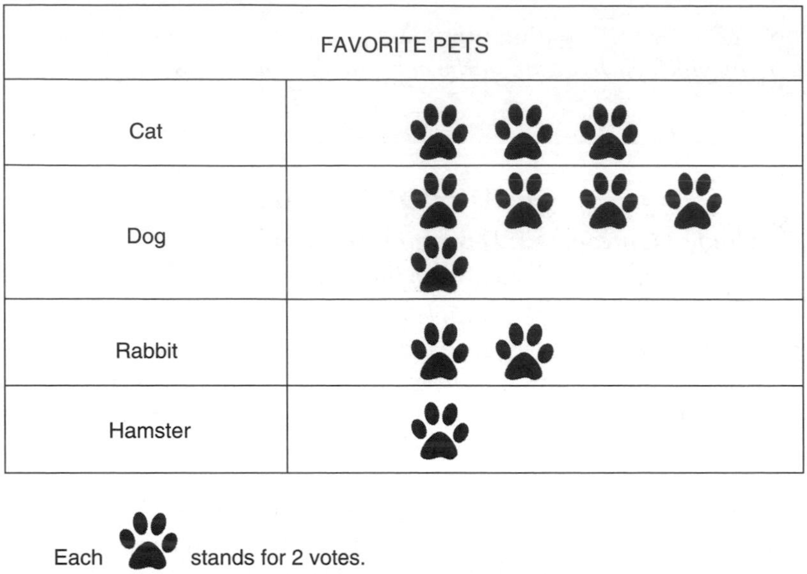

FAVORITE PETS	
Cat	🐾 🐾 🐾
Dog	🐾 🐾 🐾 🐾 🐾
Rabbit	🐾 🐾
Hamster	🐾

Each  stands for 2 votes.

Figure 7.7 Scaled Picture Graph.

My Favorite Game	
Type of Game	**Tally Marks**
Computer Game	11111
Board Game	111
Game Involving a Ball	1111111111

Figure 7.8 Table or Chart.

My Favorite Footwear				
Type of Footwear	Children's names			
Sneakers	Sarah	Daniel	Karen		
Sandals	Mary	Jean	Janice	Lynn	Alicia
Flip flops	George	Judy	Gavin	Ruben	
Crocs	Gavin	Lizzy	Joey		
	1	2	3	4	5

Figure 7.9 Bar Graph.

Once the data have been collected, it would be appropriate to categorize the information. For example, in surveying games children would choose to play, the games might be categorized into board games to play indoors, games that are played outdoors, etc. Children can then represent the data collected in a selected form (Figures 7.6–7.9). Data can be represented in two different forms and then the forms can be compared to see if one form is easier to "read" than another form. For example, children might decide to represent the data using a line plot (Figure 7.6). The same data could be represented in a bar graph (Figure 7.9). The two sets of data could then be compared.

Data for the same question could be collected at various times during the school year. For example, the question surveying how many people have pockets on their clothing on a particular day could change. Collected data for various dates could be tracked using a line graph.

Grade 3 Outcome #3: Describe the Shape and Features of a Data Set and Compare Related Data Sets

Sample Activity

With instruction, guidance, and practice, children learn how to see a set of data as a whole and describe it in general terms. They learn to focus on seeing where the data are concentrated or spread out. They also need to look for outliers, or data that are far removed from where the concentration(s) fall. In focusing on the set of data as a whole, children can begin to ask questions and find answers in the data.

Grade 3 Outcome #4: Justify Conclusions and Predictions about a Set of Data and Design a Further Investigation to Extend Conclusions and Predictions

Sample Activity

As children ask questions and attempt to answer these questions with data represented in various forms, they learn to justify their conclusions and make predictions. These predictions can lead to designing a further investigation. For example, children may decide to survey another class or children in a school to compare collected data with their original data set, or predictions could lead to designing an additional survey of their own class.

Grade 3 Outcome #5: Probability

Probability at the third grade level involves extending vocabulary focused on the likelihood of an event happening. Vocabulary should include "likely," "unlikely," "most likely," "least likely," "certain," and "impossible." Children's experiences with probability at this level should entail simple experiments with only a few outcomes. For example, children could flip a coin and record the number of times heads or tails landed upwards for X number of flips. They could also experiment with a spinner with certain sections shaded in various colors. Children could spin and record the color the spinner landed on out of X number of spins. As a whole group, and with guidance from the teacher, children can discuss the results of their experiment.

ADAPTATIONS FOR CHILDREN WITH SPECIAL NEEDS

It might be necessary to make adaptations when planning data analysis and probability lessons and activities depending on the individual needs of the children in the classroom. Several adaptations for activities could include:

- Breaking activities into smaller parts or reducing the number of steps
- Providing larger, raised, or textured objects for children who are visually impaired
- Providing larger manipulatives for children who experience difficulty in picking up smaller objects
- Positioning children who are visually and hearing impaired so they can see and hear what is going on in the classroom
- Pairing a child with special needs with a child or group of children from whom he or she can receive assistance when the teacher is busy helping others
- Creating paths in the classroom so that a child in a wheelchair can approach the graph or chart being created
- Keeping charts and graphs low enough so all children have access and can participate in the displaying of information

ADAPTATIONS FOR MATHEMATICALLY PROMISING CHILDREN

Mathematically promising children may need adaptations made to the math curriculum that challenge them. For example, a mathematically promising child might develop a survey question and collect data from multiple sections of the same grade level or all the children in the school. The data would then be compiled, graphed, and displayed to show the results of the survey question. Adaptations could include ideas from the section on gifted children under "Children with Special Needs" in Chapter 1 (p. 15, 16).

ADAPTATION FOR ENGLISH LANGUAGE LEARNERS (ELL)

Adaptations for children who are learning English as their second language could include:

- Connecting data analysis and probability concepts to a child's first language— learn important terminology in the child's first language to help connect the English words to the first-language words
- Reinforcing vocabulary with visual cues, pictures, and gestures
- Using multicultural literature, pictures, and stories that depict various cultures, especially the cultures of the children represented in the class
- Asking "wonder" questions of the children that depict cultural information for the children to discover
- Including "wonder" questions to investigate and explore from children of all cultural backgrounds
- Providing objects to sort and classify from children's cultural backgrounds
- Providing picture cues on children's recording sheets to help them remember what to do

HOME/SCHOOL CONNECTION IDEAS AND ACTIVITIES

The following ideas could be provided to parents/caregivers as ways to reinforce data analysis and probability concepts at home:

1. Make a homework schedule, activities schedule, chart of family responsibilities at home, etc.
2. Have children organize and label the work brought home and displayed on a bulletin board/the refrigerator.
3. Make grocery and other shopping lists together; organize lists into groups.
4. Organize, label, and make photo albums together.
5. Organize and label collections (e.g., coins, stamps, cards).
6. Ask "wonder" questions with family members or in the home environment, and design survey questions.
7. Collect data for survey questions from family members and relatives.
8. Sort, classify, graph, and analyze information, toys, clothing, etc. at home.
9. Represent data in various ways; find similarities and differences.
10. Analyze the data looking for concentration areas and spread-out areas.
11. Find ways to use probability vocabulary at home, including "likely," "unlikely," "impossible," "certain," and "equal".
12. Find ways to use comparison vocabulary at home, including "more than," "less than," "least," "greatest," "same as."

(Copley et al., 2010)

The National Association for the Education of Young Children (NAEYC) has an "Information for Families" website located at http://www.naeyc.org/families/. The website provides resources for families, including activities to do at home, to encourage child development.

CURRICULUM INTEGRATION

Cross-curricular opportunities involving data collection and analysis and probability are limitless. All content areas offer the opportunity to ask questions and/or poll opinions. In science class, for example, children could weigh the amount of garbage they collect in their classroom on a daily basis for a week, record the data, and graph the results. Younger children could vote on their favorite day of the school week (Monday through Friday), record the data, and graph the results. Likewise, probability terminology could also be applied to situations in just about any content area. For example, young children could look out the classroom window, study the sky, and make a prediction about the weather using the term "probably." Older children might determine the probability of rain on a given day by analyzing the percentages given with the weather forecast. For example, if the percentage chance of rain for a specific day is 10 percent, children might determine that the probability of rain on that day is low or that it is probably not going to rain.

DATA ANALYSIS AND PROBABILITY CONTENT VOCABULARY

Listed below is data analysis and probability content vocabulary that teachers could be using in their conversations with children, depending on the age level of the children. It is of utmost importance that teachers use various means to help children learn and understand the meanings of content vocabulary words as they are learning data analysis and probability concepts.

- represent, representation
- sort
- classify
- data, information
- survey
- organize
- collect, collection
- display
- analyze
- determine
- objects, manipulatives
- category, categories
- tally, tally marks
- method
- attribute, characteristic
- vote
- option, choice
- shape of data
- features of data
- graph (noun)
- graph (verb)
- horizontal
- vertical
- x-axis, y-axis
- label
- row
- column
- chart
- picture graph
- bar graph
- line plot
- scaled graph
- data table
- event, happening
- certain
- impossible
- likely, likelihood
- unlikely, not likely

LITERATURE CONNECTIONS

Children's literature can be beneficial in helping children understand concepts of probability and also in understanding how collecting information helps to answer questions that don't have an immediate answer, which, of course, is a real-world application. The following storybooks are relevant in developing these concepts for prekindergarten and kindergarten children. Fairytales provide a resource for discussing probability.

Cloudy with a Chance of Meatballs by Judi Barrett

Athenaeum, 1982

In this farcical story, the town of Chewandswallow gets weather three times a day for breakfast, lunch, and dinner.

Probably Pistachio (MathStart 2) by Stuart J. Murphy

HarperCollins, 2000

This book provides an introduction into probability as Jack thinks about the likelihood of things happening throughout the day.

It's Probably Penny by Loreen Leedy

Henry Holt and Co., 2007

Lisa and her classmates are learning about probability. Her weekend homework assignment is to make predictions about what will, might, and can't happen over the weekend.

A Very Improbable Story: A Math Adventure by Edward Einhorn

Charlesbridge Publishing, 2008

Ethan awakens one morning with a talking cat perched on the top of his head. He must win a game of probability in order for the cat to leave his head.

The Great Graph Contest by Loreen Leedy

Holiday House, 2006

Chester the snail creates a contest for Gonk the toad and Beezy the lizard to see who can create the best graph. Points are given for correct math, creativity, and neatness.

Tally O'Malley (MathStart 2) by Stuart J. Murphy

HarperCollins, 2004

The O'Malley children decide to play tally games on the long, boring ride to the beach. They keep tallies of how many different things they see along the way. Whoever ends up with the most tally marks wins the game.

Tiger Math: Learning to Graph from a Baby Tiger by Ann Whitehead Nagda

Owlet Paperbacks, 2002

After being orphaned when he was only a few weeks old, T.J., a Siberian tiger cub, is raised by veterinary staff at the Denver Zoo until he is old enough to return to the tiger exhibit area. T.J.'s growth is charted in various graphic forms in "real-world" terms.

Graphs (All Aboard Math Reader) by Bonnie Bader

Grosset & Dunlap, 2003

Gary's mom makes him take his math homework along to a family reunion after he tries to avoid the affair, using his math homework as the excuse. While at the reunion, Gary observes his relatives, collects data, and displays what he has collected in various graphic forms.

Collecting Data: Pick a Pancake (Math Monsters) by John Burstein

Weekly Reader Early Learning Library, 2003

This book provides an introduction into collecting data.

More or Less (MathStart 2) by Stuart J. Murphy

HarperCollins, 2005

Eddie uses concepts of "more" or "less" as he works the "guess the age" booth at the fair, blindfolded.

ASSESSING CHAPTER OUTCOMES

1. Think of additional activities that would be developmentally appropriate for prekindergarten/kindergarten children in meeting data analysis and probability standards.
2. What other ways could children choose an option or vote in a prekindergarten or kindergarten classroom; first to third grade classroom?
3. What other ideas do you have for displaying gathered information in a prekindergarten and kindergarten classroom; first to third grade classroom?
4. Choose an activity from the chapter, or an activity you have developed, and plan adaptations for a child with special needs. (Choose a specific disability, such as hearing or visually impaired, autistic, fine motor skills impairment, etc.)
5. Choose an activity from the chapter, or an activity you have developed, and plan adaptations for gifted children.
6. Explain how you would teach vocabulary words specific to concepts of pattern, function, and algebra to an ELL child.
7. Think of specific cross-curricular connections regarding data analysis and probability activities for prekindergarten and kindergarten children.

CHAPTER EXTENSION ACTIVITIES

1. Research additional literature, websites, and/or software programs that could be used with prekindergarten and kindergarten children to help them understand concepts of data analysis and probability.
2. Plan a grade-wide or school-wide data collection activity that would involve children collecting information, displaying the information, and analyzing it to find out the results.

REFERENCES

Barrett, J. (1982). *Cloudy With a Chance of Meatballs*. New York, NY: Antheneum Books for Young Readers.

Charlesworth, R. & Lind, K. K. (2007). *Math and Science for Young Children* (6th ed.). Belmont, CA: Wadsworth/ Cengage Learning.

Common Core State Standards Initiative: Preparing America's Students for College & Career (2010). Washington, D.C.: National Governors Association Center for Best Practices/Council of Chief State School Officers.

Copley, J. V., Jones, C. & Dighe, J. (2010). *The Creative Curriculum for Preschool: Mathematics*, vol. 4. Washington, D.C.: Teaching Strategies.

Davis, Genevieve S. & Keller, J. David (2009). *Exploring Science and Mathematics in a Child's World*. Columbus, OH: Pearson Merrill Prentice Hall.

Hutchins, P. (1989). *The Door Bell Rang*. New York, NY: Greenwillow Books.

McGrath, B. B. (2002). *The M&M's Counting Book*. Watertown, MA: Charlesbridge Publishing.

National Council of Teachers of Mathematics (NCTM) (2000). *Principles and Standards of School Mathematics*. http://www.nctm.org/standards/content.aspx?id=4294967312.

National Council of Teachers of Mathematics (NCTM) (2006). *Curriculum Focal Points for Prekindergarten through Grade 8 Mathematics: A Quest for Coherence*. Reston, VA: Author.

Pennsylvania Department of Education and Department of Public Welfare (2007). *Pennsylvania Learning Standards for Early Childhood: Prekindergarten*. Harristown, PA: Author.

Seuss, Dr. (1960). *Green Eggs and Ham*. New York, NY: Random House Books for Young Readers.

INDEX

All figures are shown by a page reference in *italics* and tables are shown in **bold**.